John Chrysostom: Embracing Greek Wisdom

Darren L. Curry

Abstract

The aim of the present study is to examine how Hellenism and Greek philosophy were received and used in arguments in the writings of John Chrysostom. The thesis is divided into five chapters of varying lengths, with the fifth chapter being the conclusion of the thesis.

Chapter 1 is divided into two major parts. Part A is the story of certain major scholarly works on the topic of Hellenism and Christianity, particularly in late antiquity. Part B turns to previous scholarship on John Chrysostom and Hellenism specifically. We discuss three particular aspects of John's reception, rhetoric, philosophy, and religious identity while also looking in interpretations from modern scholarship. This part and the chapter conclude with a general overview of the argument and an identification of research gaps.

Chapter 2 is divided into five parts. After a discussion of the identity of those called Greeks in John's corpus we proceed to analyse his extensive criticism of several aspects of Hellenism: philosophy, religion, public attitudes, and the binding power of tradition. The third part goes into the opposite direction and examines instances of John's positive references to Hellenes and Greek history. In part four we see the reception moving on from the binary of praise and criticism and we discuss examples of both praise and criticism combined, along with indifferent references to Hellenes and John's practical suggestions on how the Christians should treat the Greeks.

In Chapter 3 we examine John's embodiments of Hellenism and Christianity respectively through his comparisons of individuals. The first three parts consist of major comparisons, which are the most frequent ones in terms of the individuals compared, and minor comparisons, which are smaller treatments and usually group individuals together instead of treating them separately. The fourth part is a close analysis of Chrysostom's *Discourse on Babylas*, a treatise that includes a major comparison between Babylas and Diogenes but also provides an opportunity for John to launch a full-scale attack against Hellenism.

Finally, in Chapter 4 we will be looking into John's reception of a specific philosophical school: the Cynics. After situating John's own texts within previous Christian tradition and assessing differences and similarities, we complete the chapter by a comparison between John and the Cynics and their respective conception of a specific philosophical concept, that of *autarkeia*.

Table of Contents

1. Christianity, John Chrysostom and Hellenism: The Status Quaestionis

Christianity's engagement with late antique culture is a perennial issue that has been studied from a variety of angles and approaches. One of the aspects of this engagement is the relationship, interaction, and confrontation between Christianity and Hellenism. In this chapter, our focus will be the reception of the relationship between Christianity and Hellenism in modern scholarship, and second, the reception of John Chrysostom's role within this relationship.   John Chrysostom lived in an age when Christianity was slowly becoming the dominant religion in the Roman Empire and his attitude towards Hellenism has habitually provoked two very different responses: on the one hand, there are those who consider him someone "distinguished for furthering that fruitful encounter between the Christian message and Hellenic culture which has had an enduring impact on the Churches of East and West,"[1] and that "with John Chrysostom we see Greek culture incorporated into a newly ascendant Christianity."[2] On the other hand, he has been recently called a "champion of anti-Hellenism"[3] (whatever that may mean), a charge which we will attempt to trace as we try to see which, if either, of the two pictures described above is an accurate representation or based on an image of Chrysostom tailored to fit pre-existing conceptions. It should be obvious from the beginning that both positions suffer from certain limitations. The first position is a

---

[1] Letter of His Holiness Pope Benedict XVI on the occasion of the 16th centenary of the death of St John Chrysostom, 10 August 2007, accessed 16 December 2017, http://w2.vatican.va/content/benedict-xvi/en/letters/2007/documents/hf_ben-xvi_let_20070810_giovanni-crisostomo.html.

[2] Jacqueline De Romilly, *A Short History of Greek Literature*, trans. Lillian Doherty (Chicago: University of Chicago Press, 1985), 220. Romilly identifies the following as the assimilated elements of Greek culture: rhetorical devices, echoes of classical Greek authors (Plato, Aeschylus, Demosthenes, Homer), and images drawn from the ancient Greek poets.

[3] Niketas Siniossoglou, *Plato and Theodoret: The Christian Appropriation of Platonic Philosophy and the Hellenic Intellectual Resistance* (Cambridge: Cambridge University Press, 2008), 52. For a similar view to Siniossoglou see Frank R. Trombley, *Hellenic Religion and Christianization, vol. 1, c. 370-529* (Leiden: Brill, 1993), 341: "the most eminent scholar and anti-Hellene of the century to occupy the patriarchal throne, John Chrysostom." We will be discussing other similar views in more detail in the second part of this chapter.

sweeping judgment, which tends to forget that the encounter between Hellenism and Christianity was not always fruitful, or peaceful, for that matter.

Furthermore, it tends to imply that the two were clear, delimited categories. A subsequent outcome of the first position was the invention of the term "Christian Hellenism", commonly used to describe the Cappadocians' attempted synthesis of the two worldviews. While many scholars use the term, few have been able to define Christian Hellenism or to explain what it entails. One of the oldest definitions, and an excellent example of someone who thought of Christianity and Hellenism as delimited categories, comes from James Marshall Campbell:

> If Hellenism is one thing and Christianity is another, the Greek Fathers are of the unity of Hellenism nevertheless. When we use the term "Christian Hellenism" we are not attempting a paradox. We mean that the old Hellenic civilization finds a new lease of life, a circumscribed life, a life minus the principle of indiscriminate liberty of the reason, for instance -but yet life and growth, as distinguished from decay and final death in its pagan haunts. The principal force of Christianity comes from elsewhere, most of its ideas and sentiments are non-Hellenic, but Hellenism contributed ideas too, and above all it contributed its literary art and its intellectual method... the content of Hellenism -its Greek philosophy- furnished the intellectual frames wherein orthodoxy placed the faith for aftertimes. Without Hellenism there would have been no golden age of Patristic literature, as we conceive it on its literary side-no Basil, no Chrysostom, no Gregory of Nazianzus.[4]

The second view sometimes shows a very limited perception of what Hellenism was, and tends to equate Hellenism exclusively with pagan religious practices that had already been criticized in certain schools of Greek philosophy centuries before the emergence of Christianity.[5] It is a view shared by many modern scholars[6] and fails to

---

[4] James Marshall Campbell, *The Greek Fathers* (New York: Longmans, Green, 1929), 16-7.

[5] "The Academy, the successors of Plato ... had made such offensive comments on the morality of the Homeric gods and had even gone so far as to expel the ancient poet from his ideal state." Henry Chadwick, "Introduction," in *Origen: Contra Celsum*, ed. and trans. Henry Chadwick (1953; repr., Cambridge: Cambridge University Press, 1980), x. Plato himself condemned Homer's anthropomorphic conception of the deity in the *Republic*, 377d-387b. "The rejection of Hellenic religion did not imply a wholesale rejection of Hellenic culture." Yannis Papadogiannakis, *Christianity and Hellenism in the Fifth-Century Greek East: Theodoret's Apologetics against the Greeks in Context* (Washington, D.C.: Center for Hellenic Studies, 2012), 23. "Yet, throughout late antiquity Greekness rarely became a strictly religious identity (whether in the eyes of those who identified themselves as Greeks or those who attacked it), if a religious identity is understood to be an identity delimited by doctrinal or narrowly cultic elements alone... one is hard-pressed to find a clear instance of a "pagan" author of late antiquity who sought to limit the signification of Hellen to a religious identity in any sustained way." Aaron Johnson,

take into account a basic distinction apparent in most patristic writings: while some of the Fathers might be more sympathetic to Greek philosophy (or other aspects of classical culture) than others, almost all had an utterly negative attitude towards pagan (i.e. non-Christian) religious practices.[7] Furthermore, paganism as a religious concept is certainly not limited to ancient Greeks, who a) would not even be aware of it since it's a modern scholarly construction, and b) as an umbrella term it includes not just the religion of ancient Greeks but encompasses different religions (usually polytheistic) from different regions in antiquity.[8] Therefore, the concept of anti-Hellenism is not *necessarily* synonymous with anti-paganism. However, it is true that the age of Chrysostom can be regarded as a transition point in the development of meaning of the terms *Hellene* (Ἕλλην) and *Hellenism* (Ἑλληνισμός) and their becoming almost synonymous with pagan religious practices in Christian writings.[9] Late Antique Greek

---

Religion and Identity in Porphyry of Tyre: The Limits of Hellenism in Late Antiquity (Cambridge: Cambridge University Press, 2013), 5.

[6] Susanna Elm, "Hellenism and Historiography: Gregory of Nazianzus and Julian in Dialogue," in *The Cultural Turn in Late Ancient Studies: Gender, Asceticism, and Historiography*, eds. Dale B. Martin and Patricia Cox Miller (Durham, NC: Duke University Press, 2005), 261.

[7] In discussing Clement of Alexandria's attitude toward Greek philosophy Joseph Trigg notes that "this favourable attitude toward Greek philosophy did not extend to pagan religion, toward which Clement exhibited the same implacable opposition that characterizes all early Christian authors." Joseph W. Trigg, *Origen* (London: Routledge, 1998), 9. In certain instances, it is exactly the endorsement of pagan religion by certain philosophers (such as the Stoics) and poets that leads to Chrysostom's rhetorical outbursts against the "Greeks." Cf. R. R. Bolgar, "The Greek Legacy," in *The Legacy of Greece: A New Appraisal*, ed. M. I. Finley (Oxford: Clarendon Press, 1981), 434: "Outside the theological field the Christians' attitude to their pagan heritage remained notably ambivalent. All patristic writers, even those who are generally in favour of reading ancient literature, display a lively distrust of the pagan tradition and habitually enlarge on the dangers of corruption and disbelief."

[8] *Paganus* was the common term used for polytheists in the Latin west: "The adoption of *paganus* by Latin Christians as an all-embracing, pejorative term for polytheists represents an unforeseen and singularly long-lasting victory, within a religious group, of a word of Latin slang originally devoid of religious meaning. The evolution occurred only in the Latin west, and in connection with the Latin church. Elsewhere, "Hellene" or "gentile" (*ethnikos*) remained the word for "pagan"; and *paganos* continued as a purely secular term, with overtones of the inferior and the commonplace." Peter Brown, "Pagan," in *Late Antiquity: A Guide to the Postclassical World*, eds. G. W. Bowersock, Peter Brown and Oleg Grabar (Cambridge, MA: Harvard University Press, 1999), 625. The word itself was used in this sense by the Christians themselves, and appears first in Christian inscriptions of the early fourth century. See Robin Lane Fox, *Pagans and Christians* (Harmondsworth: Viking, 1986), 30. For the notion of monotheism in late antique debates between pagans and Christians see *Monotheism between Pagans and Christians in Late Antiquity*, eds. Stephen Mitchell and Peter Van Nuffelen (Leuven: Peeters, 2010); *One God. Pagan Monotheism in the Roman Empire*, eds. Stephen Mitchell and Peter Van Nuffelen (Cambridge: Cambridge University Press, 2010).

[9] Although N. Siniossoglou recognizes that the new meaning of the terms Hellene and Hellenism was not due to the Christians but originates from the Jewish opposition to the Hellenistic kings' attempt to

speakers sometimes used the term to describe these, but this is not always related to the broader question of Christianity's relationship to Hellenism.

At the same time, Greek language and culture, the ideals of paideia and philosophy are all major parts of Hellenism that are neglected if we equate Hellenism primarily with pagan religious practices or beliefs.[10] Any present-day treatment of Hellenism in late antiquity should also ideally incorporate discussions of notions such as ethnicity and culture, which include Hellenism as a religion but are not limited by this definition. Finally, it is important to note that the term Hellenism as used in this study does not have a strict geographical limit: Alexander's conquests and the expansion of Christianity enabled Hellenism to spread beyond Greece, making it "the only national culture that also became a transnational ideal."[11]

Therefore, this chapter will assess scholarly treatments of John Chrysostom and Hellenism, seeking to highlight the weaknesses in the two prevalent approaches. What follows is an engagement with major scholarly endeavours on two fronts: a) the relationship between Christianity and Hellenism, and b) John Chrysostom and Hellenism. The first part will include a brief overview of the debate in the early and middle 20th century since these discussions set the stage for many of the subsequent

---

convert them, he believes that the fact that the Christians accepted this connotation "illustrates the indebtedness of Christian apologetics to the Jewish opposition to Hellenism." He also claims that a major motive for the Christian opposition to Hellenism was Christianity's desire to abolish national identities and traditions and replace them with "a universal and exclusive religious identity" (*Plato and Theodoret*, 48, n. 82-83). Siniossoglou's argument can also be understood as a restatement of Julian's snarky remark that the Christians have discarded the love of ancestral traditions in *Contr. Gal.* 238D (LCL 157:390). "The word Hellenism (*Hellenismos*) takes on a new meaning in late antiquity, a meaning that proclaims in the most eloquent way possible the relation between paganism and Greek culture. For Hellenism comes to mean "paganism" itself... in later Greek [Hellenism] sometimes means paganism and sometimes Greek culture (or Hellenism as we use the word), and that *Hellenes* are sometimes "pagans" and sometimes simply "Greeks." G.W. Bowersock, *Hellenism in Late Antiquity* (Michigan, MI: University of Michigan Press, 1990), 10. Cf. Aaron Johnson, "Hellenism and Its Discontents," in *The Oxford Handbook of Late Antiquity*, ed. Scott Fitzgerald Johnson (Oxford: Oxford University Press, 2012), 437-66.

[10] An identification that has its roots in antiquity, with certain scholars proposing Iamblichus as its original proponent while others trace it to Porphyry. See G. W. Bowersock, *Julian the Apostate* (Cambridge, MA: Harvard University Press, 1978), 84. But see n. 5 above for Aaron Johnson's objections.

[11] Anthony Kaldellis, *Hellenism in Byzantium: The Transformations of Greek Identity and the Reception of the Classical Tradition* (Cambridge: Cambridge University Press, 2007), 390.

arguments, but at the same time often reflected the confessional background of the authors and the ways it influenced their positions. This will be followed by more recent discussions on the subject, which, although in many ways offering a revision and refinement of previous arguments, also tend to take one-sided positions that are still reflective of specific assumptions. In this respect, the figure of Chrysostom is emblematic of the two most common positions in scholarship on the subject: there are those who still consider Christianity and Hellenism in late antiquity as mortal enemies (with Chrysostom offering many texts towards this proposition), and those who see them as two movements which, even though they went through some difficult times in their relationship, eventually came to an irenic coexistence. Chrysostom and the Cappadocians are often used as particularly good examples of this. As we shall show, the literature on Chrysostom's reception of Hellenism tends to conform to one of these two positions, and even though one might argue that Hellenism lacks enough coherence to be treated as a movement, most of our sources treat it as such and therefore we will too.

It is important to contextualise the discussion in the broader debate about Christianity and Hellenism, particularly because this latter has been advanced on many fronts lately. This survey of the status quaestionis is a crucial starting point for this dissertation, which will argue that John Chrysostom's position vis-à-vis Hellenism is much more complex than either of the two standard accounts allow. Our proposition is that to understand Chrysostom's reception of Hellenism we need to consider the wider context of his writings in order to understand them both as responses to specific challenges (by, among others, Julian[12] and Libanius) and as individual works with different audiences in mind. We should not necessarily be looking for consistency on the subject of Hellenism in his writings, because he never aimed to be consistent on this

______

[12] Who was perceived by John as the "emperor who exceeded all who preceded him in impiety." *In Iuv. et Max.* 1 (PG 50:573).

or many other matters. One could also argue here that Chrysostom has often been misinterpreted for the exact same reason as Origen (even though in the former's case the state of the texts is infinitely better compared to most of the latter's): due to the sheer amount of his works, he is often not read as carefully as he should be, which often leads to some bold, sweeping statements on the matter. A reading of John Chrysostom which takes these factors into account will render a more nuanced account of his relationship with Hellenism and will allow us to see whether Chrysostom reflects or challenges our understanding of Hellenism in Late Antiquity.

a. Christianity and Hellenism

The question of the relationship between Christianity and Hellenism has generated volumes of scholarship in a variety of scholarly fields such as history, classics and archaeology. However, we must not forget that it has also been a divisive issue for Christian theology from the days of the early Church and ever since. As already mentioned, it has been seen through different lenses, some looking at it as a fruitful encounter and others as a conflict between fundamentally incompatible worldviews. Even so, a worldview is not just a collection of propositions about the world, but could be an attitude or mode of behaviour. Thus, for example, Paul Cartledge argues that "for a Christian, religion is essentially an individual personal, and privatized matter, a relation between a particular person's immortal soul and the Almighty. By contrast, the Classical Greeks' religion was typically focused upon relations between men collectively and the gods, and was expressed in collective, official, public rituals, above all festivals."[13] This is, in fact, an unhelpful generalisation because this particular description of ancient Greek religion could be easily used to describe Christian public rituals in late antiquity, which were also collective and official, with the Roman

---

[13] Paul Cartledge, *The Greeks: A Portrait of Self and Others* (Oxford: Oxford University Press, 2002), 169.

Emperors being participants themselves. It might also be more accurate if it were intended to be one between modern forms of Christianity compared to ancient Greek religious rites. But it still would not be absolutely applicable to Christianity in late antiquity.

Hellenism has been given various definitions throughout history, and almost all of them depended on what the relevant author wanted to emphasize as its distinct feature. Our aim in this section will be to provide a small sample of different definitions in order to become acquainted with the different perspectives and challenges Hellenism presented to the Christians of late antiquity. One of the first comprehensive definitions of Hellenism comes from Herodotus in the fifth century BC; it is a summative description that selects four features as the marks of Hellenic kinship: "then again, there is the fact that we are all Greeks—one race speaking one language, with temples to the gods and religious rites in common, and with a common way of life."[14] A little later on Isocrates would provide a very different definition in his *Panegyrikos*: "Athens has made it so that the name of the Greeks designates not a race (*genos*) but a mindset, and those are called Greeks who share in our culture rather than our common stock (*physis*)."[15] This is a classic cultural definition of Hellenism, which seems to be exclusive of any racial or ethnic elements and is usually considered as the archetype of the idea of universal Hellenism, which would only be truly actualized by Alexander. However, as A. Kaldellis has argued, Isocrates' focus was not on spreading Hellenic culture to barbarians. His definition was primarily intended for *"other Greeks* to

---

[14] Herodotus, Hist. 8.144.2 (*Historiae*, ed. N. G. Wilson, Oxford: Oxford University Press, 2015, 775; Herodotus, *The Histories*, trans. Robin Waterfield, Oxford: Oxford University Press, 1998, 539): αὖθις δὲ τὸ Ἑλληνικὸν ἐὸν ὅμαιμόν τε καὶ ὁμόγλωσσον καὶ θεῶν ἱδρύματά τε κοινὰ καὶ θυσίαι ἤθεά τε ὁμότροπα. Jonathan Hall has argued that Herodotus's emphasis on ethnic identity did not last long and was replaced by a focus on "broader cultural criteria" that defined Hellenic identity until the Roman conquest. Jonathan M. Hall, *Hellenicity between Ethnicity and Culture* (Chicago: University of Chicago Press, 2002), 226. The relationship between Hellenic religion and cultural identity and whether the use of Greek implied an acceptance of Greek religious beliefs would lead to heated debates in the patristic period, such as the one between Gregory Nazianzus and the Emperor Julian.

[15] Isocrates, *Pan.* 50 (trans. Kaldellis, *Hellenism in Byzantium*, 18).

recognize the supremacy of *Athenian culture* and specifically of his own school, which he was constantly advertising."[16]

It should also be mentioned that there are periodical distinctions in the history of Hellenism, as well as political and cultural[17], and what will mainly concern us here is the late antique and proto-Byzantine sense of Hellenism. A. Kaldellis has aptly summarized five different senses of Hellenism that would be familiar to anyone who studies Byzantine writers, and these should be kept in mind throughout this study since they are also of fundamental importance for late antique writers. They are as follows: a) the term Hellenic had sometimes a geographical connection to mainland Greece as a place of origin, and when used in that sense it did not convey anything related to nationality; b) the Hellenes were sometimes the ancient Greeks, an ancient nation mainly known through history; c) Hellenes was also the term used to denote pagans of different nationalities, Greek or otherwise[18]; d) a Hellene was also someone who spoke Greek, and this usage was neutral to other associations, religious or ethnic; e) finally, Hellenism was also the acquaintance with classical *paideia*, which included the knowledge of philosophy and an appreciation, if not usage, of rhetorical mannerisms.[19] Kaldellis' masterful study concludes that Byzantine Hellenism was both *paideia* and paganism and argues that the appeal of the classics led to the prevalence of the former over the latter. He argues for the exclusion of damnation of Hellenism from the range of

---

[16] Kaldellis, *Hellenism in Byzantium*, 18.

[17] Katerina Zacharia, Introduction to *Hellenisms: Culture, Identity, and Ethnicity from Antiquity to Modernity*, ed. Katerina Zacharia (London: Ashgate, 2008), 2.

[18] All five senses appear in Chrysostom's works. For an example of this particular sense see *In 1 Cor. hom.* 20.8 (PG 61:165; NPNF 1-12:115): "For tell me not of the present establishment, and that you have received the true religion from your ancestors. But carry back your thoughts to those times, and consider when the Gospel was just set on foot, and impiety was still at its height, and altars burning, and sacrifices and libations offering up, and the greater part of men were Gentiles [Hellenes]; think, I say, of those who from their ancestors had received impiety, and who were the descendants of fathers and grandfathers and great-grandfathers like themselves." This particular use of the term was popularized in the fourth century by authors like Eusebius and Athanasius, and from then on was used "interchangeably with *ta ethne* to designate those who were neither Jews nor Christians and who worshipped the Graeco-Roman Gods in some form." Isabella Sandwell, *Religious Identity in Late Antiquity: Greeks, Jews and Christians in Antioch* (Cambridge: Cambridge University Press, 2007), 149.

[19] Sandwell, *Religious Identity in Late Antiquity*, 184-6.

the various options on the debate between Christianity and Hellenism and identifies paideia, philosophy and national identity as the components that comprised Byzantine Hellenism. He also sees that as part of the ancient tradition of Hellenism and believes that despite what he calls the "distorting legacy" of the Fathers, the Byzantines essentially opted for the Hellenism of Plato, Isocrates, Libanius and Synesius.[20] Kaldellis' summary is extremely useful for our study since it provides us with all the different senses of Hellenism in Chrysostom's vast corpus and enables us to see which component was most important for him as a Christian writing in late antiquity.

Before we get into the different scholarly views on Hellenism and Christianity, we should mention that any discussion on the Hellenic cultural tradition in Byzantium would be incomplete without considering the other two constitutive elements of the Byzantine society, its Roman political identity and its relation to Greekness and the relation of *Romanitas* to Christianity. These issues have been the subjects of other studies, both in connection to Chrysostom and Byzantium in general, but will not concern us here.[21]

i. Nineteenth-twentieth century: Harnack and the response to Harnack

Historians of early Christianity in the early 20th century, especially Protestants such as A. Harnack, tended to see primitive Christianity as the pure religion established by Jesus and the Apostles, which was later corrupted by Hellenic influences in its doctrine

---

[20] Kaldellis, *Hellenism in Byzantium*, 397. On the other hand, Sandwell has argued that the power of *paideia* was co-opted by fourth century Christians (i.e. the Church Fathers) in their attempts to convert the Graeco-Roman elites and establish themselves as a serious intellectual force in Graeco-Roman society. Part of this effort was their interest to separate Greek culture from Greek religion. See further analysis in ibid., 152.

[21] For a concise but masterful discussion of these interconnected issues see Claudia Rapp, "Hellenic Identity, *Romanitas*, and Christianity in Byzantium," in *Hellenisms*, ed. K. Zacharia, 127-47. For a detailed study of Chrysostom's stance towards the Roman Empire see Constantine Bozinis, *Ο Ιωάννης ο Χρυσόστομος για το Imperium Romanum: Μελέτη πάνω στην πολιτική σκέψη της Αρχαίας Εκκλησίας* [*John Chrysostom on the Imperium Romanum: A Study on the Political Thought of the Early Church*] (Athens: Book Institute - A. Kardamitsas, 2003), *passim.*

and practice.[22] This process is frequently described as 'Hellenization,' and one of C. Markschies' most interesting findings in his research on the use of the term Hellenization in the twentieth century is that the word can be found in about one tenth of works by ancient historians, with the other nine tenths included in works by theologians. [23] However, the terms Hellenization and Hellenism were rarely defined with any precision, both in terms of their content as well as their chronology.[24] Scholars from Catholic and Orthodox backgrounds responded to Harnack in different ways in later decades, and in this chapter, we shall see some of these responses as exemplified in the works of Jaroslav Pelikan[25] and Georges Florovsky[26]. We will also look at how classicists and ancient historians such as Werner Jaeger[27] responded to the same issue.

In this brief survey, we will try to classify the different positions of this older generation of scholars in mostly a chronological manner, but also based on schools of thought. Jean Daniélou (and to a similar extent, Georges Florovsky) is representative of a school of thought that rejects the Hellenization of Christianity and argues instead that

---

[22] "This notion [Hellenization of Christianity] famously found its formulation thanks to A. von Harnack, according to whom Christian dogmata are the product of Greek philosophy, which was superimposed, as a sort of foreign element, upon the "pure" Gospel ground." Ilaria L.E. Ramelli, "Origen, Patristic Philosophy, and Christian Platonism: Rethinking the Christianisation of Hellenism," *Vigiliae Christianae* 63 (2009), 253 with references to Harnack's works. Cf. ibid., 258-9 for more criticisms of Harnack's thesis. It might be on this basis that G.W. Bowersock has called Hellenization "a modern idea, reflecting modern forms of cultural domination" and "a useless barometer for assessing Greek culture." *Hellenism in Late Antiquity*, xi, 7. For a summary of Harnack's arguments on Hellenization see also Christoph Markschies, "Does It Make Sense to Speak about a 'Hellenization of Christianity' in Antiquity?" *Church History and Religious Culture* 92.1 (2009), 13-5.

[23] For a history of the term Hellenization in the nineteenth century and its use particularly among German academics, including Harnack, see Markschies, "Does It Make Sense," *passim*. To Markschies' surprise, it has been used more often lately by Roman Catholic rather than Protestant theologians. However, in recent Roman Catholic works Harnack's perspective and judgment have been adopted and accepted, a phenomenon Markschies calls "protestantization of the Roman Catholic perspective". Ibid., 22-5.

[24] Ibid., 13-4.

[25] Jaroslav Pelikan, *Christianity and Classical Culture: The Metamorphosis of Natural Theology in the Christian Encounter with Hellenism* (New Haven, CT: Yale University Press, 1993). For a more specific critique of Harnack's advocacy of Hellenization, particularly on dogma, see Pelikan, *The Christian Tradition, A History of the Development of Doctrine* 1: *The Emergence of the Catholic Tradition (100-600),* (Chicago: University of Chicago Press, 1971), 45-55.

[26] Georges Florovsky, *The Eastern Fathers of the Fourth Century*, trans. Catherine Edmunds (Vaduz: Büchervertriebsanstalt, 1987).

[27] Werner Jaeger, *Early Christianity and Greek Paideia* (Cambridge, MA: Belknap Press, 1961).

Christian Platonists transformed Greek philosophy to such an extent that it is more appropriate to speak of a Christianization of philosophy.[28] Both Daniélou (and Florovsky) are espousing a synthetic view, with Christianity having the steering hand. On the other hand, Werner Jaeger looks at the process as both a Christianization of the Roman world as well as a Hellenization of Christianity. As a classicist, Jaeger views the influence as going both ways. For him, the earliest manifestation of Christian Hellenism is the use of Greek in the NT writings, which continues with the writings of the Apostolic Fathers.[29] Before Pelikan, whose arguments we will be reviewing further on, Jaeger uses the example of the Cappadocians in his discussion on Hellenism and Christianity in the 4th century and refers to their line of demarcation between Greek religion and Greek culture. Their synthesis results in a form of Christian neoclassicism, which sees Christianity as the "heir to everything in the Greek tradition that seemed worthy of survival."[30] The Cappadocians are often considered emblematic in Christian reception of Hellenism, particularly in late antiquity, and Jaeger was not the only one to see them as such.

Jaroslav Pelikan's pioneering 1993 book on Christianity and Hellenism in the works of the Cappadocians is particularly important for our discussion for two reasons: a) Pelikan, just like Harnack, was a pivotal historian of doctrine and a scholar who, through the magnitude of his works, reached far beyond his discipline and was very influential, not just to other scholars, but in public life as well; b) despite the shared Lutheran background of both authors (but not for the duration of his lifetime in Pelikan's case), they came to completely different conclusions on the subject, but their

---

[28] Ramelli, "Origen, Patristic Philosophy and Christian Platonism," 254. Cf. Morwenna Ludlow, *Gregory of Nyssa: Ancient and (Post)Modern* (Oxford: Oxford University Press, 2007), 85-6 with discussion of reasons as to the influence of Harnack's thesis within Protestantism and the utilization of a similar binary scheme (the Gospel vs Greek philosophy) by Catholic writers, specifically Daniélou.

[29] Jaeger, *Early Christianity and Greek Paideia*, 5-6.

[30] Ibid., 74-5.

respective positions still influence numerous others to this day.[31] The work can also be considered a definitive culmination of Pelikan's views on the issue, after the completion of his monumental five volumes on the history of doctrine, and whilst he was still a Lutheran. Moving beyond the binary scheme that has been previously employed to categorise the Church Fathers as either overly hostile to Hellenism or as the ones responsible for the Hellenization of Christianity, Pelikan sees the Cappadocians as authors sitting "squarely in the tradition of Classical Greek culture" *and* as "intensely critical of that tradition."[32] They are in a constant interchange as well as controversy with both the "monuments of the culture" and with "contemporary expositors of the monuments." The Cappadocians are thus both exponents of "Christian Hellenism" (particularly Basil, Pelikan argues), specifically in its literary aspects, and heavily involved in the Christian critique of Hellenism.[33] Their writings also display an awareness of both the "temptations of Classical rhetoric" and its usefulness to the Christian cause, as well as the belief that rhetoric was a common property of the Christian and the Classical tradition. In terms of their use of Classical literature, ambiguity might be the word that most closely resembles their attitude. They often ridicule myths and attribute them to demons, and are also often more vitriolic in their remarks against writers such as Homer when corresponding with people like Julian than when communicating with each other or with other Christians.[34] The Cappadocians'

---

[31] Mark Humphries with David M. Gwynn, "The Sacred and the Secular: The Presence or Absence of Christian Religious Thought in Secular Writing in the Late Antique West," in *Religious Diversity in Late Antiquity*, eds. David M. Gwynn and Susanne Bangert (Leiden: Brill, 2010), 494, included Pelikan as one of the scholars (alongside R. MacMullen, H. Chadwick, et. al.) responsible for the customary scholarly approach on the topic, "the extent to which the ancient and classical does or does not persist into the new Christian dispensation." The authors also make the pertinent observation that the opposition between pagan/classical and Christian/late antique often involves a sense of superiority of the former compared to the latter (ibid.).

[32] Although Pelikan was not the only one who avoided falling into this trap. Cf. C. J. De Vogel, "Platonism and Christianity: A Mere Antagonism or a Profound Common Ground?" *Vigiliae Christianae* 39:1 (1985), 27: "on the whole, Christian intellectuals did not take an attitude of hostility towards Greek philosophy; mostly they were positively interested, though never without critical reserve."

[33] Pelikan, *Christianity and Classical Culture*, 9-10.

[34] Ibid., 16-17.

"ambivalent identification" with Classical literature is also applicable to their treatment of Classical philosophy. Pelikan uses the example of Gregory of Nyssa to support his claim. Gregory could at the same time blame Greek philosophy for Eunomius' heretical views, whilst also accusing Eunomius of neglecting the study of philosophy.[35] One of their favourite rhetorical devices was the recitation of a catalogue of Greek philosophical schools, and the application of one or two epithets to each. This was complemented by the singling out of certain philosophers and the application of criticism to them. In Pelikan's opinion, the theology of the Greek Christian tradition from the Patristic period and onwards took shape under these encounters with Hellenism,[36] and frequently the fundamental elements of this encounter were influenced by the Cappadocians, even if their attitude was by no means uniform. Their ambiguous attitude, ranging from a positive view of the Classical language to a harsh condemnation of Greek religion, which could sometimes lead them to "align themselves... with the anticlerical, rationalistic exponents of a philosophical natural theology among pagan Greek thinkers"[37] was by no means unique or peculiar. We will see in chapter 2 how Chrysostom was also sympathetic to these very same exponents.

A similar model has been proposed by Basil Tatakis.[38] Tatakis looks at Christianity and Hellenism as two sources of philosophical thought, with Hellenism being an evolved feature stemming from classical civilization, and which, although preserving the "essentials characteristics of Greek thought", gradually faded away with the transition to a new world. This new world, as represented by the rise of Christianity, assimilated Greek thought "in form and content" as long as there were no conflicts with the faith, and Greek thought acquired a new meaning since "the foundation of the

---

[35] Ibid., 18, with references to Gregory's works.

[36] Ibid., 19-21.

[37] Ibid., 22-3.

[38] Basil Tatakis, *Byzantine Philosophy*, trans. Nicholas J. Moutafakis (Indianapolis, IN: Hackett, 2003). The original French edition is from 1949, even though it was only translated into English in 2003.

edifice that it supports is entirely different." But Tatakis correlates this development with the division between Western and Eastern Christianity, which led to the distinction between Catholicism and Orthodoxy, the latter being what he calls "the Greek conception of Christianity." As we shall see below, other scholars have made similar claims, but Tatakis sees this continuation under a different light. For Tatakis the barbarian invasions in Western Europe led to the annihilation of Hellenism in the West, where the Latin spirit then prevailed, but the embodiment of non-religious elements of Hellenism into the lives of Byzantines is one of the two constituent elements that created Byzantine civilization (the other being Christianity).[39] Finally, Tatakis extends this paradigm to Greek philosophy (which is just one part of Greek thought), where "Christianity was free to appropriate any and all of the basic elements of waning paganism, as long as these elements underwent discussion, study, and cleansing from their non-Christian foundations."[40] Tatakis is just one among many scholars who claim that Christians retained certain elements from Hellenism whilst excluding others, but aside from criterion of religion (i.e. anything that could be contrary to the faith was left out) there has not been a systematic work on what other, if any, criteria may have been operative in this process of appropriation.

It is important to note here that Tatakis speaks of an evolution within Greek thought. He does not see Hellenism in Byzantium as a continuation of classical Hellenism; his argument sees continuity in language rather than in the essence of classical thought. In this respect, he is downplaying an oft-repeated paradigm in studies on the history of Hellenism: the temptation to see Christian Hellenism as the historical evolution of classical Hellenism. This issue is particularly potent and controversial in debates on the issue of modern Greek identity, but will not concern us here.

---

[39] For a critique of Tatakis' search for an essence (in the sense of a specific, distinguishing feature) of the Byzantine philosophical tradition see Michele Trizio, "Byzantine Philosophy as a Contemporary Historiographical Project," *Recherches de Théologie et Philosophie Médiévales* 74:1 (2007), 248-57.

[40] Tatakis, *Byzantine Philosophy*, xiii.

With Tatakis we are approaching an opposite scheme to what has previously been called the Hellenization of Christianity, a reversal of the term and its construction as the Christianization of Hellenism. Georges Florovsky is a representative of this position and writing a little later than Tatakis, in the 1950's, describes it as a process of transfiguration and re-orientation: "Ancient culture proved to be plastic enough to admit of an inner "transfiguration." ... Christians proved that it was possible to re-orient the cultural process, without lapsing into a pre-cultural state, to reshape the cultural fabric in a new spirit. The same process which has been variously described as a "Hellenization of Christianity" can be construed rather as a "Christianization of Hellenism."[41] Florovsky's reorientation can be seen specifically as a response to Harnack's advocacy of a Hellenization of Christianity.[42] In this he is also followed by John Meyendorff, for whom the effort of the Church Fathers to formulate Christianity in the categories of Hellenism is a legitimate and necessary enterprise since the Christian faith needed to rethink itself in light of changing cultural patterns.[43] Florovsky qualifies

---

[41] Georges Florovsky, "Faith and Culture," *St. Vladimir's Seminary Quarterly* 4:1-2 (1955), 40. "The Christian reception of Hellenism was not just a se[r]vile absorption of an undigested heathen heritage. It was rather a conversion of the Hellenic mind and heart." Id. "Christianity and Civilization," *St. Vladimir's Seminary Quarterly* 1:1 (1952), 14. Other advocates of Florovsky's position include I. Ramelli, "Origen, Patristic Philosophy and Christian Platonism," 260-1, who makes the argument that the Fathers were "allowed to take- as they felicitously did, in the most enlightened cases- all that Greek philosophy and culture had to offer, insofar as it was compatible with Christianity" and uses the examples of Origen and Gregory of Nyssa as Christian philosophers who "sought a continuity and a synthesis without renouncing their own Christian identity" since taking over Greek philosophy did not imply a rejection of Christianity or a detachment from its Jewish root because essentially Christianity "is neither Jewish nor Greek." It is interesting to note that in Ramelli's argument the language of appropriation (allowed to take, take over) is consistently used as if the Christians writers she refers to were partaking of something that was essentially alien to them.

[42] For an analysis of Florovsky's idea of Christian Hellenism as a reaction to Harnack's Hellenization of early Christianity and their classification as two extremes stemming from the Eastern Orthodox and Liberal Protestant traditions respectively see Paul Gavrilyuk, *Georges Florovsky and the Russian Religious Renaissance* (Oxford: Oxford University Press, 2014), 201-19. For other critiques of Florovsky's position see Brandon Gallaher, "'Waiting for the Barbarians': Identity and Polemicism in the Neo-Patristic Synthesis of Georges Florovsky," *Modern Theology* 27:4 (2011), 659–91; Paul Gavrilyuk, "Harnack's Hellenized Christianity or Florovsky's 'Sacred Hellenism': Questioning Two Metanarratives of Early Christian Engagement with Late Antique Culture," *St Vladimir's Theological Quarterly* 54:3–4 (2010), 323–44.

[43] John Meyendorff, *Byzantine Theology: Historical Trends and Doctrinal Themes* (New York: Fordham University Press, 1979), 2. But others choose to emphasize the difference in forms: "The Greek Fathers are of the unity of Hellenism, certainly, ... but they are no mere echo, even in their forms, of the Greek literature that had gone before them." Campbell, *The Greek Fathers*, 10.

his statement by two admissions: a) his plea for a return to Christian Hellenism is a plea for a return to "the tradition of the Eastern Fathers as opposed to Western medieval thought", and b) he also recognizes that on certain issues the Bible and Greek philosophy are wholly incompatible, such as on the issues of creation and freedom.[44]

Therefore, if we were to briefly summarize 20th century discussions of the relationship between Christianity and Hellenism, we would say that most scholars were working mostly on a model that required a positive synthesis of the two worldviews, which is in itself a reaction against Harnack's model of Hellenic corruption of Christian dogma by its interaction with Greek philosophy. Despite minor variations on this model, it seems that the authors more commonly used to exemplify it were either the Apologists, Clement, and Origen (or any combination of the above) for the first period of the synthesis and the Cappadocians for the later period. But as we saw earlier, within this broad consensus there was a range of views as to how exactly Christianity and Hellenism came together.

ii. Twenty-first century: Hellenism and religious and cultural identity

In the early twenty-first century, there has been a resurgence of interest regarding the relationship between Christianity and Hellenism, particularly in Late Antiquity, with much of the discussion being initiated by classicists and ancient historians, as opposed to historians of Christianity and theologians. The new focus has also shifted the locus of the discussion, which is often seen as primarily a broader conflict of worldviews and ideas (along with the practices that stem from these), instead of a clash between different religions. A prime mover (although not the originator) of this argument is Niketas Siniossoglou, representative of a position that perceives the issue as a conflict between Hellenism and *Judaeo-Christianity*,[45] a term that stresses Christianity's Jewish

---

[44] Meyendorff, *Byzantine Theology*, 24, with references to Florovsky's works.

[45] This is the term used by Siniossoglou. The term Judaeo-Christian is an early modern neologism, and was characteristically used in a negative sense by Friedrich Nietzsche.

heritage over and against the Hellenic intellectual paradigm.[46] It also claims that despite the Fathers' use of Greek language and acquaintance with classical literature, their worldview was so radically different from the Hellenic worldview that no notion of compatibility is applicable. Nevertheless, they did seek to find what was useful to them and utilized it for their own (usually apologetic) purposes. In Siniossoglou's narrative, this process of ambiguous cultural appropriation reaches its culmination with Theodoret of Cyrus, who is mostly following in Eusebius' footsteps. Siniossoglou uses Theodoret as a template for his general thesis on Hellenism and Christianity in late antiquity, something that is neither fair to Theodoret himself nor particularly useful in advancing the discussion on the subject. Although Siniossoglou is not the first to argue these points, we will start with him because his radical position is characteristic of what we call the conflict model and his arguments have a forcefulness that is rarely seen in previous scholarship on the subject. Furthermore, Siniossoglou's persistent fervor in "favoring one side of late antiquity's culture wars over the other,"[47] in the most positively explicit way will show how other scholars, who also favor one side over the other, do so implicitly whilst they reach similar conclusions. As we have seen both with Adolf Harnack and with responses to him, all too often scholars have examined this issue from the other side of these very same cultural wars. Precisely because Siniossoglou's point of view is in direct contrast to earlier approaches that considered that Greek philosophy and the ideals of *paideia* were preserved and even cultivated within early Christianity, his is an argument worthy of careful consideration.

One key aspect of Siniossoglou's argument is that similarities between Christianity and certain schools of ancient philosophy such as Platonism or Stoicism can only be

---

[46] For this view see Siniossoglou, *Plato and Theodoret*, xi.

[47] Aaron Johnson, Review of Niketas Siniossoglou, *Plato and Theodoret: The Christian Appropriation of Platonic Philosophy and the Hellenic Intellectual Resistance.* Cambridge Classical Studies. Cambridge/New York: Cambridge University Press, 2008. *Bryn Mawr Classical Review* 5/5/2009. Accessed on 16 December 2017, http://bmcr.brynmawr.edu/2009/2009-05-05.html.

attributed to a common use of vocabulary, but not meaning. Christians and Hellenes might use the same words, but they are describing entirely different things. The Christian appropriation of Greek philosophy is therefore limited to external structures and words, but not its substance.[48] According to Siniossoglou, the shift in meaning of the word *philosophia* is a classic case in point. This antithesis between Christianity and philosophy occurs through a strategy devised by Christians against both their Jewish and pagan opponents: the appropriation of their own texts in order to undermine their ideas, and therefore turning their own weapons against them.[49] In this process the meaning of the text changed, and different hermeneutical strategies (such as allegory) brought forth an entirely different interpretation of the texts. The term *philosophia* is also appropriated by Christians to describe the Christian way of life and it gradually loses its original connotations. Another example of the Christians' strategy, according to Siniossoglou, is the way they used Plato and his texts: while the Neoplatonists were attempting an exegesis of the whole Platonic corpus by trying to interpret its intended meaning, Christians only sought what was useful in Plato's texts for their own religion.[50] Furthermore, the fact that sometimes the Church Fathers showed disdain and hostility towards the Greek philosophical tradition is introduced by Siniossoglou as further proof of the fact that they cannot be considered legitimate heirs of Hellenic *paideia*.[51] Finally, another factor that prevents any possible synthesis (or even

---

[48] Siniossoglou, *Plato and Theodoret*, xi.

[49] Ibid., 13.

[50] Ibid., 23. Siniossoglou calls the Neoplatonic attitude towards the platonic corpus the principal question of exegesis and describes the Christian attitude as linked to a rhetorical agenda. However, I am not entirely convinced that the Christians were the only ones with an agenda when it came to the interpretation of Plato.

[51] Siniossoglou, *Plato and Theodoret*, 54, where Siniossoglou also claims that these passages are rarely cited. Although I doubt that this is the case, every major criticism of Greek philosophy in John's corpus will be mentioned in this study. Another fact that Siniossoglou does not mention is the fact that this display of disdain and hostility, or "rhetoric of abuse" in Wilken, is not peculiar at all in the context of polemics in the fourth century. Robert L. Wilken, *John Chrysostom and the Jews: Rhetoric and Reality in the Late Fourth Century* (Berkeley: University of California Press, 1983), 122-3, provides many examples from both Chrysostom's and Julian's works and places their comments in their rhetorical contexts, while also indicating that the foes in this case were real, not imaginary.

symbiosis) between Hellenism and Christianity, at least at the philosophical level, is the latter's exclusivity, especially when it is contrasted to the universal dimensions of Hellenism.[52] Siniossoglou poses the two as completely separate entities, "neither artificial nor socially constructed."[53]

One can offer many criticisms of and counterarguments to Siniossoglou's case. For example, one can easily cite Julian using a Christian idea (the relationship between the destruction of the temple in Jerusalem and the legitimacy of Jewish law) and turning it against Christianity.[54] Allegory was by no means a Christian invention either and many non-Christians utilised it in their exegesis of ancient texts and we know of allegorical readings of Homer from the 1st cent. B.C.[55] The ecumenical dimensions that Christianity adopted from a very early stage (by using Greek, for example), which contributed to its expansion in the Roman Empire, are a fact that Siniossoglou neither mentions nor discusses.[56] Others have also mentioned certain problematic readings of Theodoret's text and the lack of analysis in terms of how Neoplatonists used (or did not use) the term "Hellene" to describe themselves.[57]

---

[52] Ibid., 106.

[53] Ibid., 238.

[54] Wilken, *John Chrysostom and the Jews*, 143. Chrysostom would not really mind the accusation. In fact, he would claim that he is just following in Paul's footsteps, as this is exactly what the latter did when conversing with the Athenians. See *Princ. Act. hom.* 1.3 (PG 51:72): Εἰσῆλθεν εἰς τὴν πόλιν ὁ Παῦλος, εὗρε βωμὸν ἐν ᾧ ἐπεγέγραπτο, Ἀγνώστῳ Θεῷ. Τί ἔδει ποιῆσαι; Ἕλληνες πάντες ἦσαν, ἀσεβεῖς πάντες. Τί οὖν ἐχρῆν ποιῆσαι; Ἀπὸ Εὐαγγελίων διαλεχθῆναι; Ἀλλὰ κατεγέλων. Ἀλλ' ἀπὸ προφητικῶν, καὶ τοῦ νόμου γραμμάτων; Ἀλλ' οὐκ ἐπίστευον. Τί οὖν ἐποίησεν; Ἐπὶ τὸν βωμὸν ἔδραμε, καὶ ἀπὸ τῶν ὅπλων τῶν πολεμίων αὐτοὺς ἐχειρώσατο.

[55] For allegorical Neoplatonist readings of Homer see Robert Lamberton, *Homer the Theologian: Neoplatonist Allegorical Reading and the Growth of the Epic Tradition* (Berkeley, CA: University of California Press, 1989).

[56] "Next to the obvious acceptance of elements of Greek philosophy operated another, underground tendency to Hellenize the Christian religion. Indeed, sometimes the fiercest opponents of traditional Hellenism were those substantially inspired by the ancient Greek spirit in its internal and ecumenical dimension." Dimitris J. Kyrtatas and Spyros I. Rangos, *Η Ελληνική Αρχαιότητα: Πόλεμος-Πολιτική-Πολιτισμός* [*The Greek Antiquity: War-Politics-Civilization*], (Thessaloniki: Institute of Modern Greek Studies, 2010), 403, my translation. The lack of these ecumenical structures, as well as other issues with the old religion and its inability to compete with Christianity after a certain point are discussed in Garth Fowden, "Polytheist Religion and Philosophy," in *The Cambridge Ancient History, vol. XIII: The Late Empire, A.D. 337-425*, eds. Averil Cameron and Peter Garnsey (Cambridge: Cambridge University Press, 1998), 559-60.

[57] Both points mentioned (with examples) in Johnson's review. See n. 47 above.

It is clear that in this debate Siniossoglou has chosen a specific side and his arguments are certainly a reflection of that. Siniossoglou's position can be labelled as the conflict model and it certainly does not lack support in scholarship. His view is just one of the most recent examples of such an argument. For example, a more radical version of this position argues that while no national, racial, social or cultural elements could prevent someone from becoming a Christian, no elements of origin or tradition could theoretically be combined with this new identity. It is also argued that with Christianity humanity was stripped from its [national] traditions, and humans became the centre of the universe and God's main preoccupation. By abandoning the Hellenic tradition of searching for God in nature or within ourselves and trying to transcend our mortal limitations, God and his representatives are now the ones concerned with human salvation, with what the authors of this position call "a characteristic tendency towards weakness (mercy, compassion, love)."[58]

Siniossoglou's argument on Christianity's appropriation of Greek culture has been previously presented by Polymnia Athanassiadi, who, despite calling John Chrysostom "a man in whom culture, literary talent and rhetorical skill combined to form the ideal late antique intellectual," also talks about an attempt by Christians such as Basil of Caesarea "to rob the Hellenes of their culture" in the way they read and interpreted Greek texts from antiquity.[59]Athanassiadi presents Byzantium as a systematic persecutor of the spirit of Hellenism. Specifically, she argues that Chrysostom's advice on avoiding the classics to parents regarding the education of children by grammarians[60]

---

[58] Kyrtatas and Rangos, *Η Ελληνική Αρχαιότητα*, 408-9. The identification of Christian virtues as signs of weakness and as the exact opposites of the classical virtues is Nietzschean in origin.

[59] Polymnia Athanassiadi-Fowden, *Julian and Hellenism: An Intellectual Biography* (Oxford: Clarendon Press, 1981), 1,10.

[60] "What is the use of sending our children to the grammarian, where, before learning their texts, they will acquire wickedness and, in their desire to receive a trifle, they will lose the most important thing, all the vigour and health of their soul?" *Adv. opp. vit. mon.* 3.11 (PG 47:367; trans. Athanassiadi, *Julian and Hellenism*, 1). Obviously, Chrysostom's view is presented completely outside its context. This phrase, in its proper context, was not a question on the value of the classics (as it is very clear that Chrysostom is discussing education), but an exhortation to parents to pay close attention to the formation of their

was not the policy adapted by the Eastern Empire. Instead, the policy chosen was one of compromise, in the sense that while the classics remained a part of the curriculum, their spirit was lost. This was a policy devised by "cunning men like Basil of Caesarea, Socrates Scholasticus and Theodoret of Cyrrhus" and safeguarded a place in the Byzantine curriculum "for the ghosts of the classical authors."[61] Similarly to Siniossoglou, Athanassiadi constructs a radical dichotomy that sees the main protagonists as cultural appropriators, conquerors of a culture that was not theirs for the taking, simultaneously persecuting and usurping Hellenism to adapt it to their purposes.[62] However, as previous criticisms of the conflict model have indicated, this approach fails to do justice to the complexity and nuances of ancient sources, whilst it has also been judged as inadequate "for any analysis of cultural conflict."[63] Others have used similar arguments to Siniossoglou and Athanassiadi. However, we think it is worthy to focus on Siniossoglou in particular because we consider him to be the logical culmination of these previous arguments, and at the same time an even more extreme proponent of the clash between Christianity and Hellenism. In his narrative, Christianity is not just appropriating texts; it is represented as being in a constant war against Hellenism, and attempts to extinguish it by any means necessary, even by turning its own weapons against it.

---

children's virtue and not to rely exclusively on their formal education, which might make them skilled in speech but wicked as individuals. However, in Athanassiadi's interpretation Chrysostom gives a warning "that the price of a cultivated mind was for the Christian the loss for his soul" (ibid., 19), which is, among other things, a complete misrepresentation of his argument.

[61] Athanassiadi, *Julian and Hellenism*, 19. Gregory Nazianzus, *Or.* 4.5 (SC 309.92) famously responded to a similar challenge by Julian, when he complained that he "barred us from rhetoric [*logoi*] as though we were stealing someone else's goods." In this respect, the appropriation argument is just a repetition of Julian's order in *Ep.* 36 (LCL 157:120) that the Christians should only teach the classics if they show appropriate piety towards the gods.

[62] Cf. Garth Fowden, *The Egyptian Hermes: A Historical Approach to the Late Pagan Mind* (Princeton, NJ: Princeton University Press, 1993), 73: "By Late Antiquity most of the leading exponents of Hellenism were orientals. Inheriting a tradition which once had professed respect for the wisdom of the Orient from a safe distance, they tipped the whole centre of gravity eastwards... Hellenism, then, was held captive by those it had conquered."

[63] Johnson, "Hellenism and Its Discontents," 438.

Finally, other scholars have described the attitudes of Christian writers of the fourth and fifth centuries towards Hellenism and classical culture as inherently opportunistic[64] and even schizophrenic, because of their simultaneous "appropriation" and condemnation of it.[65] Although these arguments can already be found in the conflict model, we refer to them separately as they do not form part of a larger narrative, as was the case with Siniossoglou and Athanassiadi. However, they do seem to rest on a fundamental assumption of a conflict between Christianity and Hellenism or classical culture.

Nonetheless, conflict is not the only model used to describe the relationship between Hellenism and Christianity.[66] There is another model, which, although realizing the varied positions of both pagans and Christians on different issues, does not believe that there was a consistent or organized pagan opposition against Christianity, as assumed in the narratives of, among others, Siniossoglou and Athanassiadi: it is a model based on the assumption of co-existence, and has been supported by Yannis Papadogiannakis.[67] It mainly sees the pagan reaction in either "covert polemical allusions" or "*damnatio* by

---

[64] Pauline Allen, "Some Aspects of Hellenism in the Early Greek Church Historians," *Traditio* 43 (1987), 371: "On the one hand, tacitly recognizing that it [Greek learning] is indispensable for the Christian; on the other, impugning it freely in arguments against the pagans." Another common *topos* to writers of the same period is the view that "Greek learning was not totally harmful, and could in fact be serviceable to the Christian" (ibid., 373).

[65] Averil Cameron, *Byzantine Matters* (Princeton, NJ: Princeton University Press, 2014), 54: "The term [Hellenism] is also commonly used instead of "classical" in discussions of the education and culture of Christian patristic writers .... Christian intellectuals and writers had a schizophrenic relation to classical culture and aspired to and sought to appropriate and exploit Greek *paideia* while at the same time condemning it."

[66] In her earlier works Averil Cameron has been critical of the models we have been describing so far and proposed alternative ways of looking at the issue: "The questions have changed, and the answers will no longer be found in the old places, whether in the traditional formulation of Christianity's "relation to" or "conflict with" classical culture or in the much-studied yet limited field of Christian-pagan polemic; we shall instead look to the broader techniques of Christian discourse and its reception in the social conditions of the empire." Averil Cameron, *Christianity and the Rhetoric of Empire: The Development of Christian Discourse* (Berkeley: University of California Press, 1991), 20.

[67] That includes both practical as well as literary opposition. Papadogiannakis is not arguing against the existence of opposition *per se*. However, he does not believe that it was a constant or that it was part of a larger scheme. As an example of the inconsistency he mentions, we could refer to the different literary attitudes towards Christians by authors like Libanius or Porphyry and their respective styles and points of opposition.

exclusion from narratives."[68] This model can be tentatively called the symbiotic model, because symbiosis primarily denotes interaction, which can at times be either irenic or polemical, but can also be both. It does not overemphasize the conflict at the expense of points of agreement and has a more inclusive understanding of the multifaceted nature of Hellenism. In this model's narrative, Hellenism included, besides pagan religious beliefs and adherence to cults, a thorough acquaintance with ancient Greek literature and a good command of the Greek language. According to Yannis Papadogiannakis, it is this multivalence of Hellenism that "rendered it inherently ambiguous and therefore subject to competing conceptualizations,"[69] thus making it difficult to draw the line between its religious and non-religious elements. He concludes that this led to a large variety of definitions and understandings of the pagan elements of Hellenism among the different Christian authors. It also points to the "intimate relations" between Greek classicism and Greek Christianity, relations that were forged through the common education that both pagan and Christian elites shared in the fourth century and the common cultural framework of the eastern parts of the Empire.[70]

Papadogiannakis' work on Theodoret is not the only one that examined the relationship through these lenses. Aaron Johnson has described Hellenism in late antiquity as a "sort of rhetorical and conceptual toolbox."[71] The educated elite of the period, which included Christians and non-Christians alike, could draw from a large variety of texts to make an argument relevant to their case, whether that was a

---

[68] Papadogiannakis, *Christianity and Hellenism*, 15.

[69] Papadogiannakis, *Christianity and Hellenism*, 23.

[70] Chrysostomus Baur, *John Chrysostom and His Time, vol. 1: Antioch*, trans. Mary Gonzaga (London: Sands, 1959), 9. These intimate relations are clearly mapped by the sober assessment of Socrates, when he talks about Julian's edict on the teaching of Greek literature: 'the Christians beginning afresh to imbue their minds with the philosophy of the heathens, this works out no benefit to Christianity, for pagan philosophy teaches Polytheism, and is injurious to the promotion of true religion.' This objection I [Socrates] shall meet with such considerations as at present occur to me. Greek literature certainly was never recognized either by Christ or his Apostles as divinely inspired, nor on the other hand was it wholly rejected as pernicious. And this they did, I conceive, not inconsiderately. For there were many philosophers among the Greeks who were not far from the knowledge of God..." *Hist. eccl.* 3.16.1 (GCS NF1:211; NPNF 2-2:87).

[71] Johnson, "Hellenism and Its Discontents," 439.

philosophical argument, an oration, writing historiography, novels, apologetic treatises, et al. One common feature of all the above is obviously the use of the Greek language. But this was not the sole tool: others, Johnson argues, included "the citation of or allusion to classical authors; mythological exempla; genealogies; ... invocation of historical figures or events; personal dress or grooming ... and, at the most basic level, generic conceptual categories for classifying the world (*genos, ethnos,* and so on)." While none of the tools was essentials for the toolbox, Hellenism itself could combine many of these for different purposes, which included the negotiation of identity, making and supporting an argument, or just displaying erudition. At the same time, Johnson emphasizes the fact that the verb *ἑλληνίζειν* as well as the term Hellene were markers of multiple identities, in both Christian and non-Christian writings (such as Julian's): it denoted religious, ethnic, and cultural identities, along with the standard topographical designation and the sense of speaking Greek.[72]

To summarize: we have referred to two models that we have been able to identify as tendencies among scholars on the subject of Christianity and Hellenism in late antiquity. One that considers the relationship through the lenses of conflict and polemic and an imbalance of power, and another that emphasizes a more even-handed interaction and symbiosis. This is obviously a broad classification, and there are numerous subdivisions and further nuances within each position. However, three points of note emerge from this discussion. First, as we have already indicated, the issue is even more increasingly important in discussions of modern Greek identity, and this is one of the reasons that Greek scholars have the lion's share in this initial survey. The reason for this is related to the model one follows and the ways it affects their position in terms of the diachronic nature of Hellenism and its existence. For example, Kaldellis' argument that Hellenism was in "limbo" for about six centuries (from 400-1000 AD)

---

[72] Johnson, "Hellenism and Its Discontents," 448.

certainly colours his interpretation of Byzantium and the way it is related to modern Greek identity. This is particularly pertinent for the conflict model. While classicists (such as Ramsay McMullen and Fergus Millar) have previously laid the groundwork by interpreting the relationship as a clash between Christianity and Hellenism, they did not always consider the implications their stance would have for interpreting Hellenism in Byzantium and modern Greece. By contrast, this question is obviously of great importance for Greek scholars, particularly when it comes to debates about ancient, medieval and modern Greek identity and their relationship to each other.

Second, despite and beyond the different models, Hellenism has a very large number of definitions. As we have seen, it has been considered (and still is) a national, cultural, philosophical and religious identity and its legacy has been contested throughout history.[73] If we aim to understand these different meanings we must primarily consider why Hellenism maintained its status as an ideal for such a long time and why it has provoked such strong reactions from people who have been either for or against it. Thirdly, however, this binary does not necessarily describe everyone's stance. There have been ancient figures that would not fit the for/against dichotomy because they could both appreciate certain aspects of Hellenism and at the same time be critical of others. It is very possible to appreciate something while being critical of it, and Hellenism's non-dogmatic and flexible nature left plenty of space for any attitude. Individuals from different sides and of varied religious persuasions might all have different senses of what exactly was bound up in the concept of 'Hellenism', and most of them did indeed, as it was a discursive category, not a clear set of things. Finally, in

---

[73] Kaldellis, *Hellenism in Byzantium*, 394. But see Cameron, *Byzantine Matters*, 56, for a critique of a scholarly tendency shared between Kaldellis, Siniossoglou and Athanassiadi, which attempts to disassociate Christianity from Byzantium and their construction of Hellenism as either a movement of rationalism and dissent (Kaldellis and Siniossoglou) or its connection with a high valuation of late antique platonism (Athanassiadi). For all three authors, Christian Hellenism is not just an impossibility, but a contradiction in terms, and it becomes more obvious in their efforts to look for Greek continuity either through a dubious link between philosophy and identity or by emphasizing the Roman identity of Orthodoxy as an oppositional power to Hellenism.

many of the scholarly treatments we have already referred to one name is notably conspicuous by its absence. John Chrysostom is usually nowhere to be found in scholarly master narratives that describe Christianity and Hellenism in late antiquity, and, if he is, it is often due to philological studies that focus on his language. We will start with this aspect of scholarship then, as it provided the starting point for further elaborations on the subject.

b. John Chrysostom and Hellenism

i. John Chrysostom and the Greek classical tradition: Rhetoric

Chrysostom's interaction with and influence by ancient Greek culture has been relatively well documented in studies that range from ancient Greek philology to patristics. While there are many studies on Chrysostom's language, relations to rhetoric and philosophy, as well as other aspects of Hellenic culture, there has been no systematic attempt to collect all these disparate elements and write a study that will provide a fair and analytic framework concerning Chrysostom's engagement with Hellenism.[74] The image of Chrysostom as the Christian classicist *par excellence* is still echoed in the assessment of one of the greatest philologists of the late nineteenth to the early twentieth century, U. von Wilamowitz-Moellendorf:

> Chrysostom is an almost pure Atticist ... All the Hellenes of his century are barbarian bunglers compared to this Syrian Christian, who merits a higher rating than Aristides, and in point of style can be compared with Demosthenes. In the Homilies ... pure Attic Greek dominates everywhere. In the great orations ... the musical periods roll out, the embellishment grows even richer, but never is there any clatter of rhyme or cadence. And this Attic style is not merely an artificial style acquired by study: it is the harmonious expression of an Attic soul. *How* anything like that is possible may be explained by him who can make the whole man comprehensible through his works. *That* it is possible, even a fleeting acquaintance can testify, and pay homage to the classic writer who is here at the same time a classicist.[75]

---

[74] In any similar endeavour, it is also important to remember that, as Raymond Laird, *Mindset, Moral Choice and Sin in the Anthropology of John Chrysostom* (Strathfield: St. Pauls, 2012), 6, argues, "In any analytical research of Chrysostom's corpus, his focus upon pastoral needs should never be overlooked."

[75] "Die Griechische Literatur des Altertums," in *Die Griechische und Lateinische Literatur und Sprache*, ed. Paul Hinnenberg (Leipzig: Teubner, 1912), 296 as cited in Baur, *John Chrysostom*, 1:305. Cf. T.D. Barnes' comment of Chrysostom as "the liveliest and most accomplished orator since

Willamowitz's emphasis in the passage above is on the aesthetic pleasure derived from reading Chrysostom's elegant Greek prose. It can also be considered an indirect response to accusations that Chrysostom was hostile to Greek learning and rhetoric.[76] The claim that Chrysostom, one of the finest rhetoricians in the history of Christianity, was hostile to rhetoric is patently absurd. Even in texts where Chrysostom seems to show hostility, it is with some of the possible outcomes of a rhetorical education and not rhetoric itself. A striking example of this subtle difference in attitude comes from *Against the Opponents of Monastic Life*: "When parents urge their children to study rhetoric (ὑπὲρ τῆς τῶν λόγων σπουδῆς), all they say are words like these: "A certain man, of low estate, born of lowly parents, after achieving the power that comes from rhetoric, obtained the highest positions, gained great wealth, married a rich woman, built a splendid house, and is feared and respected by all."[77] Furthermore, in his *Address on Vainglory and the Right Way for Parents to Bring Up their Children* John provides further information about the priorities of some parents of his day- although he does not explicitly state whether he is talking about Christians or not: "In our own day every man takes the greatest pain to train his boy in the arts and in literature and speech, but to exercise this child's soul in virtue, to that no man any longer pays heed."[78] This view might have led to certain members of his audience thinking that John espoused the

---

Demosthenes", in *The Funerary Speech for John Chrysostom*, ed. and trans. Timothy D. Barnes and George Bevan (Liverpool: Liverpool University Press, 2013), 2. A similar assessment is also almost always a feature of histories of Christian literature: "Chrysostom's speeches fascinate both by their contents and their effective eloquent presentation. His style combines the Christian spirit with Greek beauty of form." Berthold Altaner, *Patrology*, 5th ed., trans. Hilda C. Graff (Freiburg: Herder, 1960), 377.

[76] For the first accusations against Chrysostom as hostile to Greek learning and rhetoric, dating back to 1891, see Margaret Mitchell, *The Heavenly Trumpet: John Chrysostom and the Art of Pauline Interpretation* (Louisville, KY: Westminster John Knox Press, 2002), 23.

[77] *Adv. opp. vit. mon.* 3.5 (PG 47:357; *John Chrysostom, A Comparison between a King and a Monk/Against the Opponents of the Monastic Life: Two Treatises by John Chrysostom*, ed. and trans. David G. Hunter (Lewiston, NY: Edwin Mellen Press, 1988, 135).

[78] *Inan. glor. et ed. lib.* 18 (SC 188:100-2; trans. M.L.W. Laistner, *Christianity and Pagan Culture in the Roman Empire, together with an English translation of John Chrysostom's "Address on Vainglory and the Right Way for Parents to Bring Up Their Children"*, Ithaca, NY: Cornell University Press, 1951, 95).

obliteration of the rhetorical schools, and to that he pre-emptively responds as follows: "I do not say this, but let us not destroy the edifice of virtue, nor bury the soul alive. When the soul is self-controlled, no harm will come from a lack of knowledge of rhetoric (λόγων); but when the soul is corrupted, the greatest damage will result, even if the tongue is quite sharp; indeed, the damage will be greater the more skilled in rhetoric he becomes. For when wickedness gains experience in speaking, it does far worse deeds than ignorance."[79] In other words, while rhetoric is no obstacle to the virtuous life, lack of rhetorical skill should be no cause of grief to those who do want to live in virtue because it has no effect to that whatsoever. Even if John's view does not glorify eloquence, it does not show a particularly hostile attitude towards it either. Hunter is of the opinion that behind this "attack on the pursuit of rhetorical education" is Libanius and his devotion to the cult of the logoi along with the place of rhetoric in the expression of piety to the gods. Nonetheless, Hunter agrees that Chrysostom does not attack "altogether the learning or practice of rhetoric", a position he believes would be found "impractical and, indeed, self-contradictory given his own ample use of sophistic devices..." Instead, Hunter argues, Chrysostom devalues rhetoric and "strips λόγοι of any moral value."[80] In our chapter on Chrysostom's reception of philosophy we will see how he also appealed to the Greek philosophers themselves in his polemic against rhetoric.

Nevertheless, the focus of this thesis is not the language of Chrysostom, as useful as that may be, but on the actual content of this language, especially since there already are many studies on Chrysostom's use of Greek from a rhetorical and philological point of view.[81] However, these studies mostly focus on individual works and to this day "a

---

[79] *Adv. opp. vit. mon.* 3.11 (PG 47:367; trans. Hunter, *A Comparison*, 148-9).

[80] Hunter, *A Comparison*, 34-5.

[81] Besides Ameringer, for whom see n. 84 below, we will mention a small sample here: Frederick Walter Augustine Dickinson, *The Use of the Optative Mood in the Works of St. John Chrysostom* (Washington, DC: Catholic University of America Press, 1926); Mary Albania Burns, *Saint John*

comprehensive analysis of the classical elements in Chrysostom's rhetoric is yet to be written."[82] The size of Chrysostom's corpus is probably the reason that this is not something that can be easily achieved by a single person. Previous attempts to study Chrysostom and Hellenism have either been very brief (e.g. a chapter in Baur's and Papadopoulos' biographies or journal articles)[83] or served as introductions to different translations of his works in various European languages (English, French, etc.), which, with few exceptions, obviously tend to emphasize what is presented in the translated work.[84] There has also been a tendency to categorize him as someone overly hostile to classical literature, while others tend to classify him alongside Origen and the Cappadocians as those primarily responsible for striking a compromise between Christianity and Hellenism.[85] Depending on the model each scholar chooses to follow

---

Chrysostom's Homilies on the Statues: A Study of their Rhetorical Qualities and Form (Washington, DC: Catholic University of America Press, 1930); William A. Maat, *A Rhetorical Study of St. John Chrysostom's De Sacerdotio* (Washington, DC: Catholic University of America Press, 1944), as well as most introductions to the critical edition of his works published in the Sources Chrétiennes series. I think that Hubbell's assessment of Chrysostom's rhetoric is still true: "in sentence structure and in the use of figures and other ornaments of style he was a true child of his age -a Christian orator speaking with all the art of the pagan." Harry M. Hubbell, "Chrysostom and Rhetoric," *Classical Philology* 19:3 (1924), 267.

[82] Hagit Amirav, "Exegetical Models and Chrysostomian Homiletics: The Example of Gen. 6.2," *Studia Patristica* 37 (Leuven: Peeters, 2001), 311. Similarly, and in regard to classical citations within John's corpus, Samuel Pomeroy, "Reading Plato Through the Eyes of Eusebius: John Chrysostom's Timaeus Quotations in Rhetorical Context," in *(Re)Visioning John Chrysostom: New Theories and Approaches*, eds. Wendy Mayer and Chris de Wet (Leiden: Brill, forthcoming), argues that what is needed is "detailed examination of the citation techniques and rhetorical purposes of individual sets of quotations and allusions in their literary settings."

[83] Stylianos Papadopoulos, *Άγιος Ιωάννης ο Χρυσόστομος, Τόμος Β: Η σκέψη του, η προσφορά του, η μεγαλωσύνη του* [*St. John Chrysostom, vol. 2: A Study on his Thought, Contribution, and Greatness*] (Athens: Apostoliki Diakonia, 1999), 9-18. There is also a book by Christos Krikonis entitled *Σχέση Ελληνισμού - Χριστιανισμού κατά τον Ιωάννη Χρυσόστομο* [*The Relationship between Hellenism and Christianity according to John Chrysostom*], (Athens: Apostoliki Diakonia, 2012) but the title is partially misleading since the largest and first part of the book is devoted to the relations between Christianity and Hellenism *before* Chrysostom while only the second and far too brief part actually deals with the subject matter to which the title of the book refers. For a good example of the influence (or lack thereof) of a Greek author, Plutarch in this case, on Chrysostom, see Geert Roskam, "Plutarch's Influence on John Chrysostom," *Byzantion* 85 (2015), 314-63. Roskam conclusively proves that despite certain superficial similarities (such as common moral preoccupations), there is no evidence of Plutarch's influence on Chrysostom, and the parallels used by scholars in the past just show that John was familiar with the intellectual traditions of his time.

[84] Many of the introductions to the critical editions of the *Sources Chrétiennes* series as well as translations of Chrysostom into English include smaller or larger pieces discussing various aspects of Chrysostom's reception of Hellenism.

[85] Numerous expressions of the former position will be cited throughout this review. For a representative example of the latter position see Thomas Edward Ameringer, *The Stylistic Influence of the Second Sophistic on the Panegyrical Sermons of St. John Chrysostom: A Study in Greek Rhetoric*

(conflict or symbiosis), Chrysostom's texts can support both, depending on the occasion. However, this creates a very fragmented image of Chrysostom the classicist, and a further aim of this study is to collect these fragments of John's own work in an attempt to recreate an intelligible image of his fascinating reconfiguration of Hellenism through the prism of the Christian tradition. Before we proceed to the different views of scholarship on the subject, we need to mention briefly that Hellenism in the late fourth century was something different from Hellenism in Byzantium, even if some scholars have taken Chrysostom's stance towards it as indicative and axiomatic of later attitudes. In places like Antioch, its existence is highlighted not only in the writings of Libanius and others, but also in education, ethics, art and architecture, as well as everyday values and attitudes. In short, "the culture was still informed by traditional pagan values, and Christians had no reason to suppose that a Christian emperor was to be a permanent feature of the Roman Empire."[86] Wilken provides many examples of Hellenism's enduring pervasiveness on everyday life and also makes the pertinent point that it was not perceived as a separate "religion" or faith of a particular community at the time, whilst also setting the tone of life in Antioch.[87]

As we mentioned already, previous scholarship has been thorough with aspects of Chrysostom's language and studies of individual texts have increased our understanding of his reception of Hellenism. Nevertheless, the identification of the need for a comprehensive analysis that would take into account (ideally) the whole corpus is not recent, even if it has been repeated again lately. More than 40 years ago, Robert Carter

---

(Washington, DC: Catholic University of America Press, 1921), 20. Glanville Downey, *A History of Antioch in Syria: From Seleucus to the Arab Conquest* (Princeton, NJ: Princeton University Press, 1961), 42, frames Chrysostom's writings as a paradigmatic illustration of the absorption of the best elements of Greek literature and philosophy in the Christian culture of the fourth century.

[86] Wilken, *John Chrysostom and the Jews*, xvii. Cf. ibid., 18: "Antioch, in spite of its large Christian population, still retained the marks of traditional Hellenism. The city had numerous temples and pagan shrines; it celebrated the ancient festivals and games associated with the Greek gods; its shrines were still the objects of pilgrimage. Its educational system was thoroughly Greek.".

[87] Wilken, *John Chrysostom and the Jews*, 16-26, "Traditional Hellenism in Antioch." For these two points see pages 21 and 30 respectively.

suggested different types of studies on Chrysostom's theology that he thought were needed for the future.[88] What interests us here is what he calls the "third term to which Chrysostom's thinking can be related": his cultural milieu. The reasoning behind a study which examines John's cultural environment is that it will enable scholars to see what is Christian and non-Christian or culturally conditioned in Chrysostom's thought.[89] To identify the non-Christian sources behind a Christian's thought is "important theologically, since not every thought of a Christian is necessarily a Christian thought."[90] Carter believed that future studies of Chrysostom's relation to Greek culture would enable us to find out whether "alien plantings found congenial soil in Christianity" but also to identify the fundamental differences (and accidental, as he calls them, similarities) between Scripture and Greek philosophy. As far as Chrysostom is concerned, he thought that by identifying the sources behind his thought we might accurately find which influence, philosophical or biblical, "is preponderant in Chrysostom's own thinking."[91] While Carter's terminology might seem to imply a third model regarding the relationship between Hellenism and Christianity, beyond conflict and symbiosis, it did not evolve into a fully-fledged thesis since this was not the purpose of his article. Still, we cannot help but point out that Carter's thought here is a logical fallacy. Even if we were able to identify everything that Chrysostom read, it still wouldn't mean that we have found the hierarchy, according to which his sources were arranged in his mind. By the same token, the fact that Plato is the most cited author in Chrysostom's corpus does not necessarily imply that he was more engaged with Platonism than with other philosophical schools. Nonetheless, the importance of Carter's proposition lies with the fact that he thought of Chrysostom as someone worth

---

[88] Robert Carter, "The future of Chrysostom studies: Theology and Nachleben," in *Συμπόσιον: Studies on St. John Chrysostom*, ed. Panayotis C. Christou (Thessaloniki: Patriarchal Institute for Patristic Studies, 1973), 129-136.

[89] Ibid., 132.

[90] Ibid.

[91] Ibid., 133.

studying in the larger context of the relationship between Christianity and Hellenism in late antiquity, something that the grand narratives published before his article did not consider.

ii. John Chrysostom and the Greek Classical Tradition: John's Reception of Greek Philosophy and Classical Culture

While we will try to summarize the general state of research, our focus will be his relationship with ancient Greek philosophy. This is because Hellenism is often identified with philosophy, as we have seen with both Siniossoglou and Athanassiadi, and Chrysostom's stance towards it is assessed based on his various remarks on different philosophers and some of their ideas. In our case, this is not what Markschies calls "an almost randomly chosen specific phenomenon of cultural contact."[92] In Chrysostom's corpus philosophy (both as a concept and as a word) plays an important role as a major force of Hellenism and philosophers and their ideas are often referred to as paradigmatic and/or emblematic of specific cultural positions and connotations. I do not agree with Markschies that the field which examines the reception of Greek philosophy in Christian theology is always an example of a "problematical application of the term [Hellenism]", particularly since he uses it as something that often points to "theological premises and even prejudices" but as we have seen these premises and prejudices are certainly not limited to theologians.[93] When we initially deal with Chrysostom's interaction with Greek philosophy, we might reach the same conclusion that Goulven Madec did in his study on St. Ambrose and philosophy, namely that "he seems to use the language and ideas of the philosophers more as literary ornamentation than as substantial arguments."[94] One thing to be said from the outset is that it is

---

[92] Markschies, "Does It Make Sense," 26.

[93] Ibid.

[94] Goulven Madec, *Saint Ambroise et la Philosophie* (Paris: Études Augustiniennes, 1974), 175, cited in Carol Harrison, *Augustine: Christian Truth and Fractured Humanity* (Oxford: Oxford University Press, 2000), 12. "It is true that the classical *philosophy* left no deep traces in Chrysostom." Baur, *John Chrysostom*, 1:310. The reasons for this, per Baur, are three: a) Chrysostom had "no special gift for real

generally agreed Chrysostom was never as comfortable with Greek philosophy as were

Clement, Origen, or the Cappadocians.[95] For example, he certainly does not seem to

have the comfort of a Clement, who could be "combining biblical and classical

terminology or moving seamlessly from a citation of a pagan author to a similar idea in

the Bible and vice versa."[96] It is certainly difficult to see Chrysostom as an heir of the

patristic tradition of attempting to harmonize the Bible with the philosophy and

literature of Hellenism or as a Christian Hellenist in his use of philosophy in the way

that Pelikan and Jaeger present the Cappadocians.[97] But to exclude him and the whole

of the Patristic tradition from the history of Hellenism is an entirely different matter,

---

philosophy" (it is not exactly clear what Baur means by "real" philosophy), b) he gave up his education with the sophists prematurely, and c) there were no first-rate philosophers alive in Antioch or even the whole Roman Empire (ibid.). Generalisations about Chrysostom's attitude towards philosophy and rhetoric can be traced back to Edward Gibbon, who accused him of "conceal[ing] the advantages which he derived from the knowledge of rhetoric and philosophy." Ch. 32, *History of the Decline and Fall of the Roman Empire vol. 3*, (London: 1781), 468. Gibbon was willing to admit that he was a stranger to Chrysostom's voluminous production and his opinion was based on what he read from the two "most judicious and moderate of the ecclesiastical critics," Erasmus and Dupin. A variation of this thesis are the accusations of opportunism and schizophrenia we saw in the first part of this chapter. Marius Soffray, "Saint-Jean Chrysostome et la Littérature Païenne," *Phoenix* 2:3 (1948), 82, points out that the first successful overturning of the traditional opinion (that Chrysostom was overly hostile against Hellenism and philosophy) was by Anton Nägele in his article "Johannes Chrysostomos und sein Verhältnis zum Hellenismus," *Byzantinische Zeitschrift* 12 (1904), 73-113, who argued that Chrysostom deserves a place next to Origen, Basil, and Augustine for striking a compromise between Hellenism and Christianity.

[95] "Of their sentiments [the Greek philosophers] he retained little admiration when he entered the Christian life and to their writings he probably seldom recurred for recreation, but his retentive memory enabled him to point and adorn his arguments with illustrations and quotations from them." P. R. Coleman-Norton, "St. Chrysostom and the Greek Philosophers," *Classical Philology* 25:4 (1930), 305. Coleman-Norton's opinion obviously completely overlooks Chrysostom's actual engagement with philosophical ideas and emphasizes their rhetorical usefulness instead. Chrysostom was definitely more outspoken and clear about the proper order that philosophy should have in someone's life, but did not explicitly argue against its existence. For a similar argument see D. Hunter, "Libanius and John Chrysostom: New Thoughts on an Old Problem," *Studia Patristica* 22 (Leuven: Peeters Press, 1989), 133, where Hunter claims that "Greek philosophers rarely receive a positive evaluation in his works" and that Chrysostom "almost always refers to the philosophers with disdain, except in the *Adversus Oppugnatores*."

[96] Trigg, *Origen*, 9. Clement was even a proponent of the idea that philosophy was a pedagogue to the Greeks just as the Torah was for the Jews in preparation for the coming of Christ (ibid.). Josef Lössl comments that Clement's technique "creates the impression that these two are treated as equally valid sources of divine revelation" and thinks that once early Christians from a Greco-Roman cultural background distanced themselves from Judaism then the only alternative as point of reference for their past was their pagan past. Josef Lössl, "An Inextinguishable Memory: 'Pagan' Past and Presence in Early Christian Writing," in *Being Christian in Late Antiquity: A Festschrift for Gillian Clark*, eds. Carol Harrison, Caroline Humfress, and Isabella Sandwell (Oxford: Oxford University Press, 2014), 81.

[97] For this tradition as well as other challenges the Christians had to face at the time see Papadogiannakis, *Christianity and Hellenism*, 24.

and one that would need serious justification in order to do so.[98] The fact that he

despised certain aspects of the classical heritage does not obviously turn him into a

champion of anti-Hellenism. His attachment to the classical tradition, as was the case

with other contemporary authors such as Gregory of Nazianzus, was at least

ambivalent.[99] But being ambivalent is far from being an anti-Hellene by nature, as some

scholars have tried to present him.

Thus, Baur was of the opinion that John was led astray in his attacks against the

"Greeks" and the "philosophers", because what he wished was to attack "polytheism,

pagan superstition and pagan immorality" but as is often the case these later

characteristics were so intertwined with the ancient Greek heritage that it becomes

difficult to distinguish what is really attacked.[100] I. Sandwell believes that Chrysostom

"had very little time for the literature and learning of classical literature" and compares

---

[98] It may or may not be significant, but two of the references to John in the *Synaxarium Ecclesiae Constantinopolitae* mention his classical education with no hint of conflict between this and his education in Christian literature: "from the beginning of his life he acquired a great love of letters and quickly read through all pagan and Christian literature" and "he investigated all the wisdom of the Greeks and became a pupil of the sophists Libanius and Andragathius in Antioch and then of those in Athens." Entries for 13 November, transl. Barnes and Bevan, *Funerary Speech*, 164-5. The reference to John studying in Athens is obviously inaccurate. For an alternative view on the historicity of John's studies in Athens see Trombley, *Hellenic Religion and Christianization*, 333-41. One of the accusations the monk Isaac brought against Chrysostom at the Council of the Oak was that he was being too welcoming to the Greeks: "that he received pagans [Hellenes] who had done a great deal of harm to the Christians," Photius, Bibl. 59 (Photius, *Bibliothèque vol. 1*, ed. René Henry, Paris: Belles Lettres, 1959, 56; trans. Barnes and Bevan, *Funerary Speech*, 157). Barnes (ibid., n. 30) has suggested that this is "probably a reference to John's granting of temporary asylum to the eunuch Eutropius in 399." Eutropius (and the handing over of a priest to him by Chrysostom, after which he was exiled) is mentioned by name in the first list of accusations against Chrysostom brought by his deacon, also named John (ibid., 155). I think the accusation can be taken at face value: Chrysostom was responsible for the conversion of Greeks to Christianity despite the fact that they might have been hostile to Christians in the past.

[99] Anthony Meredith described this attitude as "coolness" towards the classical tradition, and contrasted it with Basil of Caesarea's defensive and cautious attitude towards Hellenism, which rejected an uncritical absorption of Hellenism but also showed an evident affection for it. According to Meredith, it was this latter attitude that enabled the culture and philosophy of Hellenism to find "its most enduring home within the austere if discriminating embrace of the Church" after the demise of the remaining pagan faculties during the fifth and sixth centuries: Anthony Meredith, *Gregory of Nyssa* (London: Routledge, 1999), 10. Gregory of Nazianzus' principle for appropriating Greek paideia has been described as a method of avoiding the thorns while plucking the roses, with revelation being the criterion for both the roses and the thorns: *Faith gives Fullness to Reasoning: The Five Theological Orations of Gregory Nazianzen*, ed. Frederick W. Norris, trans. Lionel Wickham and Frederick Williams (Leiden: Brill, 1991), 45. Frances Young believes that Chrysostom "had a strongly ambivalent locus in relation to 'Greek' (pagan) culture, and his works suggest implicit criticism of Libanius." Frances Young with Andrew Teal, *From Nicaea to Chalcedon: A Guide to the Literature and its Background*, 2nd ed. (London: SCM Press, 2010), 207.

[100] Baur, *John Chrysostom*, 1:310.

his attitude with Basil of Caesarea's careful allowance of Greek learning as a "shadow outline of Christian virtue." One of the arguments that Sandwell uses to support her thesis is Chrysostom's alleged total rejection of Greek learning.[101] Finally, Soffray is more specific about what exactly Chrysostom rejected from classical culture and argues that the one branch of Greek culture that Chrysostom rejected overwhelmingly was sophistic rhetoric, specifically its artificial and verbose elements. Nevertheless, he refuses to call him an enemy of Hellenism and claims that John was sensitive to the artistic beauty of pagan literature and favourable to the use of profane rhetoric, but without going beyond the limits of utility and necessity and by refusing to see rhetoric as an end, like the Sophists did, but as a means.[102] John was a powerful preacher, and in his homilies we find not only echoes of the Scripture but also of many Greek authors: Homer, Aeschylus, Demosthenes, and Plato.[103] In this respect, John assimilated the heritage of pagan culture and "in the spirit of that culture, he tried to speak directly to men in order to improve their lives."[104] Nevertheless, this tension has not been directly addressed in scholarship, since Chrysostom's thought is usually made to fit pre-existing conceptions rather than analysed in its own terms.

As with almost every church father, different scholars have provided a variety of interpretations on the question of Chrysostom and Hellenism. According to C. Krikonis,

---

[101] Sandwell, *Religious Identity in Late Antiquity*, 152. Cf. Duane Garrett, *An Analysis of the Hermeneutics of John Chrysostom's Commentary on Isaiah 1 - 8 with an English Translation* (London: Edwin Mellen Press, 1992), 240: "Chrysostom was well read in the classics, but his attitude towards them ranged from indifference to complete disdain. His antagonism is in part due to the artificiality of his contemporaries' imitation of the classical style, which he found irksome."

[102] Soffray, "Saint-Jean Chrysostome et la Littérature Païenne," 83-5.

[103] For complete lists of Greek authors known and cited by Chrysostom see Baur, *John Chrysostom*, 1:306 and Coleman-Norton, "St. Chrysostom and the Greek Philosophers," *passim*. Plato is obviously the one cited more than the rest, in at least thirty citations according to Baur, ibid. Baur also includes several useful assessments of Chrysostom the classicist from scholars working in the early 20th century and devotes a small but substantial chapter to this topic. They are mostly interesting because through these we can discern which aspects of Chrysostom and Hellenism interested them most and identify gaps in knowledge that need to be filled by contemporary studies. Sometimes Chrysostom's quotations of classical sources, as e.g. Plato's *Timaeus*, come through a second-hand source, in this example, Eusebius of Caesarea. For a detailed argumentation in support of this see Pomeroy, "Reading Plato," *passim*. For the influence of authors such as Aristotle and Demosthenes on John's understanding of the concept of γνώμη see Laird, *Mindset, Moral Choice and Sin*, 157-91.

[104] De Romilly, *A Short History of Greek literature*, 219.

who is the only scholar who had addressed the issue of Chrysostom and Hellenism explicitly (although in a limited way), John criticized the "pernicious fruits" of Hellenism, the neglect of ethical education and its materialist mentality.[105] He is not hostile to ancient culture, but he is not an ardent supporter either.[106] For this scholar, Chrysostom is "mercilessly whipping" the sayings of Greek philosophers due to their "wrong-headed" beliefs and their immoral lives.[107] His polemics against Greek *paideia* may also be attributed to the fact that in his time, there was a real danger of a one-sided cultivation of the mind instead of the ethos and of a secularization of Christianity instead of the evangelical fervor that characterised the movement in its infancy.[108] To summarize, for Krikonis Chrysostom did not accept the incompatibility between Christianity and Hellenism but received whatever was useful to him, such as the language, the art of rhetoric, and some moral values such as virtue, prudence, and ontological thinking.[109]

This utilitarian type of reception of Hellenism into Christianity inevitably leads to a version of Christianized Hellenism. Krikonis further argues that through logical

---

[105] Krikonis, *Σχέση Ελληνισμού - Χριστιανισμού*, 13.

[106] A similar proposition also found in Ameringer, *The Stylistic Influence*, 21: "In the heat of battle he sometimes allows his zeal to carry him too far, to censure not only the errors and vices of paganism, but profane writers and literature in general... A deeper and more sympathetic study of his sermons would have revealed the fact that, though he is unsparing in his condemnation of pagan error and immorality, he is at heart not hostile to the refining and cultural influences of antiquity." In other words, a study of the context of Chrysostom's criticisms is a pre-supposition to any attempt to pronounce him the archenemy of Hellenism.

[107] Krikonis, *Σχέση Ελληνισμού - Χριστιανισμού*, 13.

[108] Ibid., 114. For a comparison of Origen's and Chrysostom's respective uses of paideia and their development of Christian equivalents see Jutta Tloka, *Griechische Christen, Christliche Griechen: Plausibilisierungsstrategien des antiken Christentums bei Origenes und Johannes Chrysostomos* (Tubingen: Mohr Siebeck, 2005).

[109] Krikonis, *Σχέση Ελληνισμού - Χριστιανισμού*, 117. Wendy Mayer has shown Chrysostom's philosophical eclecticism on issues of social teaching that would be of concern to both pagans and Christians: "On the topic of slavery, for instance, John will on one occasion use a Stoic model to argue that slavery is an *adiaphoron*, which has no bearing on the inner virtue of the Christian. On another occasion, he construes slavery within a Platonic framework to argue that the slave is a model of a properly philosophical life that every Christian should emulate. On yet another occasion he invokes an Aristotelean view of slaves, when he argues that they are passionate, not open to impression, intractable, and not very apt to receive instruction in virtue." Wendy Mayer, "The Audience(s) for Patristic Social Teaching," in *Reading Patristic Texts on Social Ethics: Issues and Challenges for Twenty-First-Century Christian Social Thought*, eds. Johan Leemans, Brian Matz, and Johan Verstraeten (Washington, DC: Catholic University of America Press, 2011), 87, with appropriate references to Chrysostom's texts.

progression this concludes with a Hellenic Orthodoxy.[110] He also maintains that because the problems of classical Greek philosophy were the problems faced by any spiritual man, it is therefore impossible to think of Hellenism separately from Orthodox Christianity and vice versa. In a way, Krikonis seems to be thinking that the Greek spirit was absolutely indispensable for Christianity. Essentially Krikonis constructs a scheme of historical progression that begins with Classical Hellenism, is then followed by Christian Hellenism and finally concludes with Hellenic Orthodoxy (which obviously happens after the Schism of 1054), which exists to this day. Interesting as this last thesis may be, it will not concern us here, although it should be pointed out that the essential component in Krikonis' case always seems to be Hellenism. As we mentioned previously, these statements have more to do with issues in modern Greek identity than Hellenism in late antiquity. However, we see in this as well as in other works a discussion of the compatibility or incompatibility between Christianity and Hellenism, and as far as we are aware there has been no systematic attempt to answer the following questions: why exactly must these two systems of thought be compatible or incompatible? Are synthesis or antithesis the only alternatives?[111] It is hoped that this thesis will provide an initial framework that will partially give a response to these questions.

Chrysostom's engagement with Hellenism and classical culture takes place in many of his works, even in some that initially would not appear to be fit for such a purpose.[112]

---

[110] Krikonis, *Σχέση Ελληνισμού - Χριστιανισμού*,118-9.

[111] Or, in B. Leyerle's words, "whether Chrysostom was "for" or "against" classical culture." *Theatrical Shows and Ascetic Lives: John Chrysostom's Attack on Spiritual Marriage* (Berkeley: University of California Press, 2001), 207.

[112] Such as *A Comparison between a King and a Monk and Against the Opponents of the Monastic Life*. See Hunter, *A Comparison*, 2. These works alongside other similar treatises substantiates the claim of J. H. W. G. Liebeschuetz, *Ambrose and John Chrysostom: Clerics between Desert and Empire* (Oxford: Oxford University Press, 2011), 133, that "as a rule, the treatises contain more references and stylistic allusions to classical authors than the sermons." A simple skimming through the Sources Chrétiennes editions of some of John's works should be enough to show this. However, this distinction (between orally delivered sermons and literary treatises written for a smaller audience) has not been considered in discussions of John's reception of classical culture.

Overall, this engagement is usually with the personalities of the philosophers, and with some of their ideas, particularly those concerned with ethics. Chrysostom does not appeal to the philosophers too often (with the exception of the *Against the Opponents of Monastic Life*) and spends much of his time criticizing them, either for their moral failings, or, when that does not work as easily, as in the case of Diogenes, by claiming that their 'virtue' was a result of their vainglory.[113] Sometimes he would also invoke them as positive examples, particularly when he wanted to make a point about exemplary behavior and wished to show that this was not an exclusively Christian phenomenon but could also be found among the pagans.[114] His criticism also involved some of his contemporaries, such as his teacher Libanius and Julian the Emperor, and could be either implicit or explicit.[115] We should not overlook that Chrysostom's criticism against the pagans was often of a rhetorical and hyperbolic nature, nor should we ignore the historical context of many of his critiques. In the words of David Hunter,

> pagans such as Julian and Libanius were no less critical of immoral behavior than the Christian preacher. They, too, condemned the pursuit of unjust wealth. They also abstained from the sexual promiscuity associated with the theatre, dancers, and mimes. They, too, criticized the widespread practice of pederasty. Julian, in particular, was almost prudish in his observance of sexual continence, as Libanius pointed out.[116]

If that was the case, one may ask, why was there so much polemic between them? In Hunter's view, who pays particular attendance to the historical and literary context of the period, the main difference is to be found in their respective attribution of what they

---

[113] Hunter, *A Comparison*, 31.

[114] Derek Krueger, "Diogenes the Cynic Among the Fourth Century Fathers," *Vigiliae Christianae* 47:1 (1993), 37.

[115] *The Demonstration against the Pagans that Christ is God* being a case of the former and the *Discourse on Blessed Babylas* of the latter. According to Hunter, what both works have in common is "Chrysostom's apologetic arguments against the Hellenic tradition [which] involved a rejection of the moral value of Greek literature and an assertion of the moral benefits of Christianity." Hunter, *A Comparison*, 47. The lack of correspondence between Libanius and Chrysostom, despite their previous relationship, has been attributed to "Chrysostom's relative apathy for the Classics." Jaclyn L. Maxwell, *Christianization and Communication in Late Antiquity: John Chrysostom and his Congregation in Antioch* (Cambridge: Cambridge University Press, 2006), 39. One could of course argue that the surviving correspondence of both Libanius and Chrysostom is not always about the classics and this cannot possibly be the reason they did not correspond.

[116] Hunter, *A Comparison*, 55-6.

saw as the reasons for society's moral decadence: for Chrysostom, pagan culture was to be blamed for many societal evils, while for Julian and Libanius, the Christians were fundamentally responsible.[117] We also need to consider the particularities of Hellenism at the time of John Chrysostom. John's writings all come in the period after the pagan revival of Julian, who was supported by Libanius as they both claimed "the literary and cultural tradition of Greece as their own unique possession,"[118] although even Libanius was not enthusiastic about Julian's School Edict. In the works of Libanius, Julian becomes a moral paradigm that pinpoints the benefits of Hellenic culture and its pagan origins. Considering Chrysostom's extremely negative opinion of Julian, it is not surprising that his polemic would often include Libanius as well.

Other scholars have identified the influences of Greek philosophy on Chrysostom more precisely. For example, Elizabeth Clark sees Chrysostom's views on marriage and virginity as part of a discussion that borrows extensively from the traditions of Greek philosophy.[119] Clark also argues that Chrysostom sees Christian teaching "not so much as divine revelation as "philosophy,"[120] which implies that Christianity was comprised of both *theoria* and *praxis*, as were all philosophical systems. She also mentions a specific example, where John borrows Plato's image of reason as the charioteer that

---

[117] Ibid. But as D. Hunter remarks, "both pagans and Christians accepted the notion that moral conduct had apologetic value, and both sides claimed that the *paideia* on their own side produced the better results." Ibid., 58. In Chrysostom's case, his criticism against the Greeks did not prevent him from arguing against Christians in his own community, both in regard to their conduct to God and as to how their behavior affects Christianity in the eyes of outsiders. An example of this comes from *Adv. opp. vit. mon.* 1.2 (PG 47:321-2; trans. Hunter, *A Comparison*, 80-1): "For I am now forced to display our sins to all the pagans (Ἕλληνας), both those who live today and those who shall come, the very ones I am always ridiculing for their teachings no less than for the laxness of their way of life (τῶν δογμάτων οὐχ ἧττον ἐπὶ τῇ τοῦ βίου διασύρων ῥαθυμίᾳ). If any of them should realize that among the Christians there are some people so hostile to virtue and philosophy ... I am afraid that they will think that we Christians are not human, but beasts and wild animals in human for, some wretched demons, and enemies of the common nature, and they will make this judgement not only about those who are responsible, but about our entire people (ἔθνος)." The Christians in that case were the ones who opposed monasticism. This is a good example of the word *philosophia* used with a completely different way of life in mind.

[118] Hunter, *A Comparison*, 62. We should always keep in mind that Julian did not consider himself a Hellene, but a Roman, and called the Hellenes "our relatives," *Contr. Gal.* 200A (LCL 157:375).

[119] Elizabeth Clark, Introduction to John Chrysostom, *On Virginity; Against Remarriage*, trans. Sally Rieger Shore (Lewiston, NY: Edwin Mellen Press, 1983), xviii-xix.

[120] Ibid., xviii.

reins in the passions (*Phaedrus* 246A-248E) and applies it to the virgin who as a charioteer herself rules over the tongue, ears, feet, etc.[121] Clark uses this example to argue that "an appeal to revelation has here been supplanted by an appeal to Greek ethical writings."[122] The distinction between revelation and philosophy is an interesting one, although Clark does not seem to take into account the fact that the New Testament (or even the Old Testament) did not have the answer to every single problem that might arise in the Christian communities of later ages and therefore, an appeal to revelation was not always possible, unless one claimed access to extra-biblical revelation, which could often leads to charges of heresy, as for example with Montanism. Even within the context of exegesis and the fact that Chrysostom's most common exegetical device was to interpret the Bible through the Bible, there were still issues that did not necessarily have to be discussed in the context of revelation.

We can use the same argument for another of Clark's points, when she claims that "Chrysostom's treatment of riches is in strict accord with the classical praises of simple living that are more reminiscent of Stoic and Cynic diatribe than of the New Testament."[123] Our chapter on the affinities and the differences between John and the Cynics will offer a more nuanced picture to this claim, and it is our firm belief that in matters of ethics certain schools of thought within the tradition of Hellenism were riper for appropriation than others. It is not accidental that the image of Jesus as a "wandering Cynic" has been very popular among certain circles of scholars of the historical

---

[121] Clark, Introduction, xix. For the assimilation of the two platonic images of the "Wings of Love" and the "Charioteer of the Soul" in John's rhetoric see Constantine Bosinis, "Two Platonic Images in the Rhetoric of John Chrysostom: 'The Wings of Love' and 'the Charioteer of the Soul,'" *Studia Patristica* 41 (Leuven: Peeters, 2006), 433-8.

[122] Clark, Introduction, xix. Then again, if Chrysostom needed to enrich his repertoire, why would he not use examples from other popular works and stories as he does here with Plato, and why should this be thought of as supplantation? Cf. David Rylaarsdam, *John Chrysostom on Divine Pedagogy: The Coherence of his Theology and Preaching* (Oxford: Oxford University Press, 2014), 194: "[Chrysostom's] theological vision of formation was a synthesis of Scripture and classical paideia, a reading of the biblical text which was formed by and transformed Greco-Roman philosophical and rhetorical concepts."

[123] Clark, Introduction, xix.

Jesus.[124] Others have also been able to specifically identify Stoic influences in Chrysostom's critique of games and the way they could affect both bodily senses and the soul itself.[125] Clark's reading of Chrysostom, even if not always specific as to the precise philosophical influences, served as a good starting point for others to follow when discussing the influence of philosophy in Chrysostom's works.

Thus, in Wendy Mayer's most recent works Chrysostom is treated as a Christian philosopher within traditions of Greek medico-philosophical therapies, and even if he is working with a Christian framework in mind, the parameters are those of a "long-standing Hellenistic intellectual tradition."[126] For example, by comparing John and Libanius' understanding of *gnome* she concludes that what we see are two approaches "within Greek paideia", one Christian and one Greek, and with significant crossover in their approach to rhetoric as well. In treatises like John's *That No One Can Harm the Man Who Does Not Harm Himself*, Mayer sees an "understanding of the soul drawn almost entirely from a Greek *paideia*", which, even if he vehemently rejects it, implicitly influences the way he frames the Christian way of life.[127] On the other hand, Mayer does not deny the distinctiveness of John's philosophy, and identifies the following as some of its identifying marks: his appeal to the Scriptures and the biblical virtue exemplars rather than the Greek gods, philosophers, or heroes; his emphasis that philosophy is more appropriately aimed towards the heavenly rather than the earthly citizen; and his promotion of euergetism as something that needs to be directed towards the poor alone. What she claims instead is that John's "anti-intellectual stance", as

---

[124] For a description and critique of this movement see Ben Witherington III, *The Jesus Quest: The Third Search for the Jew of Nazareth* (Downers Grove, IL: InterVarsity Press, 1997), 58-92.

[125] Richard Lim, "Christianization, Secularization, and the Transformation of Public Life," in *A Companion to Late Antiquity*, ed. Philip Rousseau (Oxford: Wiley-Blackwell, 2012), 501.

[126] Wendy Mayer, "A Son of Hellenism: Viewing John Chrysostom's anti-intellectualism through the lens of Antiochene paideia," in *Intellektueller Austausch und religiöse Diversität in Antiochien 350-450/Intellectual Exchange and Religious Diversity in Antioch (CE 350-450)*, eds. Silke-Petra Bergjan and Susanna Elm (Tübingen: Mohr Siebeck, forthcoming).

[127] Wendy Mayer, "The Persistence in Late Antiquity of Medico-Philosophical Psychic Therapy," *Journal of Late Antiquity* 8:2 (2015), 338.

drawn by himself, is false, since his understanding of the role of the preacher as a medico-philosophical therapist was part of an existing intellectual tradition and not something outside of it or against it.[128]

While Clark and Mayer have placed Chrysostom firmly among traditions of Greek philosophy, Florovsky sees him as "an orator and a rhetorician" in the classical sense, while also claiming that he was not "a thinker or a philosopher."[129] Chrysostom is thus a true Hellenist who did not denounce his cultural heritage, and similarly to classical rhetoricians he was a teacher as well as a moralist and a preacher. His Hellenism is most obvious in his language and style and his writings exhibit some of the brilliance of classical Athenians like Demosthenes and Plato. At the same time, Florovsky claims, his Hellenism is not just external or superficial, even if he was never "stirred by the philosophical problems of Hellenism" or "forced to reconcile the Hellenist in himself with his Christianity." Thus, his Hellenism is also evident in his moralism, which Florovsky uses to explain the "acceptance and transformation of Stoicism by Christian ethics" and more particularly Chrysostom's contribution to this transformation in his constant efforts to teach "moral wisdom and nobility" and even his mysticism is described as "a mysticism of goodness, of good works and virtue."[130] Similarly to others, then, Florovsky emphasizes his engagement with Greek philosophical ethics and his mastery of the Greek language. However, he also explicitly calls him a rhetorician rather than a philosopher and claims that he was not particularly engaged with the philosophical problems in Hellenism.

This is an argument that has not gone unnoticed by those who follow the conflict model. There are references in Chrysostom's writings where he claims that the ἔξωθεν

---

[128] Mayer, "A Son of Hellenism."

[129] Florovsky, *The Eastern Fathers of the Fourth Century*, 241. Cf. Liebeschuetz, *Ambrose and John Chrysostom*, 251: "Chrysostom was not really interested in theology. He was basically a pastor and minister…"

[130] Florovsky, *The Eastern Fathers of the Fourth Century*, 240-1.

σοφία[131] does not even really benefit those who follow it, leaving them empty handed and without any profit.[132] The ἔξωθεν philosophers might say much, but none of it is sound.[133] N. Siniossoglou uses this reference (from his *Homilies on 1 Corinthians*) to argue that Chrysostom does not see much use in pagan philosophy.[134] However, if we look at the passage in its context we shall see that Chrysostom's argument is that the real wisdom is synonymous with the Gospel and the salvation offered by the cross, and that in comparison with that every other wisdom seems irrelevant or one might even say useless. It is relatively easy to take some of Chrysostom's statements out of their literary context and provide an inaccurate picture of his views on a range of issues, and

---

[131] The term ἔξωθεν, usually misleadingly translated as "pagan", is a reference to any kind of non-Christian wisdom, not necessarily Hellenic. Cf. a case where the term does seem to imply Hellenes: "Or haven't you heard the maxim the pagans tell: "from force of habit free will becomes second nature"," *De laud. Paul. hom.* 6.6 (SC 300:272; trans. Mitchell, *Heavenly trumpet*, 477). Cf. John referring to Moses as well versed in ἔξωθεν φιλοσοφία (of the Egyptians in this case) in *Mut. nom. hom.* 2.2 (PG 51:134). Even when used for pagans, ἔξωθεν does not carry the negative connotations that Christians would associate with paganism. It is simply a reference to those outside the Christian faith. For an example of the application of the term in the praise of widowhood among non-Christians, see *Ad. vid. iun.* 2 (SC 138:122). We should also note that the word pagan often appears in quotation marks in this thesis. This is because we usually consider it as either a wrong translation of a term that did not always necessarily mean pagan (such as Hellene or outsider) or because there are better ways to express what we mean: thus, ancient Greek philosophy is called exactly that, and not pagan philosophy, with the exception of explicit religious references in ancient philosophical writings, where one can use the term to describe pagan beliefs. Other works on Chrysostom have also indicated how problematic the term is, but for different reasons. Thus, Isabella Sandwell expresses her dissatisfaction for the use of the term pagan by referring to historians who consider it as a "Christian category that flattens out the diversity of religious experience of those in the Graeco-Roman world." She rejects other alternatives such as polytheists and her own refusal to use the term pagans comes down to the fact that it "suggests a Christian view that the world is permanently drawn into distinct, all-defining religious identities." *Religious Identity in Late Antiquity*, 10. A similar argument is also used by A. Cameron: "One gets into problematic areas with the application of the very terms "Christian" and "pagan," as though there always firm and easily detectable boundaries between them instead of a murky overlapping area." *Christianity and the Rhetoric of Empire*, 122. While I agree with both these statements, Cameron's argument can be more qualified by the observation that while "Christian" was a term used by various groups in antiquity as a way to describe themselves, we have no evidence of any group identifying as "pagan", which is purely a scholarly construct that can describe many different things. Similarly, the use of the term "Greek" does not always indicate that John is talking about ethnic Greeks. Sometimes it just refers to "those who observe the Graeco-Roman religions in the first instance, but more generally to those who don't fall within the categories 'Jew' or 'Christian.'" Johan Leemans et al., *'Let us Die That We May Live': Greek Homilies on Christian Martyrs from Asia Minor, Palestine and Syria (c. AD 350-AD 450)*, (London: Routledge, 2003), 160.

[132] *In 1 Cor. hom.* 7.1 (PG 61:55); *De stat.* 1.1 (PG 49:18).

[133] *De stat.* 19.1 (PG 49:189; NPNF 1-9:465): "the pagan philosophers have discoursed an infinite deal, and have expended a multitude of words, without being able to say anything sound."

[134] Siniossoglou, *Theodoret and Plato*, 52. Nevertheless, he is not the first to make this argument. Baur mentions several German philologists of the early twentieth century that repeatedly charged Chrysostom with "disrespect or contempt for classical education" and argued their position with reference to the fact that Chrysostom "indulges in controversy against the classic mythologies and against the moral aberrations of many philosophers." Baur, *John Chrysostom* 1:307.

therefore turn him into a champion of anti-Hellenism. It is equally easy to take other statements that favor the study of the classics and turn him into a champion of their study, such as the following:

> Every day you may find examples of these things- the succession of rulers, - the confiscation of rich men's goods… Do not our affairs resemble a kind of wheel? Read, if you will, both our own (books), and those without: for they also abound in such examples. If you despise ours, and this from pride; if you admire the works of philosophers, go even to them. They will instruct you, relating ancient calamities, as will poets, and orators, and sophists, and all historians. From every side, if you will, you may find examples.[135]

Examples of Chrysostom recommending or denigrating the classics or examples from the classical world are plentiful, but they do not mean much by themselves, unless one looks at them in their specific context: the work they appear in, its genre, potential audiences, and its place within the work itself. On the contrary, they are often used to make grand generalisations. Finally, one should also pay attention to the whole body of John's works. Only then will s/he realize that Chrysostom "was far more concerned to teach his Christians, than to polemicize against Jews and pagans,"[136] and to that we would only add that the polemic was also frequently utilized as a way of making a point to these very same Christians about what the other groups were and were not doing properly.

iii. The Question of Religious Identity

Taking John's or any other ancient author's views on any given subject out of context is often the reasoning behind grand sweeping judgments of their thought, a fault that is usually associated with older scholarship but can be found even today, although to a lesser degree. An example of this is I. Sandwell's work on Chrysostom and religious identity in Late Antiquity. Sandwell's profile of Chrysostom is one of

---

[135] *In 2 Thess. hom.* 1.2 (PG 62:472; NPNF 1-13:379). Baur's commentary on this passage is interesting, primarily because it perfectly captures John's spirit: "Chrysostom then was not ungrateful to the schools, through which he has passed; he was no fanatic, no renegade, no "embittered adversary" of classical culture." Baur, *John Chrysostom* 1:308.

[136] Liebeschuetz, *Ambrose and John Chrysostom*, 187.

someone who is not just hostile to Greek religion, but pretty much everything Greek: culture, history, moral and social values, and everything that could have been perceived as part of Greek identity. The reason Chrysostom does that, according to Sandwell, is due to his uncompromising stance in his understanding of religious and ethno-racial identity: you were either Christian or Greek in Chrysostom's time and your choice also determined your way of life. In Sandwell's argument Chrysostom was constructing a Christian identity in his attempt to define what it meant to be a Christian.[137] However, in his criticism of Sandwell's thesis, W. Liebeschuetz does not find this description helpful since it overlooks the fact that not only did Chrysostom not think that he was creating something new, but that his purpose was something much grander than the mere creation of a new identity. What Chrysostom asked from his congregation was a practical application of all Christian teaching as found in the Bible and the traditions of the Church.[138] But in Sandwell's view Chrysostom's ultimate aim was to make religion

---

[137] Sandwell, *Religious Identity in Late Antiquity*, 277.

[138] Wolf Liebeschuetz, "The view from Antioch: from Libanius via John Chrysostom to John Malalas and beyond," in *Pagans and Christians in the Roman Empire: The Breaking of a Dialogue (IVth – VIth Century A.D.)*, eds. Peter Brown and Rita Lizzi Testa (Zurich: Lit Verlag, 2011), 321-2. Liebeschuetz makes other pertinent points in his critique of Sandwell, which we will only summarize here: Chrysostom was adamant that there was only one correct belief and one correct way of life because this was the belief shared by other Christian leaders from the beginning. He also makes the case that a lot of Christian practices (such as giving alms to the poor, not going to the theatre and circus, giving up swearing, etc.) were not intended as markers of the Christians' differences from their fellow citizens, but rather as the behaviour they were taught and was considered proper; essentially, they were not different for the sake of being different, but because it is better to do what is right than what is wrong (ibid., 322). Liebeschuetz furthered his critique (*Ambrose and John Chrysostom*, 190-1) with the argument that the creation of an identity was not the purpose of preaching but its result. Thus, Sandwell's construction thesis "does not fairly describe what was going on in the minds of these men [preachers], it is not what the preachers thought they were doing, and it does not explain why congregations found their preachers' demands persuasive." We should note here that there are disagreements even among scholars who work on the basis of the conflict model, such as the debate between "essentialists" and "constructionists." For example, in a similar take on the same matter (the alleged "construction" of identities), Siniossoglou has labelled Sandwell's point of view as relativist and non-essentialist: "Christian theologians, philosophers and intellectuals in late antiquity and Byzantium certainly thought about Christianity and Hellenism in realist terms: as possessing an essential core or inalienable meaning. To study these essentialist world-views and the texts in which they are contained by adopting a relativist non-essentialist standpoint, as is commonly done in recent scholarship, means never to take Christian intellectuals, philosophical pagans and other intellectuals at their word, to assume, in effect, that they were not the persons they thought themselves to be. The intellectual and religious identities which Christians ... or pagans ... gave themselves should not be thought as unreal and should not be dissolved into constantly shifting, impersonal collective discourses." N. Siniossoglou, *Radical Platonism in Byzantium: Illumination and Utopia in Gemistos Plethon* (Cambridge: Cambridge University Press, 2011), xi-xii. Cameron, *Byzantine Matters*, 64, calls Siniossoglou's hypothesis in this work (the existence of a continuous Platonic movement within Byzantium and its role as a carrier of Hellenic identity) as part of a "clear Greek and

the defining feature of one's identity, and there could be no overlap or indeterminacy between being Christian or Greek.[139] Sandwell's idea that Chrysostom constructs a Christian identity in order to define it and in order to refute other kinds of identity is an important version of the conflict model we discussed in the first part of the chapter. But here the conflict is seen by the scholar not as something 'natural' or inherent to Christianity and Hellenism (as Harnack clearly thought); rather, the conflict is seen as a product of the way Christianity was constructed by Chrysostom.

We previously indicated that sometimes Chrysostom's attitude is also taken as paradigmatic for the literary reception of classical texts throughout Byzantium. One example of this is Ramsay Macmullen, who characterized Chrysostom as the archetypal thinker who determined the attitude of the Byzantines towards the classics for centuries following his death.[140]

---

anti-Orthodox agenda" that "depends ... on a strongly essentialist way of looking at identity." Cameron herself supports a model of "sustained challenge and redefinition" to move things forward from the positions of appropriation or existential opposition, whilst admitting that Hellenism is not enough to explain the problem of identity in Byzantium (ibid., 68). While this could potentially lead to the adoption of a third and more nuanced model to accurately describe the relationship between Hellenism and Christianity, it remains to be seen whether this could be sustainable within the context of the study of late antiquity.

[139] Sandwell's interpretation of Chrysostom's binary scheme of Christian/Greek further leads her to claim that Chrysostom allowed "no room for a non-Christian civic identity" and little room "for a non-Christian form of ethnic identification." The main reason Chrysostom even used terms such as *Hellenes* was to show the incompatibility between Christianity and Greek culture. Sandwell refers to Chrysostom's use of techniques from the classical Greek education as one of the only positive associations she finds between Chrysostom and Hellenism. All these claims finally lead to one point: that Chrysostom wanted to make Christianity the sole political, civic, ethnic and religious identity of the Christians, and that in order to do that there was not much space for religious toleration or the idea that religion is a private matter in his thought. For all these references see Sandwell, *Religious Identity in Late Antiquity*, 152-3. Cf. Maxwell, *Christianization and Communication*, 147: "Chrysostom hoped to eclipse distinctions of class or culture, by making religious identity the primary marker of difference in society." These views inevitably lead one to the conclusion that Chrysostom (and others, like Julian) were playing a game of identity politics.

[140] Ramsay Macmullen, *Christianity and Paganism in the Fourth to Eighth Centuries* (New Haven, CT: Yale University Press, 1997), 89, where we also find yet another overly negative description regarding Chrysostom's attitude towards philosophy and learning: "Chrysostom, just like earlier bishops, vaunts the wisdom of the believing unlearned over the unbelieving learned [the reason behind why Chrysostom would ever prefer the unbelieving, whether learned or unlearned, is not explained]; ridicules and rejects Plato and the other great names of the philosophic pantheon, just as Constantine had done; dismisses their teachings as mere cobwebs; and in the end approves only "rustics and ordinary folk." His is the cast of mind prevailing in the Byzantine world to come." None of the above is wrong *per se*. Chrysostom does all these things, even though his ridicule of Plato and other philosophers is not necessarily related to Constantine, as there were many other Christian writings before and after Constantine doing the exact same thing. The problem with this style of argument is that it takes one element from Chrysostom's writing, that of ridicule, and presents it as the *absolute* depiction of his

iv. Overview of the Argument: Research Questions and Future Directions

These extreme positions serve to highlight that what has been lacking in research so far is a coherent rhetorical and historical analysis of Chrysostom's views on Hellenism in an effort to provide a systematic study of a very un-systematic thinker such as Chrysostom.[141] For example: in what context is he ranting against the philosophers? Is he only criticizing them, or can we find examples of praise as well? Are the Hellenes of his time constantly disparaged? Is he really a cultural appropriator? The context in which these questions are answered is of fundamental importance, and only a contextualization of his various statements will be sufficient if we want to move beyond the dichotomies that plague the field. If we want to see how Chrysostom is relevant to modern debates on Hellenism and Christianity in late antiquity, another extended array of questions also need to be answered: how did he interpret and use Hellenism? How did he treat "external" wisdom and did he ever consider that Christianity had to "borrow" the Greek language and philosophical terminology in order to make its message more accessible to the large masses of the Roman Empire?[142] What were his views on the different schools of ancient philosophy, such as Platonism, Stoicism, Pythagoreanism and Neoplatonism, if any, and what does he approve of and reject from the Hellenic tradition?[143] How does he define his Christian identity in relation to the

---

attitude towards philosophy and the philosophers themselves. But Chrysostom, thankfully, is a much more interesting thinker than is presented in views like the one above, and his attitude, as we will be seeing, was much more varied and nuanced than Macmullen's view of him.

[141] Mitchell, *The Heavenly Trumpet*, 19, rightly emphasizes the futility of any attempts at systematization that would exclude the different literary, historical, and rhetorical contexts of his thought. In a sense, the aim is similar to Pelikan's work on the Cappadocians: "to treat their thought systematically without imposing a system upon it." Pelikan, *Christianity and Classical Culture*, 6.

[142] The reason the word borrow is in quotation marks is because the claim that Christianity borrowed the Greek language implies that it did not belong to the Christians in the first place. Even within the first generation of Christians there were believers whose native (and often only) language and culture was Greek.

[143] Beside the references from his own writings, John's antithesis to pagan religious practices is briefly mentioned in a text that is now considered the earliest of his biographies, *The Funerary Speech for John Chrysostom*: "He was unwilling to neglect the salvation even of the barbarians; he was fighting with all his might against the enemy of our salvation, now driving out impiety by the destruction of temples and idols, now introducing piety by the planting of churches," *The Funerary Speech* 60 (trans. Barnes and Bevan, *The Funerary Speech*, 74).

Hellenic and Roman cultural milieu of both Antioch and Constantinople?[144] Are his polemics against paganism a sign of cultural and/or ethnic denunciation of Hellenism?[145] Some of these questions have been asked before, and the responses have been varied.

Before proceeding to identify the exact gaps in the research, we will need to look into some of these responses because they provide both the framework and the impetus for this study. Thus, Garrett attributes Chrysostom's antagonism to the classics "in part to the grip paganism still held on people's minds."[146] Averil Cameron looks at the fight

---

[144] Whilst we can assert Chrysostom's Christian identity without any issue, things become more complicated when it comes to any assertions of his ethnicity. For example, he is sometimes referred to as a Greek-writing Syrian: Christine Shepardson, "Syria, Syriac, Syrian: Negotiating East and West," in *A Companion to Late Antiquity*, ed. Rousseau, 455. Liebeschuetz, *Ambrose and John Chrysostom*, 127, asserts that he derived "from a family of ... Western origin" due to his father's (Secundos) and sister's (Sabiniana) names. The question must be asked at this point, primarily in relation to Shepardson's claim: what makes Chrysostom a Syrian and Libanius a Hellene, considering that they were both natives of Antioch, and used Greek in both their speeches and writing? Is it just self-designation? If that is the case, Chrysostom never applied the term Syrian to himself. Even though Shepardson does not offer a response to this question, she nonetheless argues against generalizations such as calling Antioch "Greek" and Edessa "Syriac" and rightly emphasizes the place of Antioch within its Syrian environment. For another characterization of Chrysostom as a Syrian, which in this example is used as an explanation for his ample use of comparison as a literary device, see Ameringer, *The Stylistic Influence*, 68. This seems to be an issue of modern scholarship unnecessarily complicating things. In Byzantine biographies of Chrysostom, he is almost always described as a Greek from Greek parentage. See Theodore of Tremithus (c. 680), *v. Chrys.* 1.1 (*Douze Récits Byzantins sur Saint Jean Chrysostome*, ed. François Halkin, Bruxelles: Société des Bollandistes, 1977, 8): Ἦν δὲ γονέων Ἑλλήνων καὶ αὐτὸς δὲ Ἕλλην; cf. George of Alexandria (c. 680-725), *v. Chrys.* 3.2 (*Douze Récits*, 73): Πάντες δὲ ἦσαν Ἕλληνες [i.e. both John and his parents]. In the same work, we can also find an early Byzantine version of the utilitarian reception of the classics (ibid., 3.3, 78): "And he reaped what was useful among these [the ancient books, i.e. the classics], but the others he refused to touch as thorny" as well as a statement that John "mastered all of Greek education" before his return to Antioch [3.5, 88, my translation]. When describing the flames in the Cathedral that followed after John's exile, George mentions the persecutions that Johannites had to suffer from Optatus, Prefect of Constantinople at the time, who is called Ἕλλην ὢν τὴν θρησκείαν (ibid., 3.57, 236). This is particularly important due to the fact that John was also previously called a Hellene in the very same work, and indicates that the word could be used either as a description of ethnic origin or a religious persuasion and was not used to exclusively designate pagans, as is often claimed. For another reference to a Lucian who was "a Greek according to religion" and a leader of a group that violently persecuted the Johannites see *Vie anonym. du Vatic. 1669* 26.30 (Halkin, *Douze Récits*, 418). With the exception of an incident in George's *Vita* where John, whilst in Athens, strongly criticizes Hellenic religion, there is no sense of conflict or any emphasis on John's supposed anti-Hellenism in any of the Byzantine biographies. On the other hand, it is a staple feature in many works of modern scholarship on Chrysostom. For a similar false attribution of Roman identity to Chrysostom see Bozinis, *Ο Ιωάννης ο Χρυσόστομος για το Imperium Romanum*, 26-7.

[145] Other related questions could include Chrysostom's citation techniques "and rhetorical purposes of individual quotations and allusions in their literary settings," and a good starting point for Chrysostom's *Timaeus* quotations is Samuel Pomeroy, "Reading Plato Through the Eyes of Eusebius," where the question appears as well. For an extensive treatment of Chrysostom's critique of classical *paideia* along with comparisons with other Church fathers, see Nägele, "Johannes Chrysostomos," *passim*.

[146] Garrett, *An Analysis*, 240.

between pagans and Christians as a conflict over who has "the right to interpret the past" and "each side approached the task through hermeneutics."[147] Margaret Schatkin sees Chrysostom's refutation of Libanius in his *Discourse on Blessed Babylas* as a strong expression of John's anti-Hellenism. She also argues that when Chrysostom uses the word Greeks (Hellenes) as a derogatory term, as in chapter 40 of the *Discourse,* what is implied is the "linguistic and cultural legacy of pagan Greece".[148] Others have argued, that Chrysostom's polemic was not against Hellenism *per se*, but against Libanius' specific version of Hellenism and its representation of the old status quo.[149] The difference between Schatkin and Hunter's arguments is that the former sees the attacks on Libanius as part of a consistent anti-Hellenic feeling on John's part, while the latter sees it more as a personal attack that includes Hellenism because Libanius advocated for it.

Our main argument in this thesis is that Chrysostom's alleged "appropriation" of Hellenism is nothing different from what most thinkers of his era (whether they were Christians or pagans) did when it came to the reception of ancient Greek culture: they used it, interpreted it, rejected or accepted certain of its aspects and related it to their Christian beliefs in a variety of ways.[150] As Carol Harrison argued in relation to Augustine's Platonism, "to speak of Christian Platonism or Christian Neoplatonism, or indeed, Neoplatonism in Augustine's time is in reality to speak of something which did not exist. Different people interpreted, used, appropriated or rejected ideas from the

---

[147] Cameron, *Christianity and the Rhetoric of Empire*, 138.

[148] Margaret A. Schatkin, Introduction to *Saint John Chrysostom: Apologist*, ed. and trans. Margaret Schatkin and Paul W. Harkins (Washington, D.C.: Catholic University of America Press, 1985), 33, 41.

[149] See, e.g., Hunter's discussion of Libanius' connection between rhetoric (λόγοι) and religion (ἱερά) and their identification with the life of the polis: "his [Libanius'] religion was both a cultural and social conservatism; the city, its gods, and its culture were one indissoluble unity." Libanius' enduring influence on Chrysostom is also shown in the latter's virulent attacks on "that amalgam of rhetoric, religion, and civic life espoused by Libanius." See Hunter, *A Comparison*, 7-8.

[150] For example, we shall see that Chrysostom's engagement with ancient Greek philosophy goes far beyond Platonism, and includes Stoicism and Cynicism, among other schools. Furthermore, one's Christian faith did not necessarily imply a wholesale rejection of Platonism or other philosophical schools and theories. For this argument in relation to Origen see Ramelli, "Origen, Patristic Philosophy, and Christian Platonism," n. 121 at 251.

Platonists and their 'recent interpreters' in different ways, in relation to the Christian faith. And the Platonists, in their turn, criticized and evaluated Christianity."[151] And while the process of simply identifying certain philosophical influences in Christian writers by indicating the borrowing or appropriating of terms and concepts is of fundamental importance, it is also of limited value if not followed by an analysis of the re-contextualization of these same terms and concepts. In other words, we agree with Tatakis that what scholarship needs to do is "to find out whether such elements retain the same meaning, or whether they imply the same thesis within the thought of the Christian philosopher, and whether, indeed, they are presented in a new spirit, a new arrangement, or whether they serve other final aims."[152]

As we will see, some of Chrysostom's works, such as the *Discourse on Blessed Babylas and against the Greeks*, might be almost direct responses to specific works of pagan authors, such as Porphyry or Julian. Not only some of his works but also certain arguments within his corpus attest to pagan accusations against Christians that have been around for a very long time and were already counterattacked by the Apologists of the second century.[153] Julian was an avid supporter of the principle that paganism and the classical tradition formed a unified whole, and was probably not very happy that "the Christians rejected the pagan religion while seeking the classical culture with enthusiasm."[154] However, Chrysostom's polemic against the Greeks is not limited to a philosophical level or to the value of paideia, as was the case with some previous

---

[151] Harrison, *Augustine*, 13.

[152] Basil Tatakis, *Christian Philosophy in the Patristic and Byzantine Tradition*, ed. and trans. George D. Dragas (Rollinsford, NH: Orthodox Research Institute, 2007), 35.

[153] See Timothy Barnes, "Pagan Perceptions of Christianity," in *Early Christianity: Origins and Evolution to AD 600 In Honour of W. H. C. Frend*, ed. Ian Hazlett (London: SPCK, 1991), 233-4 for a discussion of Fronto's charges of Thyestean feasts (cannibalism) and Oedipodean intercourse (incest) against the Christians. Porphyry's sharp attack on Christianity was the dominant focus of the philosophical debate between pagans and Christians up until the early fifth century, when the reasons behind the fall of Rome became the central issue: see ibid., 238-40 for more information on Porphyry's anti-Christian polemic, which he considers as "the largest, most learned and most dangerous of all the ancient literary attacks on Christianity" (238). John also seems to be responding to Julian's accusations that the Christians venerate corpses by providing a detailed defence of the cult of the martyrs.

[154] Baur, *John Chrysostom*, 1:64.

apologists, but also includes a consistent and forceful attack on matters of ritual and cultic observances and, in some cases, a reference to actual conflicts.[155] The presence of a large number of sophists in Antioch, even if they were not necessarily pagan like Libanius, might have also provoked his polemics against paganism. When dealing with Chrysostom's attitude towards classical paganism and pagan philosophy during his lifetime, one should always remember the attitude their representatives had towards Christianity, which was unfriendly more often than not. As philosophers, sophists and rhetoricians were the most ardent supporters of "paganism" at the time (Libanius being an obvious example), it is not surprising to see them receiving some vitriolic remarks by Chrysostom. Considering the polemical literary environment of the time, this was a consistent attitude.[156]

Moreover, Chrysostom's challenge to Hellenism was very different from, say, Gregory of Nazianzus'. While he would surely reject (as Gregory did) Julian's identification of Greek language and literary tradition with paganism, he would disagree

---

[155] Such as John's *Letter 126 To the presbyter Rufinus*, which begins with an agonizing description of news that reached him from Phoenicia: Ἦλθεν εἰς ἡμᾶς, ὅτι πάλιν ἀνήφθη τὰ ἐν Φοινίκῃ κακά, καὶ ἡ τῶν Ἑλλήνων ηὐξήθη μανία, καὶ πολλοὶ τῶν μοναχῶν οἱ μὲν ἐπλήγησαν, οἱ δὲ καὶ ἀπέθανον (PG 52:685). Rufinus is then urged to attend to the matter as soon as possible. One of the things we can infer from the letter is that in certain areas of the empire the violence between different religions was still going strong in the early fifth century. See also *Ep.* 123 addressed to Phoenician presbyters and monks (PG 52:676-8). In *Ep.* 221 (PG 52:732-3) to the presbyter Constantius, who was also participating in the missionary work in Phoenicia and Arabia, John lists some of his duties, one of which is Ἑλληνισμοῦ τὴν καθαίρεσιν. For more information on this mission see Wendy Mayer and Pauline Allen, *John Chrysostom* (London: Routledge, 2000), 45. Other references to the same mission to the Greeks in Phoenicia occur in *Ep. 51 To Diogenes, 21 To Alphius, 53* and *69 To Presbyter Nicolaus, 54 To Presbyter Gerontius*, and *55 To the Presbyters Symeon and Maris, Priests, and Monks of Apamea*. This is how Theodoret, *Hist. Eccl.* 5.29 (GCS NF 5:329-30; NPNF 2-3:152) describes the incident: "On receiving information that Phœnicia was still suffering from the madness of the demons' rites, John got together certain monks who were fired with divine zeal, armed them with imperial edicts and despatched them against the idols' shrines. The money which was required to pay the craftsmen and their assistants who were engaged in the work of destruction was not taken by John from imperial resources, but he persuaded certain wealthy and faithful women to make liberal contributions, pointing out to them how great would be the blessing their generosity would win. Thus the remaining shrines of the demons were utterly destroyed." This could potentially explain some of the characterizations of him as an enemy of Hellenism, but does not escape the danger we mentioned previously, that is, identifying Hellenism exclusively with pagan religious practices. In *Ep.* 28 (PG 52:627) Chrysostom praises a presbyter named Basil for his zeal against the Greeks, whose error he demolishes and leads them to the truth (καταλύων αὐτῶν τὴν πλάνην, καὶ πρὸς ἀλήθειαν χειραγωγῶν). We cannot infer what exactly Basil did from the information provided in the letter.

[156] Baur, *John Chrysostom*, 1:12, 309-10. It is also possible that Julian's virulent attack against Diodore of Tarsus (in one of his letters Julian calls him "sharp-witted sophist of that creed of the country-folk," *Letter 55 To Photinus*, LCL 157:189) influenced John's criticism of paganism.

with Gregory that Hellenism simply denoted the Greek language, even if we take that statement as a rhetorical provocation.[157] His understanding of Hellenism, which was by no means uniform across his works, included a variety of aspects from classical culture, including religion, philosophy, ethics, and the significance of events from the classical past. His challenge to classical culture was not based on whether a Christian has the right to take part in *paideia* or whether Greek is the sole property of paganism.[158] It was a challenge to a certain set of values and attitudes, many of which were carried over to the Christian tradition by Greek converts.[159] Even so, we should pre-emptively warn that an image of Chrysostom constantly battling against Greek learning or as part of a general conflict between supposedly Christian and classical values is neither truthful to Chrysostom nor to the way the classics were received in the Christian East.[160] Thus, for John Hellenism implied a way of life with certain components that seemed to be indispensable in its long history, including *paideia*, the *polis* and the civic virtues that made one a good citizen. John Chrysostom's critique of Julian and Libanius' version of Hellenism, and one of the main arguments of this thesis is that the Hellenism of Julian and Libanius is just one chapter in the history of the Hellenic tradition, and certainly

---

[157] Hunter, *A Comparison*, 59. A. Cameron sees "language, and the control of language, [as] the heart of the "struggle" between pagan and Christian culture in the fourth century." Cameron, *Christianity and the Rhetoric of Empire*, 123.

[158] For an introduction to the different aspects of paganism in Chrysostom's thought see Constantine Bosinis, "What does Paganism Mean for a Church Father? An Inquiry into the Use of the Term εἰδωλολατρεία in the Rhetoric of John Chrysostom," *Studia Patristica* 47 (Leuven: Peeters, 2010): 243-8.

[159] See Robert Browning, *The Emperor Julian* (Berkeley: University of California Press, 1976), 173: "Classical culture was not just a matter of grammatical forms and literary genres. It comprised both factual knowledge- such as mythology and history- and a whole structure of values and attitudes."

[160] Mark Vessey makes the excellent point that much of this underlying tension is due to the writings of primarily Augustine and Jerome, and that in the East Basil of Caesarea's *To the Young* reflected "a comfortable consensus. Almost the only signs of friction, in the Greek sphere, between the disciplinary norms of late antique Hellenism and the profession of Christianity relate to the emperor Julian's bizarre endeavour, in 362, to ban Christians from the teaching of grammar and rhetoric ... The modern scholarly notion of a generalized conflict between Christian and classical literary values in late antiquity has no support in the Byzantine tradition." Mark Vessey, "Literature, Patristics, Early Christian Writing," in *The Oxford Handbook of Early Christian Studies*, eds. Susan Ashbrook Harvey and David G. Hunter (Oxford: Oxford University Press, 2008), 46.

does not constitute a definitive version of its manifold ideals,[161] was more direct than what most Christian writers attempted before him: besides his criticism of certain aspects of the Hellenic way of life, his most important contribution was his sustained "rejection of the pagan claim to form virtue."[162] In this process, he even counteroffered an alternative to the Hellenic way: monasticism, seen through the prism of the philosophical life. As we already mentioned, John also had to fight against the claims of Julian and Libanius, who perceived Christianity as "a return to barbarism and a rejection of culture." In this respect, they also attacked the monks, whom they considered the epitome of what was wrong with Christianity and the representatives of a spirit totally foreign to Hellenism because of their "rejection of city life and the benefits of Greek culture."[163] As D. Hunter has argued, the criticism was two-fold:

> first, they claimed that the monks embodied vices inherent in Christianity itself: a rejection of the gods, a search for virtue outside of the inherited culture, allegiance to the heavenly over the earthly city. The contempt for the monks expressed by Julian and Libanius, then, is but an extension of their hatred for the religion which was threatening the culture, religion, and way of life of the Hellenes. But by naming "misanthropy" as the monks' cardinal sin, Julian reveals that the point at issue between the pagans and the Christians is not simply whether Christianity or Hellenism produced better people. At the heart of the rival claims and criticisms is a more fundamental argument about what constitutes virtue. For the pagans, devotion to the traditional gods and to the social institutions of the Greek city was paramount in their definition of virtue. For the Christians, at least for John Chrysostom, the monks could be taken as ideals of virtue precisely because they demonstrated in their lives the secondary value of the earthly city.[164]

While D. Hunter's analysis of Julian's and Libanius' attack on monasticism and its implications about what constitutes virtue is precise for the most part, the claim about

---

[161] For its main elements see Hunter, *A Comparison*, 60: "Libanius believed that rhetoric, city life and traditional piety towards the gods were intimately connected in a single fabric of life which was Hellenism... from the earliest days of Julian's reign, and for more than twenty years afterwards, Libanius extolled the emperor Julian as the model of the social, religious, and moral benefits of Hellenism. He did this in two ways. In his orations on behalf of Julian, Libanius attributed to Hellenic paideia the formation of Julian's ascetic character as well as his pagan convictions. In Libanius' works, therefore, the emperor Julian lived on as a symbol of the Hellenic ideal."

[162] Hunter, *A Comparison*, 59.

[163] Ibid.

[164] Ibid., 65.

what virtue meant for the "pagans" fails to mention a large spectrum in the Hellenic tradition (such as the Cynics) that did not think of the gods or the social institutions of the polis as paramount to their definition of virtue. In terms of Chrysostom's defence of monasticism, Hunter further argues that besides it being largely a response to pagan critique, it also had other Christians in mind, especially the ones at Antioch "who still lead lives inextricably connected to the culture and institutions of Hellenism [and by extension the traditions of paganism]." Chrysostom's choice of the monks as the best ethical models representative of the Christian "culture", was both an answer to Hellenic critiques and an underlying message to his Christian audience. More than that, Chrysostom's presentation of the monk as the successor of the philosopher, even if "portrayed in the garb of Hellenic virtue", is an attempt at redefining what constitutes virtue: "in place of the Hellenic commitment to the city and its life, Chrysostom presented a rival, "heavenly" πολιτεία."[165]

The word philosophy will be frequently used throughout this thesis. However, a clarification should be made about how we understand and utilize the term to avoid any potential misunderstandings. Many modern accounts and histories of ancient philosophy show a tendency to look at ancient philosophy as a purely intellectual enterprise, devoid of its context as a way of life.[166] This might be an image suited to the philosophy of the Enlightenment, but it distorts ancient Greek philosophy. It is a view that sees philosophy as something antagonistic to piety (in the sense of εὐσέβεια), and while we should remember that ancient philosophers were critical of many aspects of popular

---

[165] This discussion and the references in it are based on and indebted to D. Hunter's excellent discussion of the issues at stake in his *A Comparison*, 62-6.

[166] Pierre Hadot, *Philosophy as a Way of Life: Spiritual Exercises from Socrates to Foucault*, ed. Arnold I. Davidson; trans. Michael Chase (Oxford: Blackwell, 1995), 107: "Contemporary historians of philosophy are today scarcely inclined to pay attention to this subject, although it is an essential one... they consider philosophy to be a purely abstract-theoretical activity." According to Hadot the origins of this phenomenon go back to the absorption of philosophy by Christianity and the distinction between theology and philosophy.

piety, they rarely questioned God's (or the gods') existence.[167] That is true even for

Plato,[168] who is usually considered the archetypal Greek philosopher in the discussion

on the relationship between Christianity and philosophy. Keeping in mind Pierre

Hadot's famous work on philosophy as a way of life, we shall consider how Christianity

presented itself as a philosophy that fulfilled exactly that role: a new way of life,

accompanied by a distinct set of beliefs.[169] It will then become evident that

Chrysostom's rhetorical attacks against the "Greeks" can only be discussed in the

context of competing alliances between different social groups (pagans, Jews,

Christians, heretics) and his effort to maintain the Christian faith amidst a variety of

conflicting worldviews.[170] This is an important point: we have seen that even within the

conflict model there are those who take a non-essentialist point of view in regards to

these groups (i.e. that much of what Chrysostom describes is his own construction), and

those who take a different approach and read the texts as descriptions of real identities

that reflected the world of the time as it really was. Our own approach, whilst

recognizing that, as with any rhetorical piece we should be careful in the way

Chrysostom presents Christians and other groups (as we should with others, like

Libanius), will also take his depictions seriously. This is a position that we will argue

---

[167] Trigg, *Origen*, 13.

[168] But see the qualifying statement that there is an inherent danger in trying to count Plato as a monotheist or even as a theist in the Biblical sense in Mark J. Edwards, *Origen against Plato* (Aldershot: Ashgate, 2002), 48, and 47-53 for Plato's belief in the gods.

[169] In Chrysostom's case, a new *Christian* way of life. It has been argued that he was "the earliest Christian author to employ *philosophia* with a purely Christian connotation," Laistner, *Christianity and Pagan Culture in the Later Roman Empire*, 53. Laistner succinctly summarizes the attributes of *philosophia* in Chrysostom's thought: disregard of worldly things, love of mankind, and almsgiving, ibid., 54. Garrett agrees with Laistner's point of view: most of Chrysostom's references to *philosophia* do not "designate contemplation about man and the universe but a term for the Christian way of life." He also expands the attributes that Laistner indicated: "φιλοσοφία can refer to the Christian's avoidance of materialism and greed, or to placing one's confidence not in a nation's military might but in its Christian virtue." Garrett, *An analysis*, 231.

[170] "That faith, indeed, presented itself to the ancient world not just as the *cultus* of a Jewish man-God, but as a philosophy." Trigg, *Origen*, 13. In Sozomen's account of John as bishop of Constantinople, Hellenes and heretics are persuaded by his rhetoric and unite themselves with him: Ἰωάννης δὲ ἄριστα τὴν Κωνσταντινουπόλεως ἐκκλησίαν ἐπιτροπεύων πολλοὺς μὲν ἐκ τῶν Ἑλλήνων, πολλοὺς δὲ τῶν αἱρέσεων ἐπήγετο. Sozomen, *Hist. eccl.* 8.5.1 (GCS NF 4:357). However, there is no mention of his alleged desire to abolish their national identity or, for that matter, of their identity as antagonistic to the Christian faith.

from the texts themselves, and we believe that a careful reading of the texts will prove this point.

Here we find the single most important common element between Chrysostom (and almost all Greek Patristic thinkers) and Greek philosophy: what both his homilies and the works of the philosophers describe is not a simple theoretical vision, but primarily a way of living, a practical guide to virtue. Christianity inherited from ancient philosophy not just ideas, but also a distinct set of practices and attitudes that allowed it to appropriate the word *philosophia* to describe its way of life.[171] This is not to say that these propositions agreed or they even had much in common, only that their preoccupations were largely the same. As an initial framework for that matter, I strongly agree with Meyendorff that "Greek Patristic thought remained open to Greek philosophical problematics, but avoided being imprisoned in Hellenic philosophical *systems.*"[172]

In this respect, we shall attempt to compare his understanding of certain philosophical concepts, such as *autarkeia*, with relevant arguments drawn from ancient philosophy.[173] This will allow us to have a fuller understanding of his reception of Hellenism, beyond the usual binaries of synthesis/opposition, and to see whether his arguments were part of a grander scheme against the Hellenes or simply an attitude consistent with many others from his time. A similar argument regarding Theodoret of

----

[171]For Chrysostom, the transformation of the world by Christianity is a proof of its divine origins, because earlier attempts to form a way of life out of philosophical writings have by and large been unsuccessful: "To help you see the truth of this, consider how many men wished to introduce their teachings among the Greeks and to establish a new commonwalth (politeia) and way of life. Think of such men as Zeno, Plato, Socrates, Diagoras, Pythagoras, and countless others. Yet they fell so far short of success that many people do not even know them by name. But Christ not only wrote a constitution (politeia) but even brought a new way of life to the whole world." *Adv. Iud. or.* 5.3 (PG 48:886; trans. Paul W. Harkins, *Saint John Chrysostom: Discourses Against Judaizing Christians*, Washington, DC: Catholic University of America Press, 1979, 104).

[172] Meyendorff, *Byzantine Theology*, 25; emphasis in the original.

[173] Chadwick argues that what enabled the Church to come to terms with philosophy under the Roman Empire was their common concern with ethical problems and applications: "The philosopher of the period was not expected to concern himself with an abstract and detached search for metaphysical truth, but rather with practical ethical questions." Chadwick, *Contra Celsum*, xi. While Chadwick is here referring to Origen's time, the argument is also valid for the late fourth century.

Cyrus concluded that his polemics against Hellenic arrogance were not in order to resist it but in order to radically change their worldview, in an attempt to persuade them to stop being Hellenes.[174] Chrysostom had a very pragmatic attitude towards the triumph of Christianity and the decline of paganism, especially in certain apologetic writings directed against Greeks and/or Jews: he deduced its truthfulness "from its observable worldly success," an approach that has already been used by Origen and Eusebius.[175] What remains to be determined is whether the triumph of Christianity was only due to its social and political prevalence or if it also successfully engaged with Hellenism at the intellectual level.[176] What is fundamentally at stake is the question of continuity or extinction of Hellenism, or at least some of its fundamental elements.[177] Chrysostom would probably never think of himself as someone whose writings would go on to determine the attitude of a whole civilization towards the Classics; others put him on this pedestal, but because of this his thought is usually stretched to fit the Procrustean bed of pre-existing master narratives of any given scholars' position on Christianity and Hellenism in late antiquity rather than examined in its own terms.

---

[174] Siniossoglou, *Plato and Theodoret*, 29. Others have argued that acceptance of Christianity did not involve any rejection of one's cultural heritage, since a culture could be flexible enough to accommodate a transition from one belief to another, regardless of the reasons behind the conversion. For this argument see Demetrios J. Constantelos, "The Hellenic Background and Nature of Patristic Philanthropy in the Early Byzantine Era," in *Wealth and Poverty in Early Church and Society*, ed. Susan R. Holman (Grand Rapids, MI: Baker Academic, 2008), 190.

[175] Barnes, "Pagan Perceptions," 237-8.

[176] See Siniossoglou, *Plato and Theodoret*, 234, who believes that the prevalence of Christianity in political terms does not imply that it also refuted the Hellenic philosophical arguments, and that such a conclusion is rash and precipitous.

[177] It remains to be seen which elements were maintained and which did not survive the transition from the ancient to the medieval world. Helene Ahrweiler believes that "the policing of private life by both State and Church marks the disruption of organic intellectual continuity with the ancient world despite the sporadic survival of pastoral, but mainly agrarian customs and reactions, (though these lacked any cultural impact), which provided an example of what was virtually a reflex respect for tradition, for the remote past, and which, of course, during the broad sweep of history forges certain attitudes of mind." She also mentions Hypatia's murder and Justinian's closure of the Platonic academy in Athens as examples of this disruption. For Ahrweiler the continuity of Hellenism within Christianity lies elsewhere: she sees the Christian's desire for redemption and salvation as a survival of the ancient man's struggle towards self-knowledge. In other words, a consistent dedication to and defence of freedom is the mark of Greek continuity and not the vain search for models of ancient life and customs, "the organic survival of the ancient humanistic virtue transformed into the Christian precept of universal redemption." *Problems of Greek Continuity*, trans. John Leatham (Athens: National Bank of Greece Cultural Foundation, 1998), 31.

In what follows we will be looking into three separate but interconnected threads in John's multiple receptions of Hellenism. In Chapter 2 we will look into three different discursive modes: we will start with John's negative characterizations of Greeks and their philosophy because these are not only the most prevalent but also the ones that usually set the tone in relevant scholarship. This will be followed by positive references to Greeks through praise of both famous and anonymous individuals. The chapter will end with a more complicated stance, one that combines both criticism and praise in the same place. Then in Chapter 3 we will be looking into John's embodiments of Hellenism and Christianity respectively through his comparisons of individuals from both sides. We distinguish between major comparisons, which are the most frequent ones in terms of the individuals compared (although distributed between different texts), and minor comparisons, which consist of smaller treatments and usually group individuals together instead of treating them separately. We conclude the chapter with a close analysis of Chrysostom's *Discourse on Babylas*, a treatise that includes a major comparison between Babylas and Diogenes but also provides an opportunity for John to launch a full-scale attack against the Emperor Julian and the Greeks in general. We also look into the debates surrounding the nature of the text and the way it has been considered paradigmatic in John's engagement with Hellenism. Finally, in Chapter 4 we will be looking into John's reception of a specific philosophical school: the Cynics. We start by using the same discursive categories used in chapter one and divide Christian reception of the Cynics into positive, negative, and neutral. We then situate John's own texts within previous Christian tradition and assess differences and similarities. We complete this chapter by a comparison between John and the Cynics and their respective conception of a specific philosophical concept, that of *autarkeia*.

2. Chrysostom and the Greeks: The Critique of the Past

Chrysostom's reception of Hellenism, as we argued in the previous chapter, has often been subject to overt generalisations that are often used to validate opinions on the subject of Christianity and Hellenism in general. A simplified and broad classification would be that scholarship has tended to see him as either extremely hostile against anything Hellenic, a position which also argues that this attitude was to become canonical among Byzantine writers of later times, or as someone who can be categorized together with Origen and the Cappadocians for their successful integration of Hellenism into Christian thought. Very rarely one can find a more balanced approach, although as we saw in some recent examples (e.g. some of Wendy Mayer's more recent articles) certain approaches tend to be more nuanced and even more specific as to what exactly one is talking about when discussing Chrysostom and Hellenism. Building on these approaches and inspired by the fact that previous opinions were frequently pronounced due to the focus on a single or just a few of his works, this chapter will approach the subject from a variety of angles that showcase exactly how varied and unique John's approach to Hellenism was.

After establishing some working definitions as to who Chrysostom is talking about when referring to Greeks, we will look into two main approaches in his work: instances of critiques of Hellenism (be it philosophers, customs, religious rituals, and the power of tradition) and instances of praise of Hellenism (including but not limited to historical figures, mourning rituals, philosophical ideas, etc). This will then be followed by more complex positions: examples of critique and praise within the same passage, indifferent references, and the actual treatment of Greeks by Christians in everyday life. The aim of this chapter then is twofold: on the one hand, we want to show that Chrysostom's reception of Hellenism in its different forms was far from monolithic and could be different even within the same work. If this is successfully argued, then the generalizations of the past should be put to rest and replaced by more pragmatic and textually sensitive approaches. On the other hand, it is also an initial attempt to set the stage for the next two chapters, which go into even more specific examples of this reception and contextualize the general outlines of this chapter through his paradigmatic comparisons between Christians and Greeks and his reconfiguration of a philosophical concept strongly associated with Cynicism.

a. Who are the Greeks?

Before we delve into the specific aspects of Chrysostom's varied reception of Hellenism, it would be useful to briefly clarify our persons of interest, i.e. the Greeks. If we were to distinguish the variety of meanings of the term "Hellene" (Ἕλλην) within John's corpus, we could broadly classify them in three categories: Greeks of the classical past, Greeks during Paul's time and usually in the context of John's exegesis of the Pauline corpus, and Greeks contemporary with Chrysostom himself. This chapter will mostly deal with the first and third categories, so we will briefly discuss the second as a way of introducing some of the concepts that will re-appear later. Some of the themes discussed here recur in all three categories. For example, John will usually tend to uphold Paul's loose definition of Greeks whilst also expanding it with his own understanding, such as the argument that the Greeks who persecuted Paul (or, rather, their descendants) continued to persecute Christians in later times.

When discussing Paul's various references to "Jews and Greeks" in the Pauline Epistles (it is worth remembering that for Chrysostom all 14 epistles transmitted under Paul's name were indeed written by Paul), John sometimes refers to Hellenes as certain pious individuals who did not follow Jewish customs. Thus, in his interpretation of Romans 2:8-10 ("there will be wrath and fury, there will be anguish and distress for everyone who does evil, the Jew first and also the Greek, but glory and honor and peace for everyone who does good, the Jew first and also the Greek") John thinks that Paul was talking about the times before the coming of Christ, and the one he calls Greek means not an idolater but someone who worshipped God without the Jewish observances (circumcision, Sabbaths, purifications) and who will be judged based on their conscience, which John identifies as the alternative to instruction and admonition that the Jews possessed with the Law.[1] When discussing Paul's trial before Festus (Acts 25:1-22), Chrysostom calls the latter Ἕλληνα ... καὶ ἄπιστον.[2] Festus is not an unbeliever because he is an atheist, but because he did not believe in Christ. Thus, the category of Greek, which included idolaters but also people who believed in God without observing Jewish customs, also includes unbelievers, due to their lack of faith in Christ. The Greeks are also included in a list of "servants of the devil," amongst unbelievers and tyrants who molested Paul in his ministry.[3] In essence, and according to Chrysostom, the application of the term Greeks in apostolic times meant everyone who was not Jewish, and that is why Paul was primarily sent to them whereas Peter was sent to the Jews.[4] Chrysostom, as we shall see, was also willing to recognize that some Greeks were pious while others were not. The condition of the latter would be especially problematic in the context of the final judgment, where a Christian might wonder how a Greek, who was impious (ἀσεβήσας), worshipped idols, and ignored Christ, will be resurrected as well.[5] But Chrysostom's extended definition of whom he considered a "Greek" might explain this apparent contradiction, which simply means that the Greeks (as well as all humans) will be resurrected before the final judgment but will not necessarily be saved.

---

[1] *De stat.* 12.4 (PG 49:133).

[2] *De stat.* 16.4 (PG 49:166).

[3] *De stat.* 1.6 (PG 49:24).

[4] *In fac. ei rest.* 8 (PG 51:379): Τότε τοίνυν, ἡνίκα ἐκήρυττον οὗτοι κατὰ τὴν οἰκουμένην ἄπασαν, αἵρεσις οὐδεμία ἦν· πᾶσα δὲ ἡ φύσις τῶν ἀνθρώπων δύο ταῦτα δόγματα εἶχε, τὸ μὲν ὑγιές, τὸ δὲ διεφθαρμένον. Ἢ γὰρ Ἕλληνες, ἢ Ἰουδαῖοι, οἱ τὴν γῆν οἰκοῦντες ἄπαντες ἦσαν·... Τοὺς μὲν οὖν Ἰουδαίους ἐπέτρεψε τῷ Πέτρῳ, τοῖς δὲ Ἕλλησι τὸν Παῦλον ἐπέστησεν ὁ Χριστός.

[5] *De res. mort.* 8 (SC 561:168).

This brief discussion is just a highlight of how Chrysostom could be both flexible and loose with his definition of who the Greeks were but also signifies the basis for some of his hostility. Paul was by far his favourite apostle and by considering the Greeks (since this is what he calls the Romans many times, as we shall see) responsible for his hardships and eventual death, even if they were long dead, he is already exhibiting some of the attitudes that have led some to crown him an enemy of Hellenism. It is also significant that John takes the Pauline distinction between Jew and Greek and utilises it in a way that creates an image of the world divided into these two categories *exclusively* and is only expanded with the rise of Christianity. The rise of Christianity also functions as a replacement category in what John calls healthy and corrupt doctrine. Previously, Judaism represented the former and Hellenism the latter. But the rise of Christianity represents an expansion of the corrupt category, which now includes Judaism, and its replacement by Christianity in what he understands as healthy doctrine. If we refer back to the three different categories and the discussion that will follow, we will then see that the Greeks of the classical past (such as Plato, Pythagoras, and other philosophers) comprised the proto-Greeks, but they were not the only ones. The same thing applies to Greeks contemporary with Chrysostom: these are not just Greeks by ethnicity or religious convictions. In a sense, even the heretics (such as the Arians) can be called Greeks since they exhibit what he understands as a Greek way of thinking about the world. In a way, Chrysostom both continues using Hellenes in the sense other Christians used it before him (i.e. a group separate to Christians and Jews or as a group, along with Jews, within which there are Christians, as Paul used it), but also expands on who can be classified under the category, while the antagonistic overtones in Hellenism's definition under Julian provided him with a formidable contemporary opponent.[6]

---

⁶ Raffaella Cribiore, *Libanius the Sophist: Rhetoric, Reality and Religion in the Fourth Century* (Ithaca, NY: Cornell University Press, 2013), 8.

b. Criticism of the Greeks

After this brief introduction, we can now proceed into the more specific aspects of John's critique. We will analyse this according to philosophical and religious criticism. Our division into philosophical and religious criticism is obviously artificial, and often the two categories overlap, but there is always a certain emphasis that enables us to classify each view accordingly, despite John's frequent blurring of the boundaries. Broadly speaking, by philosophical criticism we mean John's critiques against philosophers and philosophical ideas and by religious criticism we refer to his criticism of ancient Greek religion and pagan practices, even if sometimes the philosophers are treated as the enablers of these.

i. Philosophical criticism

We have already claimed that a very incomplete picture emerges when scholars argue certain things on the basis of a single or a few texts only, something that has unfortunately been the case in the past. In this dissertation, the analysis will be thematic, concentrating on the reception of different aspects of Hellenism in a much wider range of John's writings. We will begin with John's criticism of philosophical ideas, particularly metempsychosis, since metempsychosis is a prime example of a religious idea explicitly connected with philosophy.

In a curious but suggestive passage, John begins by criticizing the idea of reincarnations thus:

> For whereas their leading men [of the Greeks] affirmed that our soul passes into flies, and dogs, and brute creatures; those who came after them, being ashamed of this, fell into another kind of turpitude, and invested the brute creatures with all rational science, and made out that the creatures—which were called into existence on our account—are in all respects more honorable than we! They even attribute to them foreknowledge and piety. The crow, they say, knows God, and the raven likewise, and they possess gifts of prophecy, and foretell the future; there is justice among them, and polity, and laws. ... But when we tell them that these things are fables, and are full of absurdity, 'You do not enter (ἐνοήσατε) into the higher meaning,' say they. No, we do not enter into this your surpassing nonsense, and may we never do so: for it requires (of course!) an

excessively profound mind, to inform me, what all this impiety and confusion would be at.[7]

John offers an intergenerational criticism of Greek philosophy, mixed with criticism of certain religious practices that he attributes to the philosophers. It begins with the Platonic idea that human souls might pass onto the souls of animals after death, which is a very standard Christian criticism of metempsychosis. But, and here is a very peculiar phenomenon, this idea did not hold with the successors of Plato, who were ashamed by it, and John would probably have been aware of that.[8] Yet he decides to argue against it not because he thought of the issue as redundant but precisely because Neo-Platonists allegorized the original idea. The arguments against the successors was that what they did in place of taking things literally was an attempt to invest animals with reason and honour them more than humans. Now this might be a far-fetched criticism, but what follows that seems to be the rationalization for it, i.e. the fact that the Greeks thought that the future could be predicted by certain animals (although John mentions only birds, possibly implying the practice of ornithomancy or augury).[9] Chrysostom considers both the older and the most recent views as absurd fables, and dismisses the accusation that Christians did not really understand the higher meaning of these practices, calling them confusing and impious instead. It is quite interesting to note that when philosophy is criticized, it is almost never for its own sake, but rather because it leads to pagan religious practices[10] or because its ideas have a bad influence on public order and morals. This may be why Chrysostom does not seem to be as critical of Greek

---

[7] *In Act. apost. hom.* 4.4 (PG 60:48-9; NPNF 1-11:30-1).

[8] For Iamblichus' opposition to the idea of metempsychosis see *Iamblichi Chalcidencis: In Platonis dialogos commentariorum fragmenta*, ed. and trans. John M. Dillon (Leiden: Brill, 1973), 46, with references to relevant texts.

[9] In his homily *In Kalendas* 3 (PG 48:956) he calls the practice of observing days οὐ Χριστιανικῆς φιλοσοφίας, ἀλλ᾽ Ἑλληνικῆς πλάνης. What John considers appropriate for a Christian is not holding feasts for things like months or new moons or even Lord's days but for his whole life to be a feast. He goes on to explain that a constant feast is possible when one has a clean conscience, is nourished with good hopes, and revels in the delight of the good things to come (PG 49:955-6).

[10] *In 1 Cor. hom.* 4.4 (PG 61:36; NPNF 1-12:21).

philosophers that allegedly proclaimed atheistic ideas. In this respect, he mentions four examples: Protagoras, Diagoras the Milesian, Theodorus the Atheist, and Socrates. What these men had in common was a certain amount of influence "which comes from eloquence"[11] (δύναμιν τὴν ἀπὸ τῶν λόγων—an interesting phrase, considering the beginning of Socrates' speech in the *Apology*), were widely admired for their philosophy, and were considered to be innovators on religious matters, which brought danger to their lives, resulting in exile and even death. The reason Chrysostom mentions their example is primarily in order to exalt the accomplishment of the Apostles, who managed to overcome all these dangers, whilst also proclaiming Christ and removing the old gods from mainstream belief. However, Chrysostom's treatment of these 'atheists' also reveals the reasons behind his lack of criticism: these philosophers should not be harshly judged for refusing to believe in false gods, unlike those who actively promoted pagan religious practices (even though elsewhere Socrates is critiqued for belonging to the second category).[12] It is also important to note that Chrysostom does not critique philosophy as such: in another instance, Chrysostom admits that philosophy is a great thing, but what he means in this case is philosophy τὴν παρ' ἡμῖν. In contrast, the philosophy of τῶν ἔξωθεν is just words and myths, which do not possess true wisdom either. Ultimately, non-Christian philosophy loses its value because of its main aim: δόξα.[13]

Chrysostom's critique of the practices to which Greek philosophy led often employs the method of shaming but not naming those he criticizes. In some cases, as in the passage above, the critique is too general to be limited to one person. In other cases, his

---

[11] *In 1 Cor. hom.* 4.4 (PG 61:36-7; NPNF 1-12:21).

[12] This could possibly be a reaction to Julian's advice in his *Letter to a Priest* 301a (LCL 29:327): "For we ought not to give heed to all philosophers, not the doctrines of all, but only to those philosophers and those of their doctrines that make men god fearing, and teach concerning the gods, first that they exist, ..."

[13] *In Ioh. hom.* 63.1 (PG 59:349; trans. Goggin, *Commentary on Saint John*, 179).

criticism of specific philosophers would be particularly easy to decode but even so, he

refused to do so. The following is just one instance of this phenomenon:

> One of their lawgivers ordered that virgins should wrestle naked in the presence
> of men. I congratulate you that you are not able to bear mention of it; but their
> philosophers were not ashamed of the actual practice. Another, the chief of their
> philosophers, approves of their going out to war, and of their being held as
> common property, as if he were a pimp and they were something to indulge his
> lusts… For if those who professed philosophy among them made such laws,
> what will we say about those who were not philosophers? If such were the
> decrees of those who wore a long beard, and a serious cloak, what can be said of
> others?[14]

The laws of Lycurgus and the teaching of Plato are casually dismissed, without even

mentioning their names. The philosophers' traditional style of dress receives an ironic

mention as well, while criticism of Plato's programme for women in his ideal republic

is one of the most repeated arguments against him. Gender transgressions was a very

important issue for Chrysostom, and the criticism of Plato were not his only words on

the subject. His critique of the practice of syneisaktism among Christians was equally

devastating.[15]

As we have just indicated, John would often ascribe certain philosophical views to

the Greeks and other groups without going into much detail as to who pronounced them

or in what context. In most cases, he cites the view very briefly in order to immediately

refute it afterwards. For example, when he ascribes the view that the body was not

created by God to Greeks and heretics, he does it in a way that sets the stage for his

counter-argument, which goes all the way back to the creation of Adam and Eve.[16]

When criticizing "the insatiable desire for possessions" he mentions those who succumb

to Greek deception and follow a lifestyle where they let "all their possessions go,

keeping for themselves only a bit of a cloak and a staff, passing their whole life in this

---

[14] *In Tit. hom.* 5.4 (PG 62:694; trans. Aideen Hartney, *John Chrysostom and the Transformation of the City*, London: Duckworth, 2004, 188).

[15] Particularly in his *Contra eos qui subintroductae habent virgines* and *Quod regulares feminae viris cohabitare non debeant.*

[16] *De stat.* 4.2 (PG 49:121).

fashion and choosing to endure all this trouble and distress for the sake of people's good opinion."[17] If we were to guess the recipients of this criticism, the Cynics would be the primary candidates. This will become more obvious in the fourth chapter, where we will theorize about the possible identity of the people John is referring to here.

Sometimes he is more specific. For example, his interpretation of Acts 17:24 ("The God who made the world and everything in it, he who is Lord of heaven and earth, does not live in shrines made by human hands") is that this sentence utterly destroys and annihilates everything the philosophers say. In this case, he mentions two examples, the Stoics and the Epicureans, probably because they have previously been mentioned in Acts 17:18, and criticizes their views on the origins of the world: the Epicureans "affirm all to be fortuitously formed and (by concourse) of atoms, the Stoics held it to be body and conflagration."[18] But John argues against these cosmological ideas by claiming that there are two sufficient proofs (τεκμήρια) for the divine: that it needs nothing, and that it provides everything to everyone. In this respect, and compared to this, anything Plato and Epicurus have philosophized about God is nonsense![19] In this case his critique is based on fundamental cosmology, not on the immoral implications of the philosophy, as we have previously seen.

Generally speaking, Chrysostom considers the past to be important in scoring victories against both Greeks and Jews. This is not always necessarily related to the Christian past either, as he claims that Old Testament prophecies prove "our things to be older than theirs [the Greeks]."[20] Sometimes he will also interpret contemporary events with reference to the past as a way of showing the short-sightedness of the

---

[17] *In Gen. hom.* 20.5 (PG 53:173; Saint John Chrysostom, *Homilies on Genesis 18-45*, trans. Robert C. Hill, Washington, DC: Catholic University of America Press, 1990, 47-8).

[18] *In Act. apost. hom.* 38.2 (PG 60:270; NPNF 1-10:235). We replaced the word fire with conflagration since the word Chrysostom specifically uses here is *ekpírōsis*, a Stoic cosmological concept.

[19] *In Act. apost. hom.* 38.2 (PG 60:270).

[20] *Vid. dom. hom.* 2.3 (SC 277:98; St. John Chrysostom, *Old Testament Homilies vol. 2: Homilies on Isaiah and Jeremiah*, trans. Robert Charles Hill, Brookline, MA: Holy Cross Orthodox Press, 2003, 66).

interlocutors he often presents in his homilies. For example, when he discusses the conversion of the Philippian jailer in Acts 16:25-40, Chrysostom wants to shift the attention from the miracle to the actual conversion itself.[21] In order to do so, he presents the Greeks as saying that the jailer was "a vile, wretched creature, of no understanding, full of all that is bad and nothing else, and easily brought over to anything." They then proceed to categorize him alongside tanners, eunuchs, slaves, and women, as the kind of people that believe in these things (i.e. the things the Christians believe). Chrysostom's response to this is to point out that even then the Christians could count people such as centurions and proconsuls among their own, but, even more importantly, in the present, they count the emperors themselves. But this is not the main point he wants to make, since it is something greater he wants to talk about. His real target is "persons of no consideration (εὐτελεῖς)." Convincing people such as these about things like the resurrection, the kingdom of heaven, and the philosophical life is something exponentially more wonderful than persuading those considered wise. Chrysostom's thought can be summarized as such: "if what the philosophers would never have chosen to learn, this the slave does learn, then the wonder is greater."[22]

Chrysostom's ultimate aim is to talk about persuasion. His constant references to amazement regarding the fact that women and slaves were persuaded of these truths (as evidenced by their actions) also serves as a lesson to the Greek philosophers who were unable to persuade even their fellow philosophers. The first example is Plato, who not only was unable to persuade anyone, but also showed to his disciples the importance of not despising money by getting "an abundance of property, and golden rings, and goblets." Next up is Socrates. His legacy to his disciples was that glory should not be

---

[21] *In Act. apost. hom.* 36.2 (PG 60:260-1; NPNF 1-10:226).

[22] Cf. *In 1 Cor. hom.* 7.8 (PG 61:66; NPNF 1-12:42): "this is what especially makes the Gospel worthy of admiration; that such doctrines as Plato and his followers could not apprehend, the fishermen had power on a sudden to persuade the most ignorant sort of all to receive. For if they had persuaded wise men only, the result would not have been so wonderful; but in advancing slaves, and nurses, and eunuchs unto such great severity of life as to make them rivals to angels, they offered the greatest proof of their divine inspiration."

despised. Despite his constant philosophizing, Socrates always had an eye to fame. According to Chrysostom, one can easily see that by looking into Socrates' discourses as narrated in Plato's dialogues, with the qualifier that we believe what Plato has to say about his teacher. One can also see that these vainglorious discourses are full of irony. After this point, Chrysostom decides to leave it at that and directs his speech to the Christians again. In summary, the philosophers were not just unable to persuade people but also unable to practice what they preached. This is yet another sign of Christianity's strength versus Greek philosophy, which is also often accused of being the main enabler of paganism.

John makes a connection between philosophy and religion in many places[23] and wants to show a link between them that will enable him to charge the philosophers as fundamentally responsible for idolatry. For example, in his *Homilies on Romans* he writes that the original inventors of idolatry are the Egyptians, and Plato, "who is thought more reverend than the rest of them, glories in these masters."[24] Equally responsible is Plato's master himself, Socrates, who bids his disciples to sacrifice a cock to Asclepius. Therefore, alongside the worship of deities like Apollo and Bacchus, there is a darker side which worships creeping beasts and reptiles. Chrysostom then mentions some philosophers who lifted bulls, scorpions and dragons up in the sky, which is in itself the work of the devil who wishes to bring humans down to the worship of creeping things. The passage concludes with an attack against Plato's claim (uttered by Socrates) in *Ion* 533e-534b: "the Muse inspires men herself ... For all the good epic poets utter all those fine poems not from art, but as inspired and possessed... And what they tell is true. For a poet is a light and winged and sacred thing, and is unable ever to compose until he has been inspired and put out of his senses, and his mind is no longer

---

[23] Cf. *In Col. hom.* 6.1 (PG 62:339; NPNF 1-13:285): "Having first shaken [Paul] to pieces the Grecian observances, he next overthrows the Jewish ones also. For both Greeks and Jews practiced many observances, but the former from philosophy, the latter from the Law."

[24] *In Rom. hom.* 3.3 (PG 60:414; NPNF 1-11:353).

in him..." Chrysostom is not eager to debate the truthfulness of this claim and immediately dismisses it as absurd and ludicrous.[25] Plato might have wanted to hide his support for idolatry behind the poets and their supposed inspiration by the Muses, but Chrysostom believes he sees right through that and refuses to even engage with the argument. Even if he did, he would attribute the inspiration to demons as he does elsewhere, but this time using Plato as a supporter of his argument!

His critique of philosophy mixed with disparaging comments about the polytheistic religion was often specifically directed against its outcomes. Thus, in his *Homilies on John*, while recognizing that some of those outside the faith (ἐξ ἐθνῶν) did believe before the coming of Christ, they enjoyed none of the advantages that the Jews did. Chrysostom claims that the Greeks "never heard divine oracles- not even as much as might be spoken in a dream,"[26] which certainly sounds like an insinuation against the oracles and their inspiration. At the same time, these "pagans" were "always entangled in the myths of madmen (for that is what the philosophy of the pagans is [τοῦτο γὰρ ἡ τῶν ἔξωθεν φιλοσοφία])."[27] John would not even hesitate to use Plato to support his argument against the idea that the prophets had anything in common with soothsayers:

> We learn something else from this as well, that the inspired authors were not like the seers. In their case, after all, when the demon takes possession of their soul, it cripples their mind and clouds their reasoning, and so they utter everything without their mind understanding anything of what is said: rather, it is like a flute sounding without a musician to play a tune. This was said also by a philosopher of theirs in these words, "Just like the soothsayers and seers saying many things without knowing anything of what they say [*Apology* 22C, *Meno* 99D].[28]

---

[25] *In Rom. hom.* 3.3 (PG 60:414; LCL 164:421-3).

[26] *In Ioh. hom.* 9.1 (PG 59:70; trans. Goggin, *Commentary on Saint John*, 90). All the references in this paragraph are from this passage. Interestingly, even though John does not use the word Hellenes, Goggin translates the word for those outside the faith as "Gentiles" and again when the philosophy of those outside (the faith) is mentioned she translates it as pagans. While these translations are not wrong in this particular context, since it is very clear that John is indeed referring to the classical tradition, there are other instances where we cannot be sure that those outside the faith are always the "Greeks".

[27] *In Ioh. hom.* 9.1 (PG 59:70; trans. Goggin, *Commentary on Saint John*, 90).

[28] *Exp. in ps.* 45.1 (PG 55:184; *St. John Chrysostom: Commentary on the Psalms vol. 1*, trans. Robert Charles Hill, Brookline, MA: Holy Cross Orthodox Press, 1998, 258-9).

The exact same passage is used again in his twenty-ninth *Homily on 1 Corinthians*, but this time John has enriched his repertoire.[29] After citing Plato again, he mentions the story of a man who was divining and found himself torn by a demon. To the persons practicing these things that man says "Finally, loosen the lord [probably Apollo]. The mortal no longer makes room for the god."[30] This is a doubtful fragment from the *Chaldean Oracles* (no 225), and John has probably read it in Eusebius' *Praeparatio Evangelica* 5.9.1. This is then followed by a citation from Porphyry's *Philosophy from Oracles* ("Unbind my wreaths, and bathe my feet in drops from the pure stream; erase these mystic lines and let me go"), which is also cited by Eusebius in *Praep. Ev.* 5.9.8, in order to show the gods' willingness to withdraw upon their invocation and the oracles Eusebius cites are to that effect, as Aaron Johnson points out.[31] Chrysostom uses these examples as a starting point for his real target, the Pythia. After a very graphic description of the frenzied process by which the oracle uttered her prophecies, Chrysostom goes on to explain the differences between prophecy in Christianity and in ancient Greek religion.

Returning again to the *Homilies on John*: Chrysostom's attack on religion and philosophy is followed by an attack on the poets, whose works are called "nonsense" (λήρους) and he ascertains that they were enslaved to wood and stone. In summary: "they knew nothing useful or sound, either for doctrine or living, since their life was more impure and corrupt than their doctrine."[32] But, one may ask, how did it come to this? It was, John argues, all because of their gods, who took pleasure in every vice and enjoyed being worshipped by shameful words and deeds. This descent "to the very depths of evil" is made so that John can finally argue his point: despite all this, as if by a

---

[29] *In 1 Cor. hom.* 29.1 (PG 61:241-2; NPNF 1-12:169).

[30] Ruth Majercik, *The Chaldean Oracles: Text, Translation, and Commentary* (Leiden: Brill, 1989), 137.

[31] Johnson, *Religion and Identity in Porphyry*, 320.

[32] *In Ioh. hom.* 9.1 (PG 59:70; trans. Goggin, *Commentary on Saint John*, 90).

mechanism from heaven, they appeared shining forth (and became Christians, as one might expect).

It should be clear by now that for Chrysostom Hellenism was, primarily, a philosophical *and* religious system that entailed a different way of life and originated from a variety of sources, including the poets, philosophers, and the oracles: as such, it either led to immoral deeds, or it led to the mind being misled by deceptive oracles or by being possessed by a god (or, as John argued, a demon). However, even if that way of life was different, Chrysostom argues in his *Homilies on John*, no one has the right to condemn a man living ἐν Ἑλληνισμῷ[33]: this is because his lifestyle is merely in accord with the shameful and ridiculous gods and practices he believes in. John is also reluctantly willing to admit that there are Χριστιανοὶ τὰ φαῦλα πράσσοντες, καὶ Ἕλληνες ἐν φιλοσοφίᾳ ζῶντες, 'philosophia' here being what he considered true philosophy, i.e. a Christian lifestyle.[34] But he does not consider good behavior and seemliness to be part of virtue, so he would rather be told "of the man who endures the fierce onslaught of his passions, yet lives in an exemplary manner." If promises of the Kingdom and threat of hell cannot inspire the pursuit of virtue in the Christians themselves, John argues, he finds it extremely difficult to believe that those who do not believe in any of those things would seek to be virtuous, and if they pretend to be so, that they do it for the sake of glory. Even if some of the pagans do live virtuous lives, this would not make what John said a lie, because he is talking about the rule and not the exceptions. Again, the fact that someone is prudent and refrains from stealing does not constitute virtue because he might still be enslaved by vainglory. Indeed, no one can point to someone who, while being a pagan, "is rid of all passions and free from all evil." This is because, even those among them who were able to rise above wealth and

---

[33] *In Ioh. hom.* 28.2-3 (PG 59:164-5; trans. Goggin, *Commentary on Saint John*, 273-5). All references in this paragraph come from this homily.

[34] Chrysostom is adamant that true knowledge is only the wisdom provided by God, and that those who boast about their acquaintance with external wisdom are deficient when it comes to it. See *In 2 Cor. hom.* 12.2 (PG 61:483).

gluttony, "have most of all been enslaved by love of praise; and this is the root of all evils." We return to the same vice Chrysostom previously applied to the philosophers, only this time applied to common anonymous pagans: vainglory.

To be fair to him, Chrysostom does not consider vainglory to be an exclusively "pagan" characteristic. It can be found in equal amounts within the Christian communities, even the ones we would presume to be the farthest from it. Πάντων αἴτιον τῶν κακῶν ἡ κενοδοξία: it has turned churches upside down, spoiled political affairs, and "upsets entire homes, and cities, and peoples, and nations." It even holds power in the desert, where those who have abandoned wealth and everything worldly and subdued their bodily passions have lost everything to vainglory.[35] Vainglory is a temptation that makes no distinctions: all humans can fall victims to it.

ii. Reconstructing the beliefs of the Greeks: Religious criticism

Chrysostom's criticism of ancient Greek religious beliefs and rituals is quite varied across his works and it is not always clear whether the views he considers as "pagan" are legitimate or straw men that he uses for the purposes of his argument. In this section, we will attempt both to reconstruct the different views he expresses in many of his homilies and to see whether a coherent image of the religion of the Hellenes is possible. It is sometimes the case that the Greeks' theological opinion will be thrown into a mix that includes people like Mani, Marcion, and Valentinus, as when Chrysostom ascribes to all of them the view that matter pre-existed.[36] These same groups are also included under the collective term οἱ ἔξωθεν and their similarity this time is their utter trust in their own reasonings; contrary to this, a Christian who is vigilant will have no need of Greek *logoi*.[37] However, Chrysostom also seems to grasp

---

[35] *In Ioh. hom.* 29.3 (PG 59:170-1; trans. Goggin, *Commentary on Saint John*, 286).

[36] *In Gen. hom.* 2.3 (PG 53:30). For a similar conflation but only between Manicheans and Greeks this time, see *In Gen. serm.* 1.1 (SC 433:144).

[37] *In Eph. hom.* 23.1 (PG 62:164). In *In Col. hom.* 5.3 (PG 62:335; NPNF 1-13:282) Chrysostom contrasts faith with reasonings and their respective outcomes: "For as reasonings divide, and shake loose,

the developmental nature of Greek religion, as when he argues that the Athenians slowly incorporated other divinities, such as the ones from the Hyperboreans, Pan, and the greater and lesser mysteries (as was the case e.g. with the Eleusinian mysteries).[38]

Chrysostom repeatedly states that hyperbolic reliance on reasonings (*logismoi*) is a distinctive mark of Hellenic thought and a feature that separates it from Christianity.[39] For him, all knowledge of God presupposes faith, which in itself stands in stark contrast to questioning and doubt. At the same time, he makes clear that this is concerning the divine: "if the things asserted were human, we ought to examine them; but since they are of God, they are only to be revered and believed."[40] The lack of belief, he argues, inevitably leads to an agnostic position regarding the existence of God. To counter that, he claims that knowledge of God is only possible without any proofs or evidence (Τοῦτο πρῶτον τεκμήριον τοῦ τὸν Θεὸν εἰδέναι, τὸ πιστεύειν οἷς ἂν λέγῃ χωρὶς τεκμηρίων καὶ ἀποδείξεων).[41] Somewhat surprisingly, John brings forward the Greeks to support this last claim: he says that even they believe this, since they believed their gods and simultaneously thought of themselves as the offspring of the gods (which was their way of saying they were their descendants but did not have actual proof of that). But the gods are not the only example he brings forward. Up next is the one he calls "deceiver and sorcerer," Pythagoras, who was so revered that a simple Αὐτὸς ἔφη in relation to his sayings rendered immeasurable credence and weight to it.[42] He also mentions images of the goddess Silence (ἡ σιγὴ, but presumably he means Hesychia) in

---

so faith causes solidity and compactness." However, both reasoning and rationality are characteristics of human nature that distinguish it from the irrational creatures. See *Quod. nem. laed.* 7 (SC 103:94).

[38] *In Tit. hom.* 3.1 (PG 62:677).

[39] The heretics are also responsible for inserting their own *logismoi* into the doctrines of the Church and they are worse than poison, since poisons might harm the body but the heretics put in danger the salvation of one's soul: *Cat.* 1.24 (SC 50bis:120).

[40] *In 1 Tim. hom.* 1.3 (PG 62:507; NPNF 1-13:410).

[41] Ibid.

[42] Gregory Nazianzus has previously used this phrase against Julian and his ignorance of the *Logoi*, since the followers of Pythagoras considered it the primary and most important of their doctrines. See Susanna Elm, *Sons of Hellenism, Fathers of the Church: Emperor Julian, Gregory of Nazianzus, and the Vision of Rome* (Berkeley: University of California Press, 2012), 391.

pagan temples, whose finger on her mouth exhorted the visitors to be silent. But the real point Chrysostom is trying to make is that Greek beliefs were rightly questioned, since by nature they were conflicted reasonings, doubts, and disputations (μάχαι τῶν λογισμῶν καὶ ἀμφισβητήσεις καὶ συμπεράσματα).[43] On the other hand, the Christian beliefs were no such thing. What is it, however, that makes them different? Their origin, according to Chrysostom. Greek beliefs derive from human wisdom, but Christian ones were taught by spiritual grace. In the end, Christian doctrines are the true wisdom (τῆς ὄντως σοφίας δόγματα). Chrysostom also critiques Greek pedagogy in connection to the theme of Greek and Christian beliefs: the Greeks have no teachers or students, because in their case everyone is in conversation with one another. In contrast to that, the Christian should know from whom s/he needs to learn; s/he should not doubt, but be persuaded; s/he should not dispute, but believe.[44]

In John's *Homilies on Genesis*, the Greeks are purported to be those who were not able to move from the beauty of the sun and realize that it was God's creation, thus ending up singing its praises and treating it as a deity in its own right.[45] This could be a reference to any number of things: the status of Helios as a Titan, his identification sometimes as Apollo and other times as Zeus, or even the presence of a strong cult in Rhodes.[46] John does not make it easy for us to know exactly what he means except the

---

[43] *In 1 Tim. hom.* 1.3 (PG 62:507; NPNF 1-13:410).

[44] *In 1 Tim. hom.* 1.3 (PG 62:507; NPNF 1-13:410). But elsewhere (*In 1 Tim. hom.* 10.3, PG 62:551; NPNF 1-13:439) Chrysostom explains the necessity of teachers among Christians due to the fact that they were not who they were meant to be: "There would be no need of words [presumably Biblical exegesis] if we shone forth in our lives, there would be no need of teachers [i.e. priests] if we exhibited works. There would be no Greek if we were such Christians as we ought to be." The Christians only needed to be instructed because they did not follow the way of life derived from their beliefs. If they did, there would be no need for instructors. The sense of this is better explained by a passage in *Ad eos qui scand.* 13.1 (SC 79:188, my translation): "Tell me, what priests did Abraham have at his disposal? What teachers? What catechism? What exhortation? What advice? Then there were no written documents, no law, no prophets, none of these sorts of things." Yet Abraham needed none of these things since he showed his faith through works, possessed genuine and warm love, disregarded money and lived a life that pre-shadowed the life of the monks in Chrysostom's day. Later in the same text John uses the same argument in relation to Noah and Job.

[45] *In Gen. hom.* 6.4 (PG 53:58).

[46] For the cult of Helios see Jennifer Larson, *Ancient Greek Cults: A Guide* (London: Routledge, 2007), 158-9.

fact that he considers the Sun to have acquired a divine status among the Greeks. In any case the aim of the polemic is apologetic. John wants to reinforce the point that the Sun is just another of God's creations, and that "from contemplation of created things one should move on to the Creator."[47] But this is just one of many in a formidable catalogue of what he calls Greek impieties, which are sometimes contrasted to Christian beliefs and sometimes are not. Thus, the Christian belief in a "simple, free of parts and shape" deity is contrasted to the Greek irreverence of ascribing "an arrangement of limbs to God."[48] In fact, the Greeks' excessive trust in their own reasonings (λογισμοῖς) led them to search in bodies for the one who is incorporeal and in shapes for the one who is shapeless.[49] They also divinized their passions: thus, desire was called Venus, anger was called Mars, and drunkenness was called Bacchus.[50]

This is not the only instance where Chrysostom makes a similar accusation. He often sees the origins of idolatry in the practice of divinizing mortals (which is different from divinizing passions), and more specifically the admiration of people beyond their worth. He mentions a decision by the Roman Senate decreeing Alexander as the thirteenth God, and he contrasts that to the Divinity of Christ, who "was not proclaimed by man's decree, nor was He counted one of the many that were by them elected."[51] He also mentions the deification of Antinous, the Roman Emperor Hadrian's lover, and the naming of a city after him, as well as the fact that he was just a child when he became

---

[47] *In Gen. hom.* 6.4 (PG 53:58; Saint John Chrysostom, *Homilies on Genesis 1-17*, trans. Robert C. Hill, Washington, DC: Catholic University of America Press, 1986, 85).

[48] *In Gen. hom.* 13.2 (PG 53:107; trans. Hill, *Homilies on Genesis 1-17*, 173). John's formulation of the divine as ἁπλοῦν γὰρ καὶ ἀσύνθετον καὶ ἀσχημάτιστον is a direct quotation of Gregory of Nyssa, *De Beat.* 7.160 (GNO VII/2). Claudio Moreschini, "Gregorio di Nissa, *De beatitudinibus*, Oratio VII," in *Gregory of Nyssa: Homilies on the Beatitudes. An English Version with Commentary and Supporting Studies, Proceedings of the Eighth International Colloquium on Gregory of Nyssa (Paderborn, 14-18 September 1998)*, ed. Hubertus R. Drobner and Albert Viviano (Leiden: Brill, 2000), 240-1, calls this the usual characterization of God's nature among the Cappadocians and of Origen before them, with the qualities themselves being derived from Platonic philosophy, particularly *Phaedr.* 247a. He also provides more references in the works of the Cappadocians in n. 24, 241. Unfortunately, we cannot possibly know whether John's source was Origen or the Cappadocians.

[49] *In Rom. hom.* 3.2 (PG 60:413).

[50] *In Rom. hom.* 6.6 (PG 60:440).

[51] *In 2 Cor. hom.* 26.4 (PG 61:580-2; NPNF 1-12:402-4).

Hadrian's favourite. Chrysostom already anticipates that someone might object to these deifications and say that these were mere mortals, and their death testifies to this. But he already has an answer at hand. The devil has invented another way to deceive people: the soul's immortality (which makes the death of their physical body irrelevant), mixed with excessive flattery towards people like Alexander and Antinous. He then mentions that when Christians say that "the Crucified lives," they are faced with laughter, although it has been proclaimed by the entire world, "in old time by miracles, now by converts," and these could not possibly be the successes of a dead man. Yet when someone says, "Alexander lives," he is believed, even if there are no miracles to testify to this effect. John concedes the point that during his lifetime, Alexander achieved many remarkable things,[52] subdued nations and cities, won many wars and was victorious in battle. However, there is nothing special or new about a king winning battles with armies at his disposal, Chrysostom says, whereas the power of the Cross and its achievements throughout proclaim Christ's power everywhere. Ultimately Alexander's kingdom was torn to pieces after his death and was never restored, and the location of his tomb is still unknown along with the day he died. On the contrary, the tombs of the Apostles are in the most royal city, "more splendid than the palaces of kings" and honoured even by the Emperors themselves. He who wears the diadem implores not Alexander but the tentmaker and the fisherman to be "his advocates with God," and Constantine's burial alongside the Apostles in Constantinople shows that "what porters are to kings in their palaces, that kings are at the tomb to fishermen."[53]

---

[52] Besides these and the references to Alexander in connection to his meeting with Diogenes, Chrysostom also refers to him in the context of his discussion on the Macedonians and their fame, which, before the coming of Christ, was greater than the Romans' and in fact the latter were admired for their achievement to conquer them. Alexander may have started from a small town, but was soon able to conquer the *oikoumene* and his achievements were mentioned by Daniel and his high-mindedness and greatness of his soul was celebrated across the world. John's praise of Alexander in this instance is in *In 1 Thess. hom.* 2.1 (PG 62:399) and serves mostly as an introduction as to how the Macedonians were known everywhere, Thessaloniki being a part of Macedonia.

[53] *In 2 Cor. hom.* 26.4 (PG 61:580-2; NPNF 1-12:402-4).

The practice of divinizing mortals, besides being ridiculous compared with the (truly divine) Christ and his (human but revered) followers, also leads to unbelief towards Christ and had specific implications related to the rejection of fundamental Christian doctrines, which were often orchestrated by the philosophers. For example, in his *Homilies on Acts* Chrysostom alleges that a denial of the resurrection is combined with a further denial that God can create anything out of nothing.[54] The denial of the resurrection is also connected elsewhere with a Greek rejection of the last judgment, since Chrysostom thinks that there is no other way the world can be judged.[55] In fact, Chrysostom criticizes the fact that the Greeks reject both the resurrection and Hades as myths, whereas stories of gods fornicating are not considered myths but are believed. When one talks to them of hell, they reply back that these are myths constructed by the poets who wanted to overturn the good life (εὐζωΐα).[56] These popular beliefs are also contrasted by some with the philosophers, who "discovered something truly grand, and far better than these."

But Chrysostom will not hear it. These same philosophers are responsible for the belief in *heimarmene* as well as the rejection of providence, and that everything consists of atoms. The targets here seem to be the Stoics, Democritus and Leucippus, but John is not quite done yet. Others assign a body to God, turn the souls of humans into dogs and

---

[54] *In Act. apost. hom.* 2.4 (PG 60:31).

[55] *In Act. apost. hom.* 38.4 (PG 60:273). At this point he calls Greek ideas about creation and judgment "children's inventions, ravings of drunkards." John believed that the Greeks would only believe in the resurrection after they witness a philosophical attitude towards afflictions: "But to these things the Greeks give no heed. For (one will say) do not tell me of him who is philosophical when out of the affliction, for this is nothing great or surprising —show me a man who in the very affliction itself is philosophical, and then I will believe the resurrection," *In Heb. hom.* 4.5 (PG 63:43; NPNF 1-14:386). Elsewhere, Chrysostom explicitly states that belief in the resurrection and the last judgment is incompatible with belief in fate (εἱμαρμένη) and admits his embarrassment with having to teach Christians about the resurrection since "he who needs to learn that there is a resurrection, and has not convinced himself thoroughly that things do not happen by blind force or at random or by chance, could not be a Christian." *In Ioh. hom.* 45.4 (PG 59:256; trans. Goggin, *Commentary on Saint John*, 459). His observation about Christians holding such conflicting beliefs is interesting, considering that by that time many in his audience must have been cradle Christians. For the belief in the resurrection of Christ as a distinguishing feature between Christians and Greeks in Chrysostom's writings see Sandwell, *Religious Identity in Late Antiquity*, 69. As we will see later on in this chapter, in different places Chrysostom assumed that the last judgment and retribution was also a belief held by the pagans!

[56] *In Eph. hom.* 12.3 (PG 62:91-2; NPNF 1-13:111).

try to persuade us that we were "once a dog, and a lion, and a fish"- another reference to metempsychosis. Furthermore, even Greek philosophers in Paul's time believed that God is a body and that only pleasure is true happiness.[57] For all these reasons the Greek philosophers look like a man whose mind has been so darkened that he sees a rope and thinks of it as a serpent, an image Chrysostom probably borrows from Sextus Empiricus' *Outlines of Pyrrhonism*.[58] In sum, then, for Chrysostom, these beliefs of the philosophers are proofs of their darkened understanding both in respect of their lives and their doctrines.

The idea of *heimarmene* was consistently attacked by John in different writings and, depending on the context, for a variety of reasons. For example, in his *Homilies on Colossians* it is contrasted to the doctrine of the Resurrection and is called unjust, irrational, cruel and inhumane, whereas the latter is considered righteous since it awards everyone according to their worth.[59] Peculiarly, the ones Chrysostom accuses as accepting of *heimarmene* are those who defined pleasure as the ultimate end, i.e. the Epicureans (and John uses indolence and their lack of *nous* as the reason of this acceptance), whilst the lovers of virtue among them threw it out as irrational. Ultimately, necessity (a synonym for fate in John's corpus) was a diabolic construct so that humans would forego virtue.

John's criticism of religious Hellenism sometimes includes a direct attack on the gods of Olympus or on pagan cultic observances. When that is the case, we classify it under religious criticism since that aspect seems to be the prevailing one, even if others are included as well. As we will see in the following chapter, John often compares the

---

[57] *In Act. apost. hom.* 38.1 (PG 60:267).

[58] *In Eph. hom.* 12.3 (PG 62:91-2; NPNF 1-13:111). Sextus Empiricus, *PH* 1.33 (LCL 273:140-1). The origin of Chrysostom's image was first pointed out by William John Copeland, the translator of the Homilies in the *Library of the Fathers* series.

[59] *In Col. hom.* 2.5 (PG 62:318)

apostles and the martyrs with other humans. Nevertheless, sometimes he also compares the apostles to the Greek gods, as in the passage below:

> And what, pray you, is that Minerva of theirs, and Apollo, and Juno? They are different kinds of demons among them. And there is a king of theirs, who thinks fit to die for the mere purpose of being accounted equal with the gods. But not so the men here: no, just the contrary. Hear how they speak on the occasion of the lame man's cure. "Ye men of Israel, why look ye so earnestly on us, as though by our own power or holiness we had made him to walk? (Acts 3:12) We also are men of like passions with you. (Acts 14:14) But with those, great is the self-elation, great the bragging; all for the sake of men's honors, nothing for the pure love of truth and virtue (Ἐκεῖ δὲ πολὺς ὁ τῦφος, πολλὴ ἡ ἀλαζονεία· πάντα διὰ τὰς παρὰ τῶν ἀνθρώπων τιμάς, οὐδὲν φιλοσοφίας ἕνεκεν) ...[60]

A great number of themes emerges from Chrysostom's polemic against the Greek gods. What is primarily emphasized is their demonic nature, which is contrasted to the apostolic humility. They are also accused of suffering from *tuphos* and extreme boastfulness, which is the root cause for their seeking glory among men, instead of performing their actions for the sake of philosophy, which in this case is the literal meaning of John's Greek. The word *tuphos*[61] has a diverse range of meanings that includes vanity, pride, delusion or craziness and is a very interesting concept. The Cynics used the concept to describe a vice, of which they often accused Plato and which they saw as characteristic of the masses.

---

[60] *In Act. apost. hom.* 4.4 (PG 60:49-50; NPNF 1-11:31). Elsewhere, Chrysostom argues against the sacrificial system and cites Homer (*Iliad* 4.49), whom he simply calls "a poet of the Greeks," in support of his view that the gods of the ἔξωθεν demanded bloody sacrifices whereas the God of Christians should be worshipped through an impeccable lifestyle and with the nous only, for which see *Exp. in ps.* 50.4 (PG 55:247). He also repeats the accusation that the Greeks revel in self-references and that their gods used to be humans (διὸ καὶ ἀπὸ ἀνθρώπων ποιοῦσι θεούς): *In 1 Cor. hom.* 5.1 (PG 61:42). More specifically, the "principle and root of idolatry" is because "many after having had success in wars, and set up trophies, and built cities, and done diverse other benefits of this kind to the people of those times, came to be esteemed gods by the multitude, and were honoured with temples, and altars; and the whole catalogue of the Grecian gods is made up of such men." *De stat.* 1.7 (PG 49:25; NPNF 1-9:338). Finally, *in Post. presb. Goth.* 4 (PG 63:506), Chrysostom is yet again being consistent in his inconsistency, and declares that the Greeks made up their gods and idolatry is an outcome of their attempt to count themselves as equals to God: εἰδωλολατρεία ἐντεῦθεν γέγονεν, ὁ κολοφὼν τῶν κακῶν τῶν ἀνθρώπων, τῶν πολλῶν εἰς ἀπόνοιαν αἰρομένων καὶ ἰσοθεΐας ἐπιθυμούντων. Ἅπαντες γοῦν οἱ παρὰ τοῖς Ἕλλησι θεοὶ ὑπὸ τῶν ἀνθρώπων ἀνεπλάσθησαν.

[61] For the different meanings of the word and an interesting analysis of its use among the Cynics and the Stoics see Rene Brouwer, *The Stoic Sage: The Early Stoics on Wisdom, Sagehood and Socrates* (Cambridge: Cambridge University Press, 2014), 152-158.

Chrysostom's criticism of ancient religion is not limited to his remarks against the gods. He often refers to remnants of pagan religious practices among the Christian population and urges them to abandon them, as they go against their beliefs. In some cases, these practices seem to have nothing particularly anti-Christian about them. For example, John argued against the custom of naming children after their forebears and promoted the practice of giving them names of martyrs, bishops and apostles instead.[62] He understands that in earlier times these customs were reasonable and served as consolation for death since the departed appeared to live through the name, but this should not be the case anymore. To reinforce his argument, he brings up the examples of the righteous of the OT (Abraham, Isaac, Jacob, and Moses) who did not follow this custom either.[63] John's argument for Christian names is that by naming children after Peter or John, they will strive to imitate their zeal. While the practice by itself might initially have been harmless, the method used was characterized by Chrysostom as of questionable orthodoxy. He writes: "And do not, I pray, follow Greek customs. It is a great disgrace and laughable when in a Christian household some Greek pagan customs (ἔθη τινὰ ἑλληνικὰ) are observed; and they kindle lamps and sit watching to see which is the first to be extinguished and consumed, and other such customs which bring certain destruction to those who practice them. Do not regard such doings as paltry and trivial."[64] The purpose of the custom John is referring to is not immediately obvious, but he refers to these practices again in a homily on 1 Corinthians 4 and helps us understand the logic behind the reference: "When a name has to be given to the boy, they fail to call him after the saints. As men in older times used first to do, they light lamps and give them names. Then they assign the same name to the child as that of the lamp which

---

[62] *Inan. glor. et ed. lib.* 47 (SC 188:146).

[63] *Inan. glor. et ed. lib.* 49 (SC 188:147).

[64] *Inan. glor. et ed. lib.* 48 (SC 188:146-7; trans. Laistner, *Christianity and Pagan culture*, 108).

burns longest, inferring that he will live a long life."[65] This practice was called name divination by lamps, and even though in many cases the names given belonged to Christian saints, it was considered superstitious and common enough for Chrysostom to inveigh against it.[66]

Another example is the use of charms and amulets in Antioch, where the practice of wearing talismans with the image of Alexander the Great seems to have been popular in Chrysostom's time.[67] Isabella Sandwell argues that presenting the use of amulets as a strictly "Greek" feature helps Chrysostom in his attempt to "clarify an aspect of Christian identity", by "making a contrast with Greekness in his definition of the use of amulets as Greek."[68] This attempt to define what it means to be a Christian was a result of the Christians losing their minority status as a group excluded from mainstream society. In this respect, Chrysostom was trying to construct identities – identities that Sandwell believes did not objectively exist, but which he saw as fixed and clear-cut.

---

[65] *In 1 Cor. hom.* 12.13 (PG 61:105; trans. Laistner, *Christianity and Pagan culture*, 137-8).

[66] For more information on the practice and its survival into late Byzantium see Jane Baun, "Coming of Age in Byzantium: Agency and Authority in Rites of Passage from Infancy to Adulthood," in *Authority in Byzantium*, ed. Pamela Armstrong (London: Ashgate, 2013), 113-36, especially 120-6.

[67] *Illum. Cat.* 2.5 (PG 49:240; *St. John Chrysostom: Baptismal Instructions*, trans. Paul W. Harkins, New York: Newman Press, 190-1): "What would you say of those who use incantations and amulets and of those who tie bronze coins of Alexander of Macedon around their heads and feet? Tell me, are these the things in which we place our hopes? After our Master died for us on the cross, will we put our hope for salvation in the image of a Greek king? Do you not know how many wrongs the cross has set right? Did it not destroy death, did it not blot out sin, did it not end the power of the devil, does it not suffice for the well-being of our body? Did it restore the whole world, and yet you have no trust in it? What punishment would you not deserve? You carry around on your person not only amulets but even incantations; you bring into your house drunken and witless old hags. Are you not ashamed and do you not blush, after you have been trained in true doctrine, you have been terrified by these things?"

[68] Sandwell, *Religious Identity in Late Antiquity*, 5. Chrysostom saw his polemic against certain pagan religious practices of his day, which were also shared by some Christians, as a continuation of the apostolic project: "This is what we have to dispel and dissolve. It is night not among heretics and among Greeks only, but also in the multitude on our side, in respect of doctrines and of life. For many entirely disbelieve the resurrection; many fortify themselves with their horoscope; (γένεσιν ἑαυτοῖς ἐπιτειχίζουσι) many adhere to superstitious observances, and to omens, and auguries, and presages. And some likewise employ amulets and charms." *In 1 Cor. hom.* 4.11 (PG 61:40; NPNF 1-12:21). There is no reason to doubt Chrysostom's depiction of certain Christians in this passage. If anything, the description of believers participating in these practices would be embarrassing for any Christian preacher, and it would be more beneficial if he tried to hide the fact rather than present it in such a frank manner. We should also be reminded of B. Leyerle's pertinent remark that "despite the highly rhetorical nature of Chrysostom's treatises, we may still hope to extract from them some social data, since polemic, in order to be effective, must bear at least a stylized resemblance to observable reality." Leyerle, *Theatrical Shows and Ascetic Lives*, 11.

"For Chrysostom, people had to choose whether they were a Christian or a Greek and there was to be no space for ambiguity between the two because religious identity had to be displayed visibly in every action at all times."[69]

While Sandwell is correct that identity construction usually involves marking out differences from other groups, some of her other claims are more contentious. I agree that for Chrysostom there was "no space for ambiguity" between *being* Christian or not. Nevertheless, Chrysostom clearly refers to *actions* of the Greeks of the past, which his Christian audience could follow without problems, such as voluntary poverty. While it is true that in many of these examples Chrysostom does say that the Greeks did not have the right intention even when doing the right things, it is clear that he approves of the action itself. Hence it does not seem to be the case that, in Sandwell's words, "religious identity had to be displayed visibly in every action at all times."

This is not to deny the fact that religious identity was what primarily distinguished the different groups in Chrysostom's thought, which is well established across studies of Chrysostom: "Chrysostom hoped to eclipse the distinctions of class or culture, by making religious identity the primary marker of difference in society."[70] But Sandwell also overlooks the dimension of conversion from one belief to another and the practices that accompanied it.

As Michael Whitby argues:

> For the majority of people, conversion to Christianity could not have meant the total abandonment of all aspects of pagan practice; instead, conversion represented a coalescence of practices rather than a complete change, so that the survival of some pagan practices does not necessarily prove survival of a much more complex set of beliefs. However, a zealous Christian bishop who encountered such practices might choose to place the worse interpretation on this behaviour, either because he believed that any sign of non-Christian activity

---

[69] Sandwell, *Religious Identity in Late Antiquity*, 6.

[70] Maxwell, *Christianization*, 147.

might provide the occasion for a serious lapse or because his reputation could be enhanced by the conquest of "real" pagans.[71]

As we saw above, sometimes Chrysostom would witness Christians who actually did hold on to beliefs that were entirely in opposition to major Christian doctrines, such as the resurrection. Sandwell can also be challenged on her statement that "neither Christian nor Greek nor Jewish identity existed essentially or objectively in Chrysostom's world", therefore he had to "continually construct them out of a situation where many practices were shared by people whatever their religious allegiance."[72] First, despite the fact that people did indeed share a number of practices, there were also practices that were unique to each group and practices that, despite their similarity on the surface, took a different meaning. Furthermore, to say that these identities were not fixed is one thing; to claim that they did not essentially exist is another. If we follow that line of thought it would appear that authors like Chrysostom were arguing against smoke-screens and not real ideas. Sandwell's assertion is a result of her emphasis on religious identity, which she believes does not have an objective existence and results from boundaries constructed by human actors. But neither Greek nor Jewish identity limited themselves to their religious aspects (this is the case for centuries before but also during Chrysostom's time). Instead, I would argue that Laura Nasrallah's comment that early Christian apologists did not define Christianity "against paganism or Judaism as much as they define Christianity against certain *kinds* of other ethnic and religious practices, practices they usually attribute to the 'many' or the crowd" is much more applicable to the way Chrysostom defines Christianity.[73]

---

[71] Michael Whitby, "John of Ephesus and the Pagans: Pagan Survivals in the Sixth Century," in *Paganism in the Later Roman Empire and in Byzantium*, ed. Maciej Salamon (Cracow: Universitas, 1991), 114.

[72] Sandwell, *Religious Identity in Late Antiquity*, 5.

[73] Laura Salah Nasrallah, *Christian Responses to Roman Art and Architecture: The Second-Century Church amid the Spaces of Empire* (New York: Cambridge University Press, 2010), 6-7.

Finally, Sandwell appears to vary her estimation of the significance of amulets: she refers to Chrysostom's characterization of amulets as Greek, idolatrous or Jewish, but also claims (in the same paragraph) that he saw the use of amulets as exclusively Greek, while at the same time referring to Chrysostom's accusation against Christians who wore phylacteries as a Jewish practice![74]

This construction of identity in the case of Greek religion also involved a focus on belief as well as practice. One tactic used by Chrysostom was to single out a set of elements and identify them with the core of Greek religion. These elements included, among others, worship of the sun, water and animals, divinized humans and an association of Greek religion with philosophy.[75] John also argued that purity of life is of no benefit if one's doctrines are corrupt, while sound doctrine is not enough if one's life is immoral.[76] He also attributes many heretical teachings, particularly those of Marcion and Valentinus, to the Greeks, and considers that many of their beliefs (such as the belief that matter is uncreated) were really borrowed from non-Christian (ἔξωθεν) philosophers.[77] For example, he argues that the denial of the resurrection is a direct outcome of the belief that matter was uncreated and, if those who support that view cite "pagan" wisdom (ἔξωθεν κέχρηνται σοφίᾳ) to back up their arguments, the Christians should not be in awe but laugh at them because they are using stupid teachers. The reason John calls the philosophers stupid is because they did not deliver any "sound

---

[74] Sandwell, *Religious Identity in Late Antiquity*, 269.

[75] Sandwell, *Religious Identity in Late Antiquity*, 74. The association of religion with philosophy was also a connection Libanius made in his own works, such as in *Or.* 18.18 (LCL 451:291). Sandwell also makes the interesting observation that Chrysostom tended to ignore Neoplatonic ideas when discussing Greek religion and philosophy (ibid. 75).

[76] Οὐδὲν γὰρ ὄφελος βίου καθαροῦ, δογμάτων διεφθαρμένων· ὥσπερ οὖν οὐδὲ τοὐναντίον, δογμάτων ὑγιῶν, ἐὰν βίος ᾖ διεφθαρμένος. *In Ioh. hom.* 66.3 (PG 59:369). The discussion that follows is part of this same passage.

[77] Hagit Amirav has argued that John's opposition to Alexandrian exegesis is an illustration of how familiar he and his Antiochene colleagues were with pagan culture, since "their ideological insistence on a plain exposition of the biblical text was ... a deliberate rejection of pagan allegorical methods employed in the exposition and study of Homer." H. Amirav, *Rhetoric and Tradition: John Chrysostom on Noah and the Flood* (Leuven: Peeters, 2003), 6. This is another example of John considering the Greeks as predecessors of ideas he disapproved from other Christians.

teaching about God or about creation, but Pythagoras did not yet know things which even the widow among us understood."[78] The attack on Pythagoras is just the beginning; it is followed by an attack on Empedocles and his view on reincarnation (Fr. 117D) and an ironic statement about how these philosophers "are great men in their village, they wear their tresses long, they cast their cloaks about them. Their philosophy goes thus far. But if you look within, you see ashes and dust and nothing sound."[79]

This and similar passages from Chrysostom's corpus are often used to support arguments about his alleged hatred of Hellenism and as a prime example of his viciousness against Greek philosophy and thought. However, this point of view easily overlooks five things. First, mocking of the parochial character and dressing of the philosophers is not unheard of in the Hellenic tradition itself; in fact, mocking between philosophers in literature is abundant, as a simple skim through Diogenes' Laertius description of the shenanigans between Diogenes the Cynic and Plato would show;[80] secondly, John's focus here are the Presocratics, not each and every Greek (or even non-Christian) philosopher that has ever lived; thirdly, the argument did not begin as a diatribe against Greek philosophy but about the way Christian heretics use it against their orthodox counterparts; fourthly, criticism of people who dress as philosophers but do not really live as philosophers exists even among non-Christian authors[81] and finally, Chrysostom did not use the argument only against philosophers: elsewhere, he made the point that just as we cannot judge a philosopher based on his hairstyle or other external characteristics but on the basis of his manners and soul, or a soldier based on his

---

[78] *In Ioh. hom.* 66.3 (PG 59.369; trans. Goggin, *Commentary on Saint John vol. 2*, 224).

[79] Ibid. (trans. Goggin, *Commentary on Saint John vol. 2*, 225).

[80] See for example Diogenes Laertius, *Vit. phil.* 6.24-26, 40-41, 53, 58 (LCL 185:27ff.).

[81] See for example Julian, *Or.* 6.201a (LCL 29:57): "Therefore let him who wishes to be a Cynic philosopher not adopt merely their long cloak or wallet or staff or their way of wearing the hair, as though he were like a man walking unshaved and illiterate in a village that lacked barbers' shops and schools, but let him consider that reason rather than a staff and a certain plan of life rather than a wallet are the mintmarks of the Cynic philosophy."

uniform but on the basis of his bravery, so we cannot judge Christian virginity based on the clothing but on the way it exists in the virgin's body and soul.[82]

Later on, in his *Homilies on John* Chrysostom attacks the views of Thales, Empedocles and Anaximenes again, this time regarding the nature of the divine and the fact that they could not understand the idea of an incorporeal God; and even when they did, it was because of their contact with those he calls "our co-religionists in Egypt."[83] In essence, and in an instance of Chrysostom agreeing with previous apologists, some of the good things in Greek philosophy had their actual origins with the Hebrews.

The demonic nature of the gods that we mentioned previously is not the only instance where Chrysostom correlates the Greco-Roman religion with demons and even with Satan himself. He describes the worship of the idols as worship of "not Gods, but stones and demons,"[84] a characterization he also reserves for the Greeks themselves, while religious practices such as Greco-Roman prophecy and divination are considered signs of demonic possession.[85] The characterization of Greek religion as magical and demonic has received varied explanations from scholars. Isabella Sandwell considers it part of Chrysostom's effort to distance it from being a legitimate religious choice and also as a further proof that being Greek was something entirely incompatible with being Christian.[86] This is definitely the case with religious affiliation, a fact that Chrysostom often repeats in various instances when he mentions Jews, Greeks and heretics as

---

[82] *De virg.* 8.1 (SC 125:112).

[83] *In Ioh. hom.* 66.3 (PG 59.369; trans. Goggin, *Commentary on Saint John vol. 2*, 225).

[84] *In 1 Cor. hom.* 20.4 (PG 61:163).

[85] For the numerous references to Chrysostom's works, along with further discussion of associations of Greek religion with magic, witchcraft, and superstition see Sandwell, *Religious Identity in Late Antiquity*, 89.

[86] Ibid., 89-90. Sandwell also refers to examples where Chrysostom makes the same association with Jews and other Christian heretics and presents it as a choice of different ways of life-Greek, Jewish, or Christian. This choice in Sandwell's view was absolute and involved a number of different characteristics: social, moral, cultural and religious.

groups that the Christians have to battle against.[87] But the inspiration to do that does not originate with Chrysostom but with Paul, or at least that is what Chrysostom claims. In another attack on the idols as demons and stones that do not have any power, he considers 1 Corinthians 8:4-5 to be an attack both against philosophers as well as the simpletons among the Greeks, and the philosophers are particularly attacked for thinking that the idols have certain power in them. It is at this point that Chrysostom lays down his method: he observes that Paul is not just writing doctrine, but he does so in contradistinction to the ἔξωθεν. Therefore, when one reads the Pauline corpus, s/he should observe whether Paul is speaking abstractly or in opposition to others. The outcome of this will be twofold: "this contributes in no ordinary way to the accuracy of our doctrinal views, and to the exact understanding of his expressions."[88]

Besides his persistent condemnation of the philosophers as the intellectual enablers of Greek religion, Chrysostom often attacks certain superstitions of his day and explains them as indicative of a mentality that Christians should not subscribe to. In this respect, he criticizes the Greeks for fearing things that do not count as sins, such as filthiness of the body, care for the dead (through a fear of pollution by touching the dead body), and observation of days. At the same time, they take no account of things that are indeed sins, such as pederasty, adultery, and fornication. This contrast is followed by a caricature of superstitious characters, who resemble many of the types described by Theophrastus in Bk 16 of his *Characters*. A man might wash himself from the pollution of a dead body but would not do the same for dead works, whereas he might pursue riches with all his might and at the same time think that all this can be simply undone by the crow of a cock. Another one leaves his house and because he thinks the first person

---

[87] See e.g. *Adv. Iud. or.* 7.3 (PG 48:920). This does not apply to family life. As he argues in *Adv. Iud. or.* 2.3 (PG 48:860; trans. Harkins, *Discourses against Judaizing Christians*, 43), even if one's wife is a Hellene (pagan, or unbeliever in this text), this does not offer a sufficient excuse for a divorce: "If a man has an infidel wife, that is, a gentile, he is not forced to put her away."

[88] *In 1 Cor. hom.* 20.3 (PG 61:163; NPNF 1-12:113).

he meets is a bringer of bad luck a myriad of evils will befall him. The same one also complains when his servant puts on the left shoe first when he helps him dress up, which is considered a terrible mishap and misfortune, and the same applies when exiting the house with the left foot. Chrysostom calls these household evils. They are followed by even more examples of superstitions that happen outside the house and this time include women as well, along with the fear of certain natural animal behaviours, like the aforementioned crow of the cock or the bray of an ass or even the sneezing of a man. These superstitions show that these people behave as if possessed by the darkness and more slavishly "than all the slaves in the world." Besides his exhortation to the Christians to scorn these things, he asks them to regard only one thing as terrible: sin, and offending God.[89] At the same time, Chrysostom was aware that many Christians were equally susceptible to the very same superstitions, going as far as claiming that some deliberately avoided virgins for bringing bad luck whilst feeling joyous when meeting prostitutes on the streets.[90]

iii. Apologetic battles: the nature of society

Sometimes John uses a dialogue with a Greek as the setting for a debate about a particular issue. Wendy Mayer's recent translation of the yet unedited homily *On All the Martyrs* provides us with one such example of John apparently engaging in an apologetic effort to convince a Greek about the truths of Christianity. Whether the dialogue (or the Greek) is real or imaginary will not be our concern here: our use of the

---

[89] *In Eph. hom.* 12.3 (PG 62:92-3; NPNF 1-13:111-2). It is also the one thing that John advises his audience to be afraid of, since every other hardship can in fact have good outcomes, as per Job's example: "Let us endure the other things with courage: loss of money, bodily sickness, business reverses, abuse, slander, and whatever other trouble may come upon us. It is not the nature of these things to harm us; in fact they can give us the greatest help." *De incompr. hom.* 4 (SC 28bis:266; St. John Chrysostom, *On the Incomprehensible Nature of God*, trans. Paul W. Harkins, Washington, DC: Catholic University of America Press, 1984, 135-6).

[90] *Cat.* 1.39 (SC 50bis:128-129; trans. Harkins, *Baptismal Instructions*, 39): "I exhort both men and women to shun altogether omens and superstitions. These are foolish practices of the Greeks and of those who are still in the grip of error, this meddling of yours with the cawing of crows, the squeaking of mice, the creaking of beam; your joy on encountering those who are living disgraceful lives, while you avoid meeting with pious and devout persons, as if they were the cause of countless evils."

word apologetic as a characterization for Chrysostom's rhetoric at this point does not depend on him defending his beliefs to an actual audience who hold opposing views; rather, our use follows Amirav's definition: "An exegete whose rhetoric is more apologetic in tone seeks to encourage a sense of belonging to a particular group by contrasting it with another."[91] This definition of apologetic is more useful for our purposes since it discards the notion that the apologist needs to defend his views to a real hostile audience with the hope of converting them. But it is not just simple preaching to the converted either, since it does not always presuppose that those "converted" are equipped with a proper understanding of their faith. According to this definition, John's main purpose in this kind of text is to encourage a sense of belonging among Christians by contrasting them favourably with Greeks. Consequently, in this section of our analysis of Chrysostom's criticism of the Greeks, we will examine texts which are broadly apologetic in nature (some using dialogue, others using other forms). We will show, first, that Chrysostom *contrasts* Christian behaviour with that of the Greeks – particularly with regard to the kind of behaviour which characterises a good *polis* – and secondly, that Chrysostom *exhorts* Christians to exhibit good behaviour as a witness to their faith.

In his homily *On All the Martyrs* John is emphatic that the Greek cannot be convinced from either events of the past or the eschatological expectations of Christianity.[92] He therefore tries to argue from incidents of the present. It is worth quoting the passage in full before we proceed with our analysis:

---

[91] Amirav, *Rhetoric and Tradition*, 224.

[92] Despite the fact that elsewhere Chrysostom has no problem admitting that certain Greek eschatological ideas could be considered as εἰκόνα τινὰ κρίσεως in tandem with the Christian idea of a final judgment. The full passage is from *Adv. opp. vit. mon.* 2.10 (PG 47:347; trans. Hunter, *A Comparison*, 119): "Even if the pagans were unable to speak the truth about these things as they are, since they followed their own reasonings and certain teachings of ours which they misunderstood, nonetheless they have received a kind of image of the judgement. Among the poets, philosophers, orators, and all writers you will find speculations on these doctrines. You will hear about the Elysian Field, the Isles of the Blessed, the groves, the myrtle trees, the light air, the most pleasant odor, and the choruses who dwell there, garbed in white robes, dancing and singing hymns, and, in a word, the just desserts which await both the wicked and the good after death. How do you think both the good and the wicked

Tell me, what are you saying? He didn't resurrect the dead when he was here? Nor did he cleanse the lepers, nor drive out demons nor did he effect the rest of the things I started out mentioning? Nor after that will he come [down] from heaven and demand of each person an account of their deeds, nor will he resurrect their bodies, nor grant us incorruptibility? Well, does it seem to you that these things are a fairy tale or heap of words or pure sound? Speak! Surely what is both present and visible doesn't seem to be a fairy tale. For instance, the Churches everywhere in the world that multiply the sea of piety; the choruses of virgins; the ranks of monks; the diverse and perfected social group within the Church of people who conspicuously practice moderation in marriage, of people who practice patience in widowhood; the patronage focused on the poor; the ranks of priests; the obedience of the emperors; the philosophy of foreign people. Surely these things aren't a fairy tale? Surely these things aren't part of the future and the past?[93]

In his willingness to convince the Greeks, if they were really the intended audience of this homily, Chrysostom is willing to put aside certain apologetic motifs that we can, by and large, consider as some of the central tenets of Christian doctrine: Jesus' signs, which represent the past of Christianity, and his role in the eschatological times as both a judge and as the one who provides resurrection and incorruptibility to humans, which represent the future.[94] His apologetic trope in this instance is consciously present-oriented and pragmatic. What is essentially said is this: you can overlook the past and the future if you wish, but you can definitely not overlook what is happening right now. Churches are being built everywhere, virgins and monks are multiplying by the day, and the Christians are well known for their moderation in marriage and patient endurance of widowhood. He implies that Christians took the patronage system in the classical *polis* (which could provide for anything, from public events such as horseraces to war funds

---

live after reflecting on these things? Are there not some persons who, even if they prosper in this life without pain and with great pleasure, upon reflection are struck, as it were, by the whip of conscience and by the expectation of the frightening things that await them? And, yet, good people, even if they should suffer a thousand misfortunes, have "a hope which nourishes" them, as Pindar says, and which does not allow them to feel the present misfortunes." Besides an extensive knowledge of Greek eschatological ideas, this passage also shows that John was willing to admit that the weight of conscience and the hope for the future things was present in Christians and non-Christians alike, ideas that he could be very sympathetic with, even if disagreeing in the details about what the eschaton will look like.

[93] *In mart. omn.* 14 (John Chrysostom, *The Cult of the Saints*, trans. Wendy Mayer with Bronwen Neil, Crestwood, NY: St Vladimir's Seminary Press, 2006, 251).

[94] The resurrection of Christ was a very popular apologetic tool, especially among the early Apologists. However, Chrysostom's reluctance to use it in this case could have much to do with M. Ludlow's comment that "addressing queries about the *possibility* of resurrection seemed to miss the fundamental pagan concern: *why* should resurrection be a good thing to hope for?" Morwenna Ludlow, *The Early Church* (London: I.B. Tauris, 2009), 42, italics in the original.

and everything in between) and focused it on the poor, whether they were fellow citizens, foreigners, or slaves.[95] The emperor's Christian faith also gets an honorable mention, although Julian's recent example could easily be used as a counterargument. The reality of all these things, Chrysostom believes, ultimately proves that Christianity is not a fairy tale, whether or not the Greeks are willing to engage with its past and/or future.

It is notable that some of the things Chrysostom mentions are distinctively Christian (e.g. virgins and monks); others are examples of Christians using a social institution – like marriage, almsgiving or patronage – better than the Greeks. Therefore, I do not believe that he was against the institution of the *polis* in principle but rather had a different set of beliefs as to what made a *polis* great: "So Isaiah has instructed both the leaders and all his hearers quite a bit about philosophy in teaching them not to place confidence in the city's greatness, its defence works or its military hardware, but in the virtue of their own people."[96] Here Chrysostom encourages a sense of belonging to a particular group – Christians – by contrasting their vision of the polis with that of earlier citizens – Greeks, even if many of these Christians were from a Greek background. These Christians are simply being asked to reconsider what constitutes virtue for their particular *polis*: its humans, and their way of life.

---

[95] Liebeschuetz's summary of the differences between Christian giving and traditional munificence is excellent and provides the necessary framework for us to understand John's comment on the Christian patronage of the poor: "Christian charity was not directed towards fellow citizens or political supporters but towards the poor, whoever they might be. It was given to them precisely because they were poor or sick, and because God wants Christians to look after those in need... The idea that the poor and the sick and the old ought to be helped because they were there, and were God's creatures, is not classical... Christian charity did not provide amenities like shows and baths and colonnades which were of benefit to rich and poor alike. It was focused on basic needs of food and shelter. Christian giving was quite independent of the secular institutions of the city." J. H. W. G. Liebeschuetz, *Barbarians and Bishops: Army, Church, and State in the Age of Arcadius and Chrysostom* (Oxford: Clarendon Press, 1990), 187.

[96] *Comm. in Is.* 3.2 (SC 304:152; trans. Garrett, An Analysis, 81). Cf. *De stat.* 17.4 (PG 49:179; trans. Mayer and Allen, *John Chrysostom*, 115): "When you wish to praise the city, don't tell me about its suburb, Daphne, nor about the number and height of its cypress trees, nor its springs of water nor the numerous people who live in the city, not that its market-place is frequented with great freedom right until very late in the evening not of the abundance of market goods. All these things belong to the senses, and last for the duration of this present life. But if you can call on virtue, gentleness, almsgiving, vigils, prayers, common sense and wisdom of spirit- adorn the city with these qualities."

Besides comparing the behaviour of Christians and Greeks, Chrysostom also analyses the difference Christianity could make to a Greek who converted. The example of a female prostitute and the changes that Christianity brings to her life after baptism serve as an example of the transformative and effective nature of the Christian faith. To contrast that with Hellenism Chrysostom brings up one of his favourite examples of Hellenic ineffectiveness: the case of Plato and his failed attempts to convert the tyrants of Syracuse into following his doctrine. Plato's failure[97] is directly in contrast to the power of the cross: "the philosopher ... didn't have the power to convert a single tyrant when he sailed so vast a sea ... but the power of the cross convinced everyone: Romans, foreign people, fools, ordinary citizens."[98]

Hellenic ineffectiveness is one of his favourite themes, and in another apologetic work, *Against the Jews*, he contrasts a variety of things he regarded as failures with Christian successes. He mentions, for example, the failure of several philosophers (Zeno, Plato, Socrates, Pythagoras, Diagoras) who tried to introduce different *politeiai* among the Greeks but failed, with the subsequent result that many people hardly remember them.[99] On the contrary, Christ's *politeia* has been diffused to the whole *oikoumene*. In an abrupt turn of speech, Chrysostom asks about the number of miracles Apollonius of Tyana performed, before proclaiming that all his deeds were "a fraud, a vain show, and devoid of truth,"[100] because they vanished and disappeared in an instant.

---

[97] The Greek philosophers' failures are also contrasted with the success of the Christian project as was initiated by the Apostles, a project far more radical than Plato's republic that involved "disturbing ancient customs, and removing their father's landmarks." *In 1 Cor. hom.* 4.9 (PG 61:37; NPNF 1-12:20). After Chrysostom, other Christian authors continued stressing the failures of Plato and the other philosophers and exploiting their disagreements. In his study of Theodoret Papadogiannakis argued that "the failure –moral and otherwise- of Greek philosophers illustrates that the superiority of Christianity is based on the practice of virtue rather than cultural affiliation." Papadogiannakis, *Christianity and Hellenism*, 103.

[98] *In mart. omn.* 15 (trans. Mayer, *Cult of the Saints*, 252).

[99] *Adv. Iud. or.* 5.3 (PG 48:886). The following discussion is based on the same passage.

[100] Ibid. (trans. Harkins, *Discourses Against Judaizing Christians*,105). Apollonius of Tyana is mentioned again when John discusses the opinions of some who thought that Christ was a magician and mention him in the same context as Apollonius: ""But what about the man from Tyana?" someone says. "That man was a cheat and a charlatan and he was renowned." Where, and when? In a tiny part of the world, and for a short time, then he was quickly snuffed out and perished, leaving behind neither a church

Anticipating that some from the audience might object to Christ being mentioned in the same sentence as Plato, Zeno, Pythagoras and Apollonius, John says that he does so out of consideration to the Jews, who think of Christ as a mere man, and uses the example of Paul who did not use the Scriptures when conversing with the Athenians but used their altar to the unknown God as the basis for his speech.

Another theme in Chrysostom's comparison of Greek and Christian public behaviour is pagan cult. For example, in his homily *On all the Martyrs*, the power of the cross, which was previously contrasted to Plato's failure, also served to eliminate the pagan cults. These receive a very graphic description by Chrysostom:

> whereas before this there were altars and temples and burnt sacrifices everywhere, and cult statues and festivals full of shamelessness and dances of demons and the Devil reveling in the cities, and the tyranny of drunkenness and furnace of licentiousness and the flame of wickedness arose from all quarters, after the cross's power all this was removed.[101]

Chrysostom's tirades against blood sacrifices have to be particularly seen in the light of Julian's restoration of sacrifice as a central feature of Graeco-Roman religion and Libanius' emphasis on it in many of his orations.[102] Chrysostom's claim that burnt sacrifices are being replaced by spiritual sacrifices and the wilderness has become more law-abiding than the cities, even resonates with Libanius' claim that Christianity "has quenched the sacred flame: it has stopped the joyful sacrifices: it has set them on to spurn and overthrow your altars: your temples and sanctuaries it has closed, or

---

nor a people, nor any other such thing." *De laud. Paul. hom.* 4.8 (SC 300:198; trans. Mitchell, *The Heavenly Trumpet*, 461). The polemic against Apollonius might have its origins in Libanius' reference to him as a pagan hero. See Cribiore, *Libanius the Sophist*, 56-8. For the survival of a cult devoted to Apollonius in Byzantium well into the seventh century and beyond see Helen Saradi-Mendelovici, "Christian Attitudes Toward Pagan Monuments in Late Antiquity," *Dumbarton Oaks Papers* 44 (1990), 57.

[101] *In mart. omn.* 15 (trans. Mayer, *Cult of the Saints*, 252). In *De laud. Paul. hom.* 4.8 (SC 300:198-200) Chrysostom specifically mentions the silence of specific cult locations, such as the temple of Zeus in Dodona in Epirus and the sanctuary that contained a temple and oracle of Apollo in Claros, on the coast of Ionia.

[102] For the particular references in Libanius' works see Sandwell, *Religious Identity in Late Antiquity*, 95. Libanius was willing to offer unqualified support to Julian's religious restoration project. For the relevant texts see ibid., 217.

demolished, or profaned, or given to harlots to dwell in."[103] Chrysostom's rhetoric is surely intended to encourage Christians' sense of belonging to a distinct group which rejected blood sacrifice.

The victory of the cross brings with it a great number of societal changes that John links in *On All the Martyrs* with monasticism: people are now subverting their stomachs, controlling their desires, consider money to be filth, and shape their souls on top of mountains. The focus here is certainly on desert asceticism and how it affected the society in general. The reason for the presentation of this idealized picture of the society of his time becomes more obvious when it is compared with the situation before the coming of Christianity: people married their mothers, men had sex among themselves, prostitution and adultery were all prevailing, and what was worse, according to Chrysostom, some of these things were considered law while others were considered religious observance. This obvious reference to the story of Oedipus is, as Wendy Mayer points out, an attempt by Chrysostom to promote "mythology as part of the Greek past."[104] It also aims to distance Christians from that past.

Chrysostom's caricature of Greek society is completed by an attack on one of his favourite targets, theatrical shows, and their role as "schools for immorality."[105] Theatrical shows were a constant thorn in Chrysostom's side, and we should elaborate a little on why he perceived them as something fundamentally incompatible with the Christian faith. In one of his very graphic descriptions about the state of humanity before the coming of Christ, John describes one of the reasons for his regular denunciations of the theatre:

---

[103] *Or.* 17.7 (LCL 451:217). The polemic against sacrifice is further proof that it had played a major role in Christianity's battle against Graeco-Roman religious practices. Before detailing exactly what Christianity inflicted on paganism, Libanius begins by declaring its victory (ibid.): "A creed which we had until then laughed to scorn, which had declared such violent, unceasing war against you, has won the day, after all."

[104] Mayer, *Cult of the Saints*, 253.

[105] n. 17 in ibid.

In their indecent night-time gatherings, women were admitted to the performance. There you could see the obscene sight of a virgin sitting in the theatre during the night, amidst a drunken crowd of young men madly revelling. The festival was actually the darkness, and the abominable deeds practiced by them.[106]

The first point that is observable is Chrysostom's claim to be shocked regarding the presence of women in theatres, but, as A. Hartney has pointed out, the truthfulness of that claim does not really matter.[107] What does matter is that one of his factors in explaining the decline of ancient society seems to be the "lapse in behavioural boundaries between the sexes."[108]

Secondly, the theatres and the behaviour of the spectators become a source of negative role models for his congregation, who were nonetheless very familiar with the great plays of the past. John takes this familiarity for granted when he attacks the plot of some of the greatest plays of the past without actually naming them, because he is sure that most of those attending know them already:

One man loved his stepmother, and a woman her stepson, and as a result hung herself... And would you wish to see a son married to his mother? This too happened among them, and what is most horrible, although it was done in ignorance, the god whom they worshiped did not prevent it, but permitted this outrage against nature to be committed, even though she was a member of the nobility... The wife of a certain man fell in love with another man, and with the help of her adulterer, killed her husband on his return home. Most of you probably know the story. The son of the murdered man killed the adulterer, and after that his mother, and then he himself went mad, and was haunted by the furies. After this the madman himself murdered another man, and took his wife for himself.[109]

---

[106] *In Tit. hom.* 5.4 (PG 62:693; trans. Hartney, *John Chrysostom and the Transformation of the City*, 186). We will be citing Hartney's translation of John's criticisms against theatrical shows because although she used the Nicene and Post-Nicene Fathers series as the basis of her translations, her slight revisions make the text slightly more comprehensible to a modern audience.

[107] Hartney, *John Chrysostom and the Transformation of the City*, 186.

[108] Ibid. B. Leyerle similarly interprets Chrysostom's obsession with Plato's "proposed marriage legislation, which pricked his ire every time he thought about it" as primarily taking issue with its "proposed reduction of social distinction between the sexes." Leyerle, *Theatrical Shows*, 72.

[109] *In Tit. hom.* 5.4 (PG 62:693; trans. Hartney, *John Chrysostom and the Transformation of the City*, 186).

This brief tour de force describing the plots of some of the greatest plays in ancient Greek literature[110] and the dismissal of their subject matter do give the impression that he might have disparaged "Greek society as a whole, rather than merely the mythical heritage of this society."[111] John's attack on the theatre was, as Blake Leyerle has argued, "part of a far larger cultural critique," and particularly his culture's "emphasis on display."[112] Ruth Webb theorizes that Chrysostom's opposition was "informed by the fierce asceticism that had driven him to live as a hermit for several years."[113] Webb also sees this critique as a development of the Classical tradition of moralizing critiques, with the additional element of characterizing the theatre as non-Christian and demonic, and argues that what Chrysostom has in common with other Christian writers like Augustine and Tertullian is a "rejection of fiction, the refusal to grant an autonomous status to theatrical representation, and the denial of the boundaries between theatre and life."[114] However, other boundaries seem to be being blurred in this text: this seems to be another instance where the lines between the mythological and the historical past are unclear, and I would argue that this is exactly Chrysostom's intention. Despite his acknowledgment of his audience's familiarity with drama, and the understanding that these plays are all part of their common and inherited culture, Chrysostom wants them to realize that this behaviour belongs to their pre-Christian past. To drive his point even closer to home, he even argues that if this was the conduct of those who were supposed to be virtuous (even if it was for the sake of appearances), what was then the conduct of the *hoi polloi* who mostly lived in obscurity? If Chrysostom ignored "the more complex plot motivations behind each of the listed events" and instead presented them as

---

[110] The texts Chrysostom is referring to are *Hippolytus, Oedipus Rex*, and the trilogy of the *Oresteia*, as identified in Hartney, *John Chrysostom and the Transformation of the City*, 186.

[111] Hartney, *John Chrysostom and the Transformation of the City*, 186.

[112] Leyerle, *Theatrical Shows*, ix.

[113] Ruth Webb, *Demons and Dancers: Performance in Late Antiquity* (Cambridge, MA: Harvard University Press, 2008), 7.

[114] Ibid., 200.

"heinous crimes prevalent in this decadent society,"[115] it is because his intention was not to be a literary critic but a preacher. In order for him to emphasize the debauchery of the past, he picks a fair number of stories that most people of his time would know and treats them as history in order to prevent the Christians from participating in theatrical shows and thus being tempted to imitate the behaviour they saw in the plays. Even if Chrysostom was not seriously concerned that this was about to happen, he still did not want the audience to draw the wrong lessons. Finally, Chrysostom's words are also an attack on theatrical shows as the traditional loci that "ensured the dissemination of the traditional canon even among those without formal schooling."[116] Someone might say that in an ideal Christian world Chrysostom would replace these dramatic performances with Christian sermons, which would ensure the dissemination of the Bible instead of the Greek classics, but he never claimed as much.

Theatrical shows were not the only focus of attack related to the classical past. Homosexuality and its Greek origins was another. Chrysostom's commentary on Romans 1:26-7 attempts to trace Paul's charge of homosexuality back to the Greek past. John begins by mentioning a law of Solon as quoted by Plutarch: "He also wrote a law forbidding a slave to practise gymnastics or have a boy lover, thus putting the matter in the category of honourable and dignified practices, and in a way inciting the worthy to that which he forbade the unworthy."[117] However, homosexuality was not so much honourable but rather shameless, Chrysostom argues. He attributes the practice to the Athenians specifically, "and Solon who is so great among them."[118] He argues that the books of the philosophers are full of this disease, but interestingly does not mention certain criticisms against the practice from the philosophers themselves, as in Plato's

---

[115] Hartney, *John Chrysostom and the Transformation of the City*, 187.

[116] Leyerle, *Theatrical Shows*, 4.

[117] Plutarch, *Sol.* 1.3 (LCL 46:407).

[118] *In Rom. hom.* 4.2 (PG 60:419; NPNF 1-10:357).

Laws 1.636, where both the Spartans and the Cretans are criticized for it. Chrysostom compares the youth who are involved in the practice to whores, whose plight is more miserable because at least whoredom is lawless, but at least not contrary to nature, whereas homosexuality is both. John considers them as worse than murderers, since death is a better option than living like this, and no other sin is equal to this. Whereas the murderers break the connection between the soul and the body, the homosexual man ruins both.[119] Chrysostom's words become harsher after this point, but for the purposes of our discussion it is interesting to note that his reference to Greek homosexuality is ostensibly only due to the fact that he wishes to trace the phenomenon back to its origin. But after mentioning Solon and his law, he transitions into the present tense and speaks about it as something that is still present and needs to be dealt with. This is not the only reference to this law. The second reference[120] mentions the law on pederasty specifically and further claims that there were houses where pederasty was practiced openly. He even goes on to mention *paidika*, erotic songs addressed to young boys, for which certain lyric poets were famous, such as Ibycus, but without mentioning their actual subject matter, i.e. passion for boys. However, his condemnation of homosexuality has an apologetic function in both texts: it is a way of reinforcing the Christians' identity rather than a real attempt to dissuade Greeks from such behaviour in the present.

Nevertheless, dramatic performances and homosexuality would not be the worst aspect of a pagan's past, according to Chrysostom. The epicentre of the problem, of which drama and homosexuality were just a part, was an entirely different way of life – a way of life which is connected to the Greeks' past. In another apologetic text, his *Demonstration against the Pagans that Christ is God*, Chrysostom identified two factors as the most difficult aspects in the process of conversion from a non-Christian faith to Christianity: habit and pleasure (we will return to habit below). He does not

---

[119] *In Rom. hom.* 4.2 (PG 60:419; NPNF 1-10:357).

[120] *In Tit. hom.* 5.4 (PG 62:693)

identify the former religion as paganism, but from the description of their past it is obvious that this is the religious system he has in mind. Part of this past are the people who taught the pagans their way of life: "their fathers, grandfathers, great grandfathers, their ancestors, their philosophers, and public speakers."[121] Despite the difficulty of rejecting one's past, the people were persuaded to do so and accept a new and very difficult one. This new way of life also entailed some major changes: "from luxurious living ... to fasting; from the love of money ... to poverty; from wanton ways ... to temperance; from anger ... to mildness; from envy ... to kindliness..." John insists that the people who converted to the Christian faith were not different kinds of human beings that lived outside of this world. They were very much part of this world and its ways until they were won over to the Christian way of life, which is defined, from among other things, by poverty. To the question as to who won them over, Chrysostom's answer is typical: "eleven men [for some reason John does not include Matthias] ... [who] were unlettered, ignorant, ineloquent, undistinguished, and poor. They could not rely on the fame of their homelands, or any abundance of wealth, or strength of body, or glorious reputation, or illustrious ancestry. They were neither forceful nor clever in speech; they could make no parade of knowledge." The message is clear. It does not matter if they had none of these things, because they had the power of Christ and all the virtues John mentioned before, and thus were able to win people over. At the same time, they also had to define themselves against the licentious Greek way of life, which included dishonour, drunkenness, greed, luxury and pomp.[122] John's targets in this instance are twofold: on the one hand, a strong connection to a glorious past through ancestry that led people to arrogance; on the other, a way of life taught by these very same predecessors. Christians are able to reject both, because they belong to

---

[121] This and the quotes that follow are from *C. Iud. et Gent.* 12.6-9 (PG 47:830; trans. Harkins, *Apologist*, 240-1).

[122] See also *De res. mort.* 2 (SC 561:122).

a different community which, even if it lacks illustrious (from a worldly point of view) predecessors, teaches its members the exact opposites of the vices mentioned above.

There are other examples of a similar appeal to the Greeks' past. One of Chrysostom's favourite phrases from the Platonic corpus are the words of the Egyptian priest who speaks to Solon in *Timaeus* 22b: "you Greeks are always children: there is not such a thing as an old Greek." But in his interpretation of the sentence the Egyptian's phrase is taken as a way to explain the behaviour of the Greeks of his time. Just like children who do not care when important things are discussed, so are the Greeks. When Christians talk to them about the Kingdom of God, they laugh. When you take away their wealth, just like when you take away things from a child, they cry. Finally, just as children have no shame and expose themselves, so the Greeks wallow "in whoredoms and adulteries."[123] This is not the only case where Chrysostom uses either an opinion or an event of the past and applies it to his own context.

Another one of John's arguments against the Greeks of his time stems from contemporary events and the attitude exhibited by the Christians: in this example, the monks during the statues riots.[124] The *parrhesia* of the monks, as effective in front of humans as it is in front of God, is proof for John that the older stories of the Christians, those concerning Peter, Paul, and John, are true. On the contrary, the behavior exhibited by the philosophers at that time also proves that the older stories of the Greeks about their philosophers are false. In fact, even if the Scriptures did not exist this would not

---

[123] *In 1 Cor. hom.* 4.4 (PG 61:38; NPNF 1-12:22). For other uses of the same platonic passage see Pomeroy, "Reading Plato Through the Eyes of Eusebius." In this case Pomeroy claims that Eusebius is not John's source, particularly since John does not use it, as Eusebius did, to claim that the Greeks stole their philosophy from the Hebrews. Besides the portrayal of Greeks as immature children, they are also sometimes presented as the enemies of the Bible or of the Christians themselves, as in *In 1 Cor. hom.* 6.3 (PG 61:52; NPNF 1-12:32): "for the books [of the Bible] are with their enemies, and through the zeal of certain Greeks they have been transferred into the Greek tongue."

[124] In 387, after the announcement of an imperial tax in Antioch, and the subsequent destruction of statues and portraits of the Emperor Theodosius and his family. For more information on the events as well as John's response to it see Frans van de Paverd, *St John Chrysostom, the Homilies on the Statues: An Introduction* (Rome: Pontificium. Institutum Studiorum Orientalium, 1991).

present a problem, since the actions of the monks exhibit the apostolic virtues without any need to resort to their writings.[125]

The discussion of the Greeks' past leads John to discuss the whole nature of kinship. Psalm 144:7 ("Stretch out your hand from on high; set me free and rescue me from the mighty waters, from the hands of aliens") provides Chrysostom with the opportunity to discuss what he considers true kinship and who is kin and who an alien. To this extent, he provides a working definition, which he goes on to explain: "This person … is kin who is registered in the same country as I and shares the same table rather than the one related by race (γένει προσήκων)."[126] This is followed by his oft-repeated statement that the earth is not our home, before bringing up the story of the Good Samaritan, where he claims that the gap between the Samaritans and Jews was not by nature and exhorts the Christians to consider everyone their neighbour when it comes to doing good. But when it comes to truth the distinction between kin and alien comes back again. Chrysostom argues that the law of truth takes precedence even before blood relations, and a brother from the same parents that does not share the law of truth is "more savage than the Scythian."[127] On the other hand, if one is a Scythian or a Samaritan and a believer of the truth at the same time, then he/she is more related to us than the one who was born from the same parents![128] Chrysostom concludes this section by providing an alternative definition as to who is really a barbarian: the Christians should think of barbarians "on

---

[125] *De stat.* 17.2 (PG 49:175; trans. Mayer and Allen, *John Chrysostom*, 110): "Because of the fact that they've become successors of the apostles as far as their piety is concerned, they have consequently received the apostles' frankness of speech as well. Because of the fact that they were brought up in the same laws, they've consequently emulated the apostles' virtue. The result is that we've no need of writings to demonstrate apostolic virtue, when the facts themselves are crying out and the pupils are pointing to their teachers. We've no need of words to demonstrate the nonsense of the pagans, and pusillanimity of their philosophers, while facts present and past are crying out that everything of theirs is a fable, a theatrical trick, and play-acting." Chrysostom's attacks on the philosophers can be understood as an attack primarily on their prestige and as part of his attempt to re-define philosophy and ascribe the title to the monks instead, and their respective behavior during the riots provides him with the opportunity to do just that. For this point see Maxwell, *Christianization*, 32.

[126] *Exp. in Ps.* 144 3 (PG 55:461; trans. Hill, *Commentary on the Psalms* vol. 2, 327).

[127] Ibid.

[128] He says so explicitly again in *In 1 Thess. hom.* 2.3 (PG 62:404; NPNF 1-13:331): "Friends, that is, friends according to Christ, surpass fathers and sons."

the basis not of language or race but of mindset and spirit (μὴ ἀπὸ τῆς γλώττης, μηδὲ ἀπὸ τοῦ γένους, ἀλλ' ἀπὸ τῆς γνώμης καὶ τῆς ψυχῆς)." What marks a human being, after all is ὅταν δογμάτων ἀκρίβειαν ἔχῃ καὶ πολιτείαν φιλόσοφον.[129] In this respect, the Christians are explicitly called an ἔθνος.[130]

In these apologetic battles on the nature of society Chrysostom had a fairly consistent apologetic strategy, which encouraged a keen sense of Christian belonging, by stressing the contrast between Greeks and Christians. Christians are better in their morals (homosexuality, attendance of the theatre) and in their public contribution to the polis (alms, rejection of sacrifice); where Greek religion is a failure, Christianity is a success; although Greeks have a strong sense of attachment to their past through their ancestral lineage and through teaching, Christians reject that for the stronger and better kinship of the Gospel. Although there are points when he admits that Greeks show virtue and Christians fail, on the whole, the point of the comparisons is to show the superiority of Christianity.

iv. Apologetic battles: the power of public Christian behaviour

A second aspect of Chrysostom's apologetic strategy is to exhort Christians to behaviour which will contrast favorably with that of the Greeks – or to avoid behaviour which is worse. In both cases the aim is similar to what we mentioned in the section above, i.e. to show that Christians could stand on a higher moral ground not only on the basis of doctrine but also through their public attitudes.

Chrysostom was also not afraid to argue against national pride, primarily on the basis that humans are all strangers in this world. In his *Homilies on Matthew*, in order to back his claim that things such as national pride are utterly contemptible, he brings

---

[129] *Exp. in Ps.* 144 3 (PG 55:461; trans. Hill, *Commentary on the Psalms vol. 2*, 327). While Chrysostom often used the scheme of Greek/Barbarian in his rhetoric (e.g. *Post. presb. Goth.* 1, PG 63:501), he also provided, as we can see in the example above, alternative definitions.

[130] *In Act. apost. hom.* 1.4 (PG 60:19; NPNF 1-11:5): "How then was our religion (ἔθνος, lit. nation) instituted?"

forward the support of the philosophers of the Greeks, who also call them external (ἐκτὸς) and rank them in the lowest place.[131] At the same time, the source of Greek pride itself, which Paul took down, is the strength of sophistries and syllogisms.[132] Unfortunately, Chrysostom laments, the same cannot be said for some of the Christians of his day. They are utterly incapable of defending their faith and "it is this that prevents the pagans from quickly realizing the absurdity of their error."[133] It also allows the pagans to despise the Christian doctrine, consider the Christian teaching as deceitful and foolish, and blaspheme Christ as εἴρωνα καὶ ἀπατεῶνα "who makes use of the stupidity of the majority to advance His deceit." Ultimately, Christians are responsible for this blasphemy due to their unwillingness to speak on behalf of the truth and do not think of these matters as important but concern themselves with the things of the earth instead.

This is not the only instance where Chrysostom engages with the topic of the apologetic value of virtue and conduct. In his forty-third *Homily on Matthew* the Christians are reminded that, just like the apostles, their conduct will determine how they are perceived by the Greeks. As with their illustrious predecessors, they need to be "gentle, pure from wrath, from evil desire, from envy, from covetousness, rightly fulfilling all our other duties," since not even the resurrection can appeal to the Greeks as much as a person practicing philosophy.[134] In his *Homily on Pelagia* he is even more explicit about the kind of conduct that brings shame to the Christians and allows the Greeks to criticise them. Once the festival of the martyr is over, many Christians are "running off to drinking and pub-crawling", thus disgracing the festival itself and losing their right to be frank. What John means by frankness (παρρησίαν) in this instance is the fact that Christians can shame the Greeks with an apologetic argument stemming from

---

[131] *In Matt. hom.* 9.5 (PG 57:181).

[132] *In 2 Cor. hom.* 21.2 (PG 61:543).

[133] *In Ioh. hom.* 17.4 (PG 59:112; trans. Goggin, *Commentary on Saint John*, 170). The rest of the references in this paragraph are from the same work.

[134] *In Matt. hom.* 43.5 (PG 57:463-64; NPNF 1-10.277).

the example of Pelagia herself: the fact that so many years after her death, a single girl is able to attract such a large population in her memory, and that no passage of time has been able to interrupt this custom. This is what should ideally happen. But, as John indicates, "if they [the Greeks] were to catch sight of what happens in the festival, we would be stripped of the majority of praise."[135]

One of Chrysostom's most commonly utilized arguments in his frequent exhortations to Christians to behave in a manner worthy of their name is the fact that their attitudes, particularly the ones in public, can be seen and judged by members of other communities, usually the Greeks and the Jews. It is often the case, Chrysostom claims, that even a minor scandal involving a few Christians can lead to a judgment against the whole community. To make this point visible to the Christian community, he is always providing plenty of examples of what he considers to be shameful behaviour, which provides ammo to those he calls unbelievers. Thus, a Christian frequenting a Church and turning up to horse races is a cause for Greeks and Jews to think that Christians are hypocrites. The same is the case when they see a Christian behaving with indifference.[136] If a Greek enters a church and finds women adorned with gold and pearls he will say that the church of the Christians is a show and a myth, and that despite Paul's teaching that "women should dress themselves modestly and decently in suitable clothing, not with their hair braided, or with gold, pearls, or expensive clothes" (1 Timothy 2:9) the opposite impression is given in practice.[137] The reason that Greeks often disbelieve the things the Christians say is because their actions go contrary to their beliefs, and, Chrysostom claims, it is what the Christians do rather than what they say that the Greeks receive as a demonstration. Therefore, when they see Christians "building ourselves fine houses, and laying out gardens and baths, and

---

[135] *De Pelag.* 3 (PG 50:582-583; trans. Mayer, *'Let us Die That We May Live,'* 155).

[136] *In Gen. hom.* 7.1 (PG 53:62).

[137] *Ne tim. hom.* 1.5 (PG 55:507).

buying fields, they are not willing to believe that we are preparing for another sort of residence away from our city [on earth]."[138]

To take Chrysostom's condemnations of Christian hypocrisy as indications of the tensions between "the ideals of the Christians Church and the way that ordinary Christians were actually living their lives" is perfectly acceptable, since Chrysostom himself acknowledges that much. But some scholars have used these examples as proofs of the fact that in the fourth century, as Sandwell puts it, "large numbers of people were apathetic or indifferent to Christianity or… saw Christianity as something they only had to adopt in name." This is an imaginative leap that becomes even larger when "the problematic nature of sermons as a source" is admitted.[139] Later on, Sandwell makes the case that in Chrysostom's audience we are not necessarily looking at people who were apathetic or indifferent towards religion but rather people who had a "a different idea from Chrysostom about the place religion should have in their lives and the extent to which being Christian should impact on them."[140] Similarly, Ruth Webb argues (regarding Christians who attended the theatre despite John's condemnation) that "these ordinary Christians need not necessarily be considered as 'semi-Christians' (as Chrysostom himself termed them) or as 'lukewarm converts', but as Christians who had different ideas about where to draw the boundary between the acceptable and the unacceptable."[141] There is no possible way of knowing that though, even if Sandwell makes a good point that sometimes Chrysostom was presenting his audience "in starker terms than was really necessary and that the gap he presents between his ideals of religiosity for his audience and what they were actually doing might not have been as

---

[138] *In Matt. hom.* 12.5 (PG 57:207-8).

[139] Isabella Sandwell, "John Chrysostom's Audiences and His Accusations of Religious Laxity," in *Religious Diversity*, eds. Gwynn and Bangert, 525.

[140] Sandwell, "John Chrysostom's Audiences," 526-7.

[141] Webb, *Demons and Dancers*, 200.

wide as he suggests."[142] A further point that can be made in relation to both Sandwell's and Webb's arguments is that their claims not only cannot be empirically verified but also create a gap between the beliefs of an alleged clerical elite ("the Church") and those of ordinary people, which, yet again, cannot be substantiated on the basis of Chrysostom's claims only.[143] To repeat something we have said before: Chrysostom had nothing to gain by presenting the Christians behaving like this. Thus, we are more often inclined to take him at his words than not.

Another troubling issue was the irrational fear of death among some Christians. Chrysostom's argument[144] is against excessive wailing, lamenting and weeping; in order to convince his audience, he praises what he finds commendable in the Greeks' way of mourning in order to correct Christian behavior. The first arguments he uses are unreservedly Christian: death is a sleep, and the proof we have of the resurrection should prevent anyone from excessive mourning.[145] But not only do some Christians mourn excessively, but they go beyond that and add more to the crime: they hire female Greek mourners to sing dirges and rouse the passions during the funeral. He contrasts that attitude with the Greeks (παῖδες Ἑλλήνων), who, even without knowing anything about the resurrection, still find appropriate words of consolation such as 'be brave, for you cannot change what happened or alter it with lamentations.'[146] Chrysostom also refers to a custom of the Greeks to wear crowns and white garments when their children died, which they do, he claims, "that they might reap the present glory." By contrast, the

---

[142] Sandwell, "John Chrysostom's Audiences," 526.

[143] Liebeschuetz, *Ambrose and John Chrysostom*, 19, makes a similar argument in relation to the writings of philosophers and moralists: "The thoughts of intellectuals and what 'ordinary' people believe about the meaning of their religious practices interact. It can even be argued that the writings of philosophers and philosophical moralists often represent a systematic and logical arrangement of the thoughts and values that are current among some, or even most, of their unphilosophical contemporaries."

[144] Over many texts but here specifically in *In Matt. hom.* 31.3-4 (PG 57:373-5).

[145] *In Matt. hom.* 31.3 (PG 57:374).

[146] Ibid.

Christians cannot stop behaving like women despite the glory that lies ahead of them.[147]
The Christians should be ashamed for their behaviour because the words they hear are better but their attitudes do not actually reflect it. They also impede the preacher's work, since the Greeks do not pay attention to his words about the resurrection and instead look at what the Christians are doing.[148]

Margaret Alexiou has pointed out that Chrysostom refers to Greek hired mourners in eight homilies and commentaries and the reason he regarded these practices as dangerous was not "only because of its insidious effects on others, but also because, as Chrysostom understood, in the initial stages before Christianity was firmly established, such pagan customs were 'fatal to the Church'."[149]

The ultimate aim of commending appropriate Christian behaviour in apologetic contexts is to show the Greeks of what goods they have been deprived, even if he is addressing himself to Christians. But in order for this to happen, Chrysostom thinks that the Christians need to exhibit a certain set of behaviors: gentleness, purity from wrath, evil desire, envy, and covetousness.[150] In other words, to practice what constitutes Christian philosophy, which is more effective in attracting the Greeks than the resurrection of a dead man; the latter only leads to amazement, but the former will profit them and abides forever.[151] Chrysostom believes that what he asks from the Christians is nothing burdensome. He insists that he is not telling them not to marry or to disengage from the city and its public affairs, but rather that they show their virtue in its midst. He even goes as far as to say that he approves more of this than those who occupy the

---

[147] *In Matt. hom.* 31.4 (PG 57:375; NPNF 1-10:203-4).

[148] *In Heb. hom.* 4.5 (PG 63:42).

[149] Margaret Alexiou, *The Ritual Lament in Greek Tradition*, rev. Dimitrios Yatromanolakis and Panagiotis Roilos, 2nd ed. (Oxford: Rowman & Littlefield, 2002), 28. In *In Heb. hom.* 4.5 (PG 63:43) Chrysostom threatens those who hire wailing women with a long excommunication from the church, applying to them the same punishment as the idolaters, since they bring idolatrous practices to the faith.

[150] *In Matt. hom.* 43.4 (PG 57:463).

[151] Ibid. (PG 57:464).

mountains, i.e. the monks, due to the fact that the behavior of Christian laypeople in the cities was more beneficial to Christianity overall.[152] After all, Chrysostom argues, "no one after lighting a lamp puts it under the bushel basket, but on the lampstand, and it gives light to all in the house" (Matthew 5:15).

In the conclusion to one of Chrysostom's *Homilies on Romans* he is arguing about the need for Christians to lead Christian lives in order to convince the Greeks in the form of a dialogue. The Greek very successfully criticizes the Christians' actions that are in conflict with their beliefs. But in this case, Chrysostom's focus is not simply on what the Christian says to the Greek, but on how he can correct him. The conversation takes place through a series of antithetical schemes: when the Greek sees the Christian philosophizing about the Kingdom of Heaven and disregarding the things of this life, he will wonder how is it possible to be afraid of hell and the calamities of this life at the same time. This will inevitably lead him to a series of questions: "If you are in love with the Kingdom, how is it you do not look down upon the things of this life? If you are expecting the awful judgment, why do you not despise the terrors of this world? If you hope for immortality, why do you not scorn death?"[153] These are the things, Chrysostom claims, that scandalize the Greeks. If the Christians are to defend themselves from these accusations, they need to do it by actions, not words. Blasphemies against God come from bad lives, not from questions. Chrysostom insists that the only way the Greek would be convinced that the Christian commandments are feasible and achievable is by their practice, which some Christians never do. Indeed, when they are examined about this, they point to the monks in the desert as exemplars of the Christian way of life.

Chrysostom argues that people who point to others whilst they are unable to display the Christian way themselves should be ashamed to call themselves Christians. He also points out the source of this shame: why does one need to go to the mountains and the

---

[152] Ibid. (PG 57:463-4).

[153] *In Rom. hom.* 26.4 (PG 60:642; NPNF 1-11:533).

deserts in order to live like a Christian, the Greek would ask, and he would inquire instead to see a man who has a wife and children and is also able to pursue wisdom. Christ's commandment to "let your light shine before others" (Matthew 5:16), means everywhere, not just mountains, deserts, and wildernesses. Chrysostom is explicitly clear that his comments do not mean to disparage the monks, but rather embarrass those who live in cities and have banished virtue from them. All he wants to do is to introduce the philosophy of the desert to the cities, which will release the Greek from being scandalized and allow the Christians to enjoy numerous rewards.[154] In other instances, such as in his *Homilies on 1 Timothy*, Chrysostom makes the same point, but rather than putting the arguments in the form of a dialogue, albeit an imaginary one, he is direct about what he thinks is wrong with Christians of his day.[155]

v. Breaking the Habit

We have already mentioned several instances where Chrysostom uses stories from the Greek past in the context of his homilies in order to support the point he is arguing in each particular situation. More specifically, Chrysostom uses the concept of συνηθεία (custom, habit) to explain Hellenic resistance to the power of the Gospel, both in his

---

[154] *In Rom. hom.* 26.4 (PG 60:643-4; NPNF 1-11:533). For a contrast between the impiety the cities were filled with before the Incarnation and the current situation where even the desert (i.e. the monks) philosophizes see *Fil. ex se nihil fac.* 3 (PG 56:252). Statements such as these have been recently interpreted as an indication that Chrysostom wanted to turn the whole world into a monastery. For this position see Kaldellis, *Hellenism in Byzantium*, 136.

[155] *In 1 Tim. hom.* 10.3 (PG 62:551-2; NPNF 1-13:440): "We admire wealth equally with them, and even more. We have the same horror of death, the same dread of poverty, the same impatience of disease, we are equally fond of glory and of rule. We harass ourselves to death from our love of money, and serve the time. How then can they believe? From miracles? But these are no longer wrought. From our conversation? It has become corrupt. From charity? Not a trace of it is anywhere to be seen. Therefore, we shall have to give an account not only of our own sins, but of the injury done by them to others... There have been great men, it may be said, amongst us, but "how," says the Greek, "shall I believe it? for I do not see anything like it in your conduct. If this is to be said, we too have had our philosophers, men admirable for their lives." "But show me another Paul, or a John: you cannot." Would he not then laugh at us for reasoning in this manner? Would he not continue to sit still in ignorance, seeing that the wisdom we profess is in words, not in works? For now, for a single halfpenny you are ready to slay or be slain! For a handful of earth you raise lawsuit after lawsuit! For the death of a child you turn all upside down: I omit other things that might make us weep; your auguries, your omens, your superstitious observances, your casting of nativities, your signs, your amulets, your divinations, your incantations, your magic arts. These are crying sins, enough to provoke the anger of God; that after He has sent His own Son, you should venture on such things as these."

time as well as in the NT era. Among the Greeks, he claims, "great was the tyranny of the custom."[156] In their case, it starts as prejudice and a hardening of their attitudes that ultimately leads to their erroneous opinions. He wants to make it explicit that he is not just talking about one or two people. Those bound by custom include "sophists and orators, and fathers, and grandfathers, … all nations of Barbarians and all tribes of the Greeks, and wise men and ignorant, rulers and subjects, women and men, young and old, masters and slaves, artificers and husbandmen, dwellers in cities and in countries; all of them."[157] Later on, he repeats some of the categories, and mentions the Pythagoreans and the Platonists specifically, as he already expects the question: do you really think that all these people have been deceived and that twelve fishermen and tentmakers are wiser than all of them? To support his point on the tyranny of the custom he mentions two examples: the Jews and Plato. In regard to the Jews, he mentions their demand of garlic even though they had the manna, and their continual longing for Egypt, despite their status as slaves there. Similarly, the example from the ἔξωθεν is Plato, and his belief that everything about the gods is fallacious. Despite this belief, he condescended to popular feasts and rituals, both because of his inability to contend with custom and having learned this from Socrates. Even the suspicion that Plato was about to innovate led him to an unsuccessful attempt to implement what he really desired, his *politeia*, and he subsequently lost his life.[158]

The discussion then moves to Chrysostom's own time, and to the men he sees as prejudiced in their impiety, who, when charged with being Greek (ἐπειδὰν ἐγκαλοῖντο Ἕλληνες ὄντες), blame their fathers, grandfathers, and great grandfathers. The argument goes full circle again and closes with a saying from the ἔξωθεν: this is why they call habit second nature. As with many other cases, we cannot be sure of the

---

[156] *In 1 Cor. hom.* 7.6 (PG 61:63; NPNF 1-12:40).

[157] *In 1 Cor. hom.* 7.7 (PG 61:63; NPNF 1-12:40).

[158] *In 1 Cor. hom.* 7.7 (PG 61:64). Chrysostom seems to believe that Plato's involvement in the politics of Syracuse was what caused his death, although this is not confirmed in other sources.

origins of John's phrase. The section concludes with a connection between doctrines and habit, and how much more rooted habit becomes when it is considered as part of a belief system, and this is why "a man would change all things more easily than those pertaining to religion."[159]

In various places Chrysostom is more specific about the kinds of habits he would like the Christians to move away from. One example he uses is that of marriage. He recognizes that marriage is an honourable thing for Christians and non-Christians alike. But he also recognizes that the strong appeal of custom has introduced Greek elements that he finds objectionable: "For dancing, and cymbals, and flutes, and shameful words, and songs, and drunkenness, and revellings, and all the Devil's great heap of garbage is then introduced."[160] He understands that many people will find his objections ridiculous and will accuse him of disturbing ancient laws. As he has said before, the deceptive power of custom is great, and even if only a few listen to what he has to say then he will be content. In this case his argument is not against custom *per se*. If a custom is evil, it should not even be done once, but if it is good, then he allows for it to be done constantly, whatever its origins, Greek or Christian. His problem is not with marriage, but with the things that accompany it: painting the face, coloring the eyebrows, and so forth.

This is followed by an attack on customs that come after the wedding, and are related to childbirth. He mentions nursemaids in the baths smearing a child's forehead with mud in order to protect it from the evil eye and envy.[161] In this case, he wonders why the adults practising this custom do not do it to themselves, when it is more likely that they will be envied. Indeed, why do they not cover their whole bodies with mud while they are at it? He is not surprised to find such practices among the Greeks, but he

---

[159] *In 1 Cor. hom.* 7.7 (PG 61:63-4; NPNF 1-12:40).

[160] *In 1 Cor. hom.* 12.5 (PG 61:103; NPNF 1-12:69).

[161] *In 1 Cor. hom.* 12.5 (PG 61:106; NPNF 1-12:71).

finds deplorable that Christians do the very same things. His solution is the application

of the sign of the cross instead of this and an exhortation to understanding that even

minor things can be a "source of great evils."[162] Throughout this attack on bad custom

John is not willing to concede ground to those who make a joke out of him: "the

derision I can bear, when any gain accrues from it. For I should indeed be worthy of

derision, if while I was exhorting to contempt of the opinion of the many, I myself, of

all men, were subdued by that feeling."[163] But as we saw, he can also be flexible. When

he realized that an entire custom cannot be uprooted that easily, he could come up with

solutions that would Christianize it until a time where it simply would not be necessary.

vi. Interpreting Chrysostom's criticism of the Greeks

In section b of this chapter, we have analyzed some of the most common ways in

which Chrysostom attacks the Greeks. His usual method of operation is utilizing

examples from both Greeks of the classical past as well as his contemporaries and the

ideas attacked range from philosophical propositions (like Plato's *politeia*), religious

concepts connected with philosophy (like reincarnation) to everyday customs that have

been around for quite a long time and which he considered objectionable from a

Christian point of view. Chrysostom's constant attack on certain aspects of ancient

Greek culture has been called "ironic", considering that he shared many opinions with

those he allegedly despised.[164] For example, his sentiments towards ancient drama are

very similar to those of Plato in the *Republic*, where he "disparaged Greek epic poetry

on the account of its portrayal of men and gods performing immoral deeds."[165] As we

will see in the chapter that examines his relationship to the Cynics, Chrysostom also

shared a number of their views on issues of social justice. In light of this fact, why is

---

[162] Ibid.

[163] *In 1 Cor. hom.* 12.5 (PG 61:103; NPNF 1-12:69-70).

[164] Hartney, *John Chrysostom and the Transformation of the City*, 188.

[165] Ibid.

John so violently opposed to certain aspects of the Hellenic intellectual heritage?[166] Is he opposed to 'being Greek' as a whole and in itself, or is he opposed to certain aspects and consequences of being Greek? This question is one of the driving forces behind this thesis, and our conclusion will be a preliminary attempt to answer that question based on the sources we examined. Before that, in what remains of this chapter, we will show that there are other places where Chrysostom appears to be more positively or neutrally disposed towards the Greeks. As we will see in these other references, we can tentatively argue that the correct response to the question above is that Chrysostom opposes certain aspects and consequences of 'being Greek' but in many other circumstances has no issue with giving credit where credit is due. There is nothing peculiar about the fact that the number of times he does that is smaller than his criticisms. He was, after all, a Christian.

c. The praise of Hellenism

While Chrysostom often uses the Greeks and their ancient society as negative examples that highlight the case he is trying to make, there are other instances where he compares them with other groups and either praises them or at least argues they are better than the other group/s he is discussing.[167] One tactic is to use the example of a Greek or Greeks to shame his audience into better behaviour. Thus, when discussing the power that habits hold in our minds, and wanting to show that changing to another (good) habit is easy, he mentions two stories about Demosthenes: one regarding how he cured his lisping, and another on how he was able to stop his shoulders from shrugging up and constantly moving. The reason he uses these stories need not be guessed, as he

---

[166] Hartney has framed the problem in two different ways, without attempting to provide a solution: "Is he [John] deliberately sabotaging the intellectual heritage of his audience in order to replace it with a Christianized version of 'philosophy'? Or is he merely employing the rhetorical cliché of simplicity, which proved so effective and popular a weapon in the Christian armoury?" Ibid.

[167] Something that he also does in respect to other groups, like the Jews. For examples of positive comments on the Jews see Wilken, *John Chrysostom and the Jews*, 126 n.9.

immediately explains it afterwards: "for since you are not persuaded out of the Scriptures, I am compelled to shame you by them that are without."[168]

Elsewhere Chrysostom pursues the same tactic with a comparison between heretical virgins and "pagans":

> Oh, you are more wretched than the pagans (Ὦ καὶ Ἑλλήνων ὑμεῖς ἀθλιώτεροι)! For even if the horrors of hell await them, nevertheless the pagans (Hellenes) here and now at least enjoy the pleasures of life; they marry, enjoy what money buys and indulge themselves in other ways. Yet for you there is torture and hardship in both worlds: in this one when you are willing, in the next when you are not. No one will reward the pagans (Hellenes) for fasting and practicing virginity, but neither is punishment in store for them. You, on the other hand, instead of receiving the multitude of praises you were expecting will pay the supreme penalty.[169]

The discussion is obviously about fasting and virginity, and Chrysostom recognizes that these phenomena can be found outside Christianity, in both heretical and pagan communities. What is different in each case is the outcome, with the heretical virgins expected to receive a harsher punishment:

> For fasting and virginity are neither good nor evil in themselves (οὔτε καλὸν καθ' ἑαυτὸ οὔτε κακόν) but from the purpose of those who practice them comes each of these qualities (ἀπὸ τῆς τῶν μετιόντων προαιρέσεως ἑκάτερον γίνεται). The practice of this virtue is unprofitable for the pagans (Hellenes); they earn no wage because they did not pursue it out of fear of God. As for you, because you fight with God and slander the objects of his creation, not only will you go unrewarded, you will even be punished. You will be ranked with the pagans for your opinions since you have denied as they do the true God and have introduced polytheism. Yet they will fare better than you because of their way of life. Their penalty will be limited to not receiving any good, but for you there will be the additional punishment of suffering evil. While it was possible for them to enjoy everything in the present life, you will be deprived both now and later.[170]

---

[168] *In Matt. hom.* 17.5 (PG 57:263; NPNF 1-10:119).

[169] *De virg.* 4.1 (SC 125:102; trans. Shore, *On Virginity*, 5-6). Bernard Grillet uses the term "Grecs" in the French translation of the Sources Chrétiennes edition, in contrast to the English translation that replaces it with the word pagans. This chapter's title is telling: Ὅτι καὶ Ἑλλήνων ἀθλιώτεροι κατὰ τὴν παρθενίαν οἱ αἱρετικοί! The heretics in this case seem to be the Marcionites, Valentinians and the Manicheans, since Chrysostom mentions their founders in the previous chapter of the same work, although he could have others in mind as well. This is not the only instance of Chrysostom comparing the beliefs of Greeks and heretics. In his homilies *On the Incomprehensible Nature of God* he made the case that the iniquity of the Anomoeans regarding the divine nature was even more excessive than the one of the Greeks since the latter did not try to define the divine nature or give it a name. Even "in their speculations on the nature of incorporeal beings, the Greeks did not set down a complete definition of this nature but gave an obscure statement and description rather than a definition." *De incompr. hom.* 5.37 (SC 28bis:302; trans. Harkins, *On the Incomprehensible Nature of God*, 153).

[170] *De virg.* 4.2 (SC 125:104; trans. Shore, *On Virginity*, 6).

When discussing the classification of the heretical virgin, and her contempt for marriage and married people, Chrysostom wonders about what group she can be associated with. He mentions the Jews first, but dismisses the idea since they honour marriage and do not allow the practice of virginity. The Christians are mentioned next, but this idea is dismissed as well, by citing Hebrews 13:4 ("Let marriage be kept honourable in every way..."), which John attributes to Paul. The pagans are the last group remaining, but even in that case the heretical virgin is found wanting. Chrysostom approvingly cites Plato's dicta that "he was good who made all of this" and "no envy over anything is born in what is good" as evidence that the heretical virgin would even be rejected by the pagans.[171] On the contrary, she is even more irreverent than the pagans; this is due to the fact that she calls God wicked and thinks of him as the creator of wicked works (αὐτὸν πονηρὸν καλεῖς καὶ πονηρῶν ἔργων δημιουργόν). Since she cannot be associated with any of these groups, the only one that remains to share her opinion is the Devil himself, since even his angels recognize that God is good.[172]

As part of this series of comparisons, John not only mentions Plato, but quotes him with approval. These positive references are not just mere indications of Chrysostom's acquaintance with classical literature. They also challenge claims that, as A. Hartney puts it, "Chrysostom liked to ignore classical literature unless he was mocking its

---

[171] Λείπεται δὴ μετὰ τῶν Ἑλλήνων ὑμᾶς στῆναι λοιπόν. Ἀλλὰ κἀκεῖνοι παρώσονται πάλιν ὑμᾶς ὡς ἀσεβεστέρους. Πλάτων μὲν γάρ φησιν «ὅτι ἀγαθὸς ἦν ὁ τόδε τὸ πᾶν συστησάμενος», καὶ «ὅτι ἀγαθῷ οὐδεὶς περὶ οὐδενὸς ἐγγίνεται φθόνος.» *De virg.* 8.2 (SC 125:116; *On Virginity*, 10). The quotations are from *Timaeus* 29a and 29e. Samuel Pomeroy interprets this citation as Chrysostom's attempt to show that "widespread agreement that the source of all things is good, and that the biblical narrative corroborates this notion." Pomeroy, "Reading Plato Through the Eyes of Eusebius." Pomeroy also mentions that despite the fact Chrysostom is citing a text that many would consider sacred to Greek culture, he does not bring up the issue of "its religious or ethnic ownership", since his purpose was not to "construct" an identity at this point. Papadopoulos, *John Chrysostom vol. 2*, 15, sees the citation of these passages as a form of Pauline concession from John to his audience, considering that they are taken out of their original context, which is evident by the fact that Plato and Chrysostom would have very different understandings of the meaning of ἀγαθὸς.

[172] Ibid., providing Mark 2:24 and Acts 16:17 as evidence for the last claim.

baseness and immorality."[173] Chrysostom neither ignored nor just mocked classical literature, unless we only choose to read and cite passages that prove this point. Our references to his work will show that Chrysostom had a much more nuanced stance towards the classics, which certainly included mocking them, but did not do so exclusively.

Indeed, this is not the only example of John citing Plato with measured approval. As we will see in the next chapter, there are plenty of examples where he criticizes him, especially when he compares him with Christians. Nevertheless, there is a striking passage in which John praises Plato, along with Socrates, Diogenes, Aristides and Epaminondas.[174] We will be looking at the praise of Diogenes in more detail in our chapter on John and the Cynics. But it will be interesting to look at the other cases and see what exactly draws John's admiration and praise. The passage begins with a comparison between Plato and Dionysius, the tyrant of Sicily. It is a matter of fact, John argues, that Plato is more illustrious and praised than Dionysius. This despite the fact that "the tyrant ruled the entire world, lived in luxury, and spent his days amid great wealth, bodyguards, and other vanity, but Plato spent his time in the garden of the Academy, watering, sowing, eating olives, laying out a cheap table, and being free of all this vanity."[175] It is interesting to note that while in other passages John ruthlessly criticizes Plato for his alleged vanity, in this example he shows him completely free of it in comparison with the tyrant. Another interesting omission, intentional or not, is the lack of reference to Plato's teaching in the Academy, among the other activities

---

[173] Hartney, *John Chrysostom and the Transformation of the City*, 36. For another example of this point of view see Hill, *Introduction to St. John Chrysostom: Commentary on the Psalms vol. 1*, 22: "Despite his reputation in antiquity for classical scholarship, exemplified by his mentor Libanius's vain hope to have him as his successor and by the odd reference in this commentary to Homer and Plato, his nod in the direction of "the scholars" seems at best deferential, probably disparaging, hardly sympathetic."

[174] *Adv. opp. vit. mon.* 2.5 (PG 47:339-40).

[175] *Adv. opp. vit. mon.* 2.5 (PG 47:339-40; trans. Hunter, *A Comparison*, 106-8). All references below come from the same passage. This and other references from Chrysostom's corpus only reinforce the point that sweeping judgments about his total negativity to classical scholarship are of little help when discussing the relations between early Christianity and Hellenism.

mentioned. John goes on to mention Plato's sale as a slave, which "actually seemed admirable even to the tyrant himself. Such is virtue! Not only through its actions, but also through the misfortunes it suffers, it prevents itself and those who practice it from being forgotten or consigned to oblivion." In this instance, Plato's attitude is a prime example of virtue, which ultimately leads to the everlastingness of his name.

This story is followed by a comparison between Socrates and king Archelaus of Macedon. Again, the king is living in great wealth whereas Socrates has only one garment and lives on bread, which he received from others, because he was so poor. The way these men lived is also a determining factor in the glory they possess during John's time: "For the names of those men, Plato and Socrates, are known to many, whereas Dionysius and Archelaus are virtually unknown." These philosophers' claim to illustriousness is also attributed to the fact that they chose a "private life free of business and did not wish to get close to the government."[176] One cannot but notice the contradiction with Chrysostom's claims elsewhere: in comparison to the apostles, the philosophers are virtually unknown. In this comparison, it is the kings who are unknown instead. In order to make his point here, John intentionally omits the fact that Plato eventually returned to Sicily to tutor Dionysius II (son of the tyrant mentioned before) in his attempt to become the archetypal philosopher-king.

Chrysostom's reference to government leads into a small diatribe about those involved with politics: "those who become famous are not the ones who live in wealth, luxury, and abundance, but rather those who live a life of poverty, simplicity and modesty." To illustrate this point, he has two concrete examples in mind. The first is Aristides, to whom the Athenians gave a public funeral and who was much more

---

[176] However, elsewhere John does mention Plato's wish "to strike out a new form of government ... not by changing the customs relating to the gods, but merely by substituting one line of conduct for another" and then goes on to mention his exile from Sicily and his sale as a slave. In this case Plato is used as an example of how much easier it is to innovate in political rather than religious affairs, especially in the case for someone like Plato, whose proposals were in a book and did not create any obligation to the lawmakers to put them into practice. *In 1 Cor. hom.* 4.4 (PG 61:36; NPNF 1-12:20).

illustrious than Alcibiades, even though the latter was "outstanding in wealth, family, luxury, rhetorical power, bodily strength, nobility of birth and everything else." The other example is Epaminondas, who only had one pair of clothes and was thus unable to attend the assembly of the Thebans when called there due to the fact that he had to wash them before he could go. Nevertheless, he was far more illustrious than the generals who did attend the assembly. This assessment of Epaminondas' character is in accord with the opinion of other ancient historians who praised him for his simple and ascetic lifestyle and his disdain for material wealth.[177] In John's opinion both examples serve to prove that "fame and splendour do not reside in places or in clothes or in dignity or in power, but only in virtue of soul and philosophy." Again, despite the fact that Aristides and Epaminondas had plenty of power during their lives, what John emphasizes is that their fame was not because of that but due to their spiritual attributes.

Another instance of John agreeing with and appealing to the philosophers is in some of his polemics against rhetoric. His argument is that many "pagan" philosophers (ἔξωθεν φιλοσόφοις) cared little for education ὄντες ἀμαθεῖς.[178] This is why they spent all of their lives concerned with the ethical part of philosophy, which is why they "lived a brilliant life and became famous." The philosophers he mentions in that category are Anacharsis, Crates and Diogenes, who were either Cynics themselves (the latter two) or considered forerunners of Cynicism. All these had no taste for letters, John claims, and some even say that Socrates did not either, a view that John does not completely advocate and thus mentions it with the disclaimer of "some say". After citing part of Socrates' speech in Plato's *Apology*, John comes to the point he wanted to make all along: "rhetoric (εὐγλωττία) is not appropriate for philosophers, or even for grown men; rather, it is an ostentatious display of adolescents at play." Chrysostom reinforces his

---

[177] See Xenophon, *Hellen.* 7.5 (LCL 89:323-5); Diodorus, *Hist.* 9.11 (LCL 375:73); 15.88 (LCL 389:199).

[178] For this and the other references in this paragraph see *Adv. opp. vit. mon.* 3.11 (PG 47:367-8; trans. Hunter, *A Comparison*, 148-50).

point by saying that this view is not only shared by all the other philosophers but even by the one who surpassed them all (Plato), since he believed that "such decoration was shameful for the philosopher."[179] At the same time, he recognizes that these arguments were more convincing to a pagan than a Christian, since the former chase after the glory of the crowd, but still think that eloquence is really nothing. The passage is concluded with John posing a hypothetical question: if even the "pagans" loathe eloquence, why are Christians willing to despise their spiritual needs in order to achieve it? As we have seen before, Chrysostom posed the same question in relation to the purposes of education in his day.

Chrysostom's praise of the philosophers sometimes takes a more general form that allows him to commend them without actually naming them. Thus, to support his argument that "no one cures evil by evil, but evil by good"[180], he describes it as a conclusion reached by Greek philosophers (who remain nameless). The point he is trying to make yet again is that Christians should be ashamed that there is such virtue among the Greeks, even though their philosophy is inferior. What follows then is a catalogue of these virtues: "many of them have been wronged and have borne it; many have been falsely accused and have not taken revenge; they have been plotted against and have shown kindness." In fact, Christians should be in awe because if some Greeks' way of life is found to be superior to theirs, their punishment will be more severe. The Christians are then reminded about the benefits they have received because of their faith: "for, when we who have shared in the Spirit, we who are in expectation of the

---

[179] However, elsewhere Chrysostom accuses Plato of betrayal of Socrates' principles on that matter: "Yet see how very ridiculous [Plato] is. That which he has represented his master as avoiding, on the ground that it is disgraceful, and unworthy of philosophy, and the work of striplings, this he himself has practiced most of all." *In Ioh. hom.* 2.3 (PG 59:32; trans. Goggin, *Commentary on Saint John*, 19). A basic difference between this passage and the one mentioned in the main text is that in the former case Plato is compared to Paul, and, as with every case of a Christian being compared to a "pagan" in Chrysostom's writings, there is always a need to downplay certain elements of the pagans' personalities in order to make the Christians appear superior.

[180] *In Ioh. hom.* 51.3 (PG 59:286; trans. Goggin, *Commentary on Saint John vol. 2*, 42). Every reference in this paragraph is from this passage.

kingdom, we who live virtuously for a heavenly reward, we who do not fear hell, we who are bidden to be angels, we who enjoy the benefit of the Mysteries, when, I repeat, we do not overtake them in practicing the same degree of virtue, what pardon shall we have?" The presumed answer is that there will be no pardon. Either way, Chrysostom concludes his praise by urging the Christians to leave aside all "bitterness and anger and passion." This is yet another instance of John praising Greeks not for their own sake, but as a method of inspiring shame in his Christian audience.

Chrysostom also sometimes appealed to some views of Greek philosophers to reinforce his arguments and show that his point is not only based on Jewish or Christian precedent but can also be found elsewhere, usually among the Greeks. Thus, when he wants to make the point that greed is the worst of all evils, he first appeals to the ἔξωθεν, who call it the citadel of all evils, and then to 1 Timothy 6:10. The reference here is probably to Diogenes the Cynic, who, according to Diogenes Laertius, called greed the metropolis of all evils.[181] John also refers to anonymous philosophers when he wants to teach the Christians about the worthlessness of things in this life. Christians should be reproved and ashamed by the examples of those who exercise external wisdom, who were able to discern the shabbiness of this world and abstained from it. These philosophers have actually shown to the Christians that without any promise of future rewards (which the Christians aspired to), they were still able to keep away from vices.

They did not expect any wealth, yet they subscribed to poverty, simply because they knew that poverty is better than wealth. They did not hope in any sort of future life when they abandoned luxury and followed a strict discipline, but they did so only because they learned the true nature of things as well as the fact that the strict training

---

[181] *In Matt. hom.* 63.4 (PG 58:608); Diogenes Laertius, *Vit. phil.* 6.50 (LCL 185:52). The difference in John's quotation is that he claims they called it ἀκρόπολιν κακῶν, whereas Diogenes is said to have called it μητρόπολιν πάντων τῶν κακῶν.

of the soul goes together with the health of the body.[182] Chrysostom is also willing to cite popular sayings in support of his arguments. When he wants to make a point that luxury and sobriety cannot coexist, he quotes from Arsenius' *Apophthegmata*: "A fat belly does not produce a subtle mind."[183]

When Chrysostom wants to talk about conjugal relations between a husband and a wife, and the role of patience in case one marries a raucous wife, he uses the example of Socrates and his wife Xanthippe. In this example, she is presented as evil, loquacious, and a drunkard, and Socrates is cited as having said to some who asked how can he endure her, that she enables him to have his home as a school and training ground for philosophy, adding "for I shall be to all the rest meeker being here disciplined every day." Chrysostom is profoundly sad to find that the Greeks can be so much more philosophical than the Christians, and advises them, in case they end up with unsuitable partners, to "try to be like this philosopher."[184]

Finally, Hellenism is also praised in the context of comparison between the attitudes of Hellenes (famous or not) and ordinary Christians in their everyday lives. One such example comes from Chrysostom's lament regarding how Christian women mourn the deaths of their loved ones. He accuses them of putting on a show, some of them due to grief, others due to their vanity and still others to attract the male gaze. This is how he describes their lamentation: they are "baring their arms, tearing their hair, making scratches down their cheeks,"[185] and other things he does not mention. John's first problem with this attitude is how it appears to the Greeks, who might ridicule the Christians and think of their teachings as myths. The way the Christian women behave,

---

[182] *In 1 Cor. hom.* 8.5 (PG 61:74-75).

[183] *In 1 Tim. hom.* 13.4 (PG 62:569; Arsenius, *Apophthegmata* 5.22a, in *Corpus Paroemiographorum Graecorum vol. 2*, ed. Ernest Ludwig von Leutsch and Friedrich Wilhelm Schneidewin, Hildesheim: Georg Olms, 1958, 337).

[184] *In 1 Cor. hom.* 26.7 (PG 61:224; NPNF 1-12:156-7).

[185] *In Ioh. hom.* 62.4 (PG 59:346; trans. Goggin, *Commentary on Saint John*, 174). Cf. *De Laz. conc.* 4.2 (PG 48:1020).

John argues, resembles more the maenads than believers in God and will ultimately lead the Greeks to laugh and believe that there is no resurrection and that the Christian teachings are lies and jokes. The core of the problem appears to have been a lack of attention to the Biblical text, because if these Christian women believed that their beloveds' lives have not ended but they have been transferred to a better life instead, they would not mourn them as if they no longer exist. If they believed in the resurrection they would never utter such words as "I will never see you again; I will never have you back again."[186] The result of this behaviour is that the Hellenes would come to believe that all Christian teachings are fables and if the Christians do not believe in their most important doctrine "how much more must this be true of the rest of their piety." In his attempt to inspire shame in his audience, John contrasts this attitude to the Greeks, who do not behave like women (οὐχ οὕτως Ἕλληνες γυναικίζονται)[187] and "many among them have lived according to the precepts of true wisdom."

To prove his point, he goes on to cite three examples from Greek history that show true philosophical behaviour in the face of death, of which two have women as protagonists! The first is a reference to Plutarch's *Sayings of Spartan women*, and the passage John cites is from a section on sayings of women whose names did not survive. In Plutarch's version, upon hearing that all her five sons lost their lives in battle for Sparta, the woman simply says to the messenger "I did not inquire about that, you vile varlet, but how fares our country?"[188] After learning that it was victorious, she gladly accepts the death of her sons. John's reference to the incident is a little different: in his example, the woman has only one son, and her question is "but how are the fortunes of

---

[186] *In Ioh. hom.* 62.4 (PG 59:347; trans. Goggin, *Commentary on Saint John*, 174).

[187] Interestingly, one of Libanius' stereotypes against Christianity was that it was a religion for women, and in *Or.* 16.47 (LCL 451:241) Christian males are accused of avoiding discussions of the doctrines of Plato and Pythagoras under the advice of their mothers, women and housekeepers: "So, whenever there is any mention of Plato and Pythagoras, you put forward the excuse of your mother, your wife, your housekeeper, your cook, and your lasting trust in doctrines like theirs, and you have no qualms about the qualms that such doctrines inspire, but you follow the lead of those you should command."

[188] Plutarch, *Sayings of Spartan Women* 7 (LCL 245:463).

the city getting on", which essentially has the same meaning as the question above, but might indicate a different source due to the difference in the number of sons. Chrysostom's next example is a story about Xenophon (who is called a philosopher) from Diogenes Laertius' *Lives of the Philosophers*. The story is about the participation of Xenophon's sons, Diodorus and Gryllus, at the Battle of Mantinea in 362 and his reaction after he learnt that Gryllus was killed during the battle. This is how Plutarch describes it: "On this occasion Xenophon is said to have been sacrificing, with a chaplet on his head, which he removed when his son's death was announced. But afterwards, upon learning that he had fallen gloriously, he replaced the chaplet on his head."[189] Chrysostom omits the detail that Xenophon was sacrificing when he found out about his son's death, but uses the rest of the story as an example of how a Hellene showed such exemplary behaviour upon learning about the death of his own child.[190]

His final example comes from Sparta yet again,[191] particularly the famous exhortation of Spartan women to their sons that they should return either carrying their shields (thus implying they would be alive and not have fled the field of battle) or carried on them (the implication being in this case that they would be dead). Although John refers to this story as an example of Greeks giving up their sons and daughters to be sacrificed in honour of demons, he still considers it as a true example of practising philosophy, which some Christians do not follow. The conclusion to these stories is yet another mention of the principle of the reverse practice of doctrine: those who do not subscribe to a specific doctrine act like those who believe in it, while those who do

---

[189] Diogenes Laertius, *Vit. phil.* 2.54 (LCL 184:185).

[190] John, in stark contrast to Julian, believed that these writings could teach ἀνδρείαν, φρόνησιν, δικαιοσύνην to Christians, as we see in these examples. On the other hand, Julian could not possibly fathom that reading the Bible would ever make anyone φρονιμώτερος οὐδὲ ἀνδρειότερος οὐδ' ἑαυτοῦ κρείττων, *Contr. Gal.* 229E (LCL 157:386).

[191] Could we possibly explain John's inclination to use examples from Sparta as a reaction to Libanius' dislike of its values as expressed in *Or.* 64.8 (trans. Johannes Haubold and Richard Miles, "Communality and Theatre in Libanius' Oration LXIV *In Defence of the Pantomimes*," in *Culture and Society in Later Roman Antioch*, ed. Isabella Sandwell and Janet Huskinson, Oxford: Oxbow, 2004, 28)? "Prosperity has furthered the growth of many cities and Hellenes and barbarians alike assign great value to being wealthy. The Spartans were convinced by their laws that poverty is stronger than riches."

believe in that doctrine do not perform the actions they should due to their belief in said doctrine. Although the Greeks know nothing about the resurrection, they still perform the actions that "should be performed by those who know about it, while those who do know about it [the Christians] act like those who are ignorant of it."[192] Chrysostom was not afraid to call attention to the fact that in some instances the Greeks practised true philosophy in a more genuine way than some of the Christians, and did not hesitate to point that out, despite his alleged "anti-Hellenism."

It is interesting to note that all three examples Chrysostom invokes are related to deaths on the battlefield. This may be because these kinds of deaths can provide him with agonistic and heroic motifs. That would be true, except for the fact that his emphasis is not on the people that actually died, but rather the reaction of those related to them. The heroes in the stories as Chrysostom narrates them are the mother and the father who hear about the death of their sons and deal with it in the appropriate, Christian-like manner, not the sons who die in defence of their homeland. We saw that John could find some positive exemplars on how to face death among the Greeks. But how did he deal with one of the most famed deaths in antiquity? Could he make an example out of that?

We are talking, of course, about the death of Socrates, which does not impress Chrysostom, who uses it as a negative example when comparing attitudes from Greeks and Christians in contempt of death. He indicates that he can bring forward ten thousand from within the Church that would drink the hemlock if it was lawful at the time of the persecutions. Socrates was not free to decide whether to drink the hemlock, John argues, whereas the Christian martyrs endured suffering on their own volition when they could choose not to. It is obvious that Socrates' refusal to flee is not mentioned here, since it would not serve his argument. Socrates' age is also mentioned,

---

[192] *In Joh. hom.* 62.4 (PG 59:347; trans. Goggin, *Commentary on Saint John*, 175).

as Chrysostom finds it ironic that he decided to despise life when he was seventy, "if this can be called despising ... For to die by hemlock is all as one with a sleeping man's continuing in a state of sleep. Nay even sweeter than sleep is this sort of death, if reports say true."[193]

There are also other instances where John criticises *all* Christians and scorns them for their behaviour when compared to the Greeks. While his praise is often paired with a backhanded comment about the *motive* of the Greeks' actions, he still finds it preferable to what the Christians are doing. Thus, the Greeks have practised an exemplary philosophy of life, but for the sake of δόξα.[194] Equally, the Christians ought to practise every virtue more intensely and not for glory but to fulfill the will of God, a condition that John recognizes they often do not satisfy. The Christians should despise money for the sake of Christ but they do not; on the contrary, the Greeks make little account of their lives and during wars even give their children over to demons (an argument Chrysostom has already used when mentioning the Spartan women). At the end of his argument Chrysostom cannot but admit his shamefulness and astonishment (αἰσχύνομαι καὶ ἐκπλήττομαι) over the fact that he can obviously see some pagans despising money whereas *all* Christians get frenzied over it (παρὰ δὲ ἡμῖν μαινομένους ἅπαντας). The hyperbolic nature of this statement leads Chrysostom to a quick qualification: even if there are Christians who scorn money, they are still enslaved by other passions, such as θυμῷ and βασκανίᾳ, which leads him to a very pessimistic closing: πρᾶγμα δύσκολον, καθαρὰν φιλοσοφίαν εὑρεῖν.

In conclusion, it appears that John had no trouble using and citing examples from the classical world when he wanted to make certain points, and when he did so he was even willing to praise the philosophers or even anonymous Greeks for their attitudes

---

[193] *In 1 Cor. hom.* 4.4 (PG 61:35; NPNF 1-12:19).

[194] For the passage discussed in this paragraph see *In Ioh. hom.* 84.3 (PG 59:458-9; trans. Goggin, *Commentary on Saint John vol. 2*, 425-6). This is an example of combining both criticism and praise, which will be the focus of the next section.

and views. This by itself is not significant. But when seen in the context of modern arguments against John as the archetypal Christian anti-Hellene, it provides a useful counterexample that shows the one-sidedness of these points of view. The rest of this chapter (section d) will introduce some examples to show that Chrysostom's attitude is even more complex. Having looked into examples of both praise and criticism towards Hellenism (sections b and c), we shall briefly look into three related attitudes: one that combines praise and criticism together, one that shows indifference and one that recommends how Greeks should be treated. Finally, we will examine concepts which Chrysostom inherits from Hellenism.

d. Further complexity

i. Praise and Critique of Hellenism combined

We have already seen many instances where Chrysostom will criticize or praise the Greeks either as individuals or for their beliefs.[195] In most of these cases he is doing one or the other. But there are instances where he can do both within the same homily, and it is with these that we will deal in this section. For example, John is prepared to admit that some of the Greek philosophers despised wealth and death,[196] but with a caveat: they only did so in order to show off to others, and that is why their hopes were empty. Their paradigm is used in an exhortatory fashion: if the Christians are not even able to do what they did, how do they expect to be saved? The transgression of a Christian is much greater than that of a Greek, since the latter has lost all hope anyway.[197]

---

[195] At one point (*In 2 Tim. hom.* 4.3, PG 62:622) he will also praise the Greek language as "admirable and beautiful."

[196] *In Tit. hom.* 5.2 (PG 62:689) also mentions that while many of the ἔξωθεν philosophers despised money, virtually none of them was indifferent to women, which is proof enough for John that greed is worse than lust since the latter is implanted in our nature. Despite the fact the he was the one using the example of the philosophers, he quickly turns the discussion to Paul since he is addressing the Church and in this case, it is more appropriate to choose examples from the Scriptures rather than from those "outside."

[197] *In Matt. hom.* 14.9 (PG 57:235). See *In Matt. hom.* 21.3 (PG 57:299-300; NPNF 1-10:147) for another reference to Greeks voluntarily stripping themselves of their possessions, "though not in a proper spirit," and an exhortation to Christians to not appear inferior compared to Greek philosophers.

In his seventh *Homily on Genesis* he talks about the misuse of reason among the Greeks. The piece begins with an observation: the Greeks fell into error (ἐπλανήθησαν). The observation is followed by a procedural list: a) they entrusted everything to their own reasoning; b) refused to acknowledge the limitations of their nature; c) let their imagination run wild; d) exceeded the measure of their capabilities, and e) lost the status they laid claim to. And what exactly was that status? This is where Chrysostom's praise, albeit brief, begins: they received the gift of reason and preeminence from the Creator himself, whilst they also outranked *every* other visible creature (λόγῳ τετιμημένοι καὶ τοσαύτην προεδρίαν λαβόντες παρὰ τοῦ δημιουργοῦ, καὶ τῶν κτισμάτων ἁπάντων τῶν ὁρωμένων τιμιώτεροι). The praise of what one assumes to be intended for Greeks of the past is followed by an attack on the Greeks of both past and present: they fell into ἀλογίαν and ended up worshipping "dogs, monkeys, crocodiles ... even onions and more worthless things than that." But this was just the beginning: "following this extreme they went on to call sticks and stones gods, and divinized all the visible elements; once, you see, they strayed from the right path, they fell headlong and were cast into the very depth of wickedness."[198] Despite the negative conclusion, John's praise is not minimal. His anthropology is defined by the concept of the λόγος being the distinctive mark that separates humans from all other animals. Simply put, a human is, above all, a logical (or rational) animal.[199] In this sense, the Greeks were preeminent

---

[198] *In Gen. hom.* 7.6 (PG 53:68; trans. Hill, *Homilies on Genesis 1-17*, 102).

[199] *Vid. dom. hom.* 4.1 (SC 277:140; trans. Hill, *Homilies on Isaiah and Jeremiah*, 81): "What is it, rather, by which the human being is distinguished from the beasts? Language (Τῷ λόγῳ): on this score the human being is also a rational being (διὰ τοῦτο καὶ λογικὸν ζῷόν ἐστιν ὁ ἄνθρωπος). Hill (ibid., 128) believes that Chrysostom is trying to flatter his audience for being attentive to his homilies by using a Stoic expression. Jean Dumortier identifies the origins of the phrase λογικὸν ζῷόν as Stoic (SC 177:141) as well, with references to Chrysippus, Marcus Aurelius, Epictetus and Artemidorus. John uses a similar definition in *In 1 Tim. hom.* 13.4 (PG 62:569), which he attributes to the ἔξωθεν: Οἱ ἔξωθέν φασι ζῷον λογικὸν, θνητὸν, νοῦ καὶ ἐπιστήμης δεκτικόν. The attributes of humanity in this definition, although not all at once, can be found in Aristotle, *Trop.* 112a and 128b. It appears verbatim in Sextus Empiricus, *PH* 2.5 (LCL 273:168-9): Ἄλλοι ἔφασκον ἄνθρωπον εἶναι ζῷον λογικὸν θνητόν, νοῦ καὶ ἐπιστήμης δεκτικόν. The Loeb editor attributes the definition to Peripatetics and Sceptics. Interestingly, it is one of the many definitions included by Sextus, the others belonging to Plato, Epicurus, Socrates, and Democritus. However, John chooses this one over the others, possibly because, as we also saw above, he could make it work from a Christian point of view. The sentence also appears verbatim in ps-Basil, *Adversus Eunomium* 4 (PG 29:688). Even when Chrysostom wants to escape the narrow definition of humans as

above everyone else, because they possessed the gift of *logos* to such an extent that it distinguished them from other humans.

In this passage, the fact that John refers to onion worship among the Greeks might seem particularly strange. At the same time, in his *Homilies on Matthew* he calls ancient Egypt "her that was the slave of cats, that feared and dreaded onions." This is yet another instance of Chrysostom being loose with the application of the word Hellenes and using it both as an ethnic and as a religious appellation.[200] Similarly, in the context of Chrysostom admonishing Christian women not to paint their faces and bringing biblical figures in support of his argument, he mentions Leah, Jacob's wife, who "although she was uncomely ... continued to preserve the lineaments thereof undisfigured" and did this despite the fact that she was brought up by Greeks.[201] This usage becomes clearer in John's interpretation of Romans 2:10, where he talks about Greeks before Christ's coming: "But by Greeks he here means not them that worshipped idols, but them that adored God, that obeyed the law of nature, that strictly kept all things, save the Jewish observances ... such as were Melchizedek and those around him, such as was Job, such as were the Ninevites, such as was Cornelius."[202] Furthermore, in the context of a comment on Romans 2:8-9, John mentions the countless evils that Greeks have suffered in this world, as recounted in both the histories written by the ἔξωθεν as well as the Scriptures. This is then followed by a question: "For who could recount the tragic calamities of the Babylonians, or those of the Egyptians?" This is yet another example of the name Hellenes used in a religious rather

---

rational animals, since this is the primary definition provided by those outside the faith, he still makes the point that we are not just rational animals; we are, or at least we should be, more than that. Cf. *Illum. cat.* 2.1 (PG 49:232; NPNF 1-9:165): "For a man [human in the original] is not merely whosoever has hands and feet of a man, nor whosoever is rational only, but whosoever practices piety and virtue with boldness."

[200] *In Matt. hom.* 8.5 (PG 57:88; NPNF 1-10:51).

[201] *In Matt. hom.* 30.5 (PG 57:369-70; NPNF 1-10:199).

[202] *In Rom. hom.* 5.3 (PG 60:426; NPNF 1-10:363).

than an ethnic sense.[203] Sometimes, what might appear as a criticism of Hellenism on the surface, ends up being something entirely different due to what we perceive as Chrysostom's inconsistency. However, this might be an overly complex explanation of this problem. Chrysostom was no historian or classicist, and expecting him to abide by their rules as a pastor might just be us asking for too much. His comment is better understood within the context of early Christian critiques of Greek religion as coming from other cultures, including the Egyptians, which allows them to be homogenised in this way.[204]

ii. Indifference to Hellenism

Chrysostom's references to classical authors or ideas were not always positive or negative. There were times when he mentions historical personages, events, and ideas without making any value judgments. Thus, in his *Commentary on Isaiah* Chrysostom briefly mentions Socrates and Demosthenes and notes that prior to the coming of Christ even philosophers and rhetoricians had to serve in the army and fight in the battlefield.[205] Furthermore, in the same work Chrysostom cites a phrase from Demosthenes' *On the Embassy* and calls him simply one of those outside the faith (τις καὶ τῶν ἔξωθεν).[206] This attitude of Chrysostom has been interpreted in different ways. For example, D. Garrett considers it as a standard feature of John's attitude towards classical authors and contrasts it with the attitude of other fathers: "Overall, Chrysostom's attitude towards the masters of antiquity is cool. Some other fathers cannot but admire them and wonder if they might have been Christians unaware, that is, men who by their wisdom and moral life proved themselves to be part of God's

---

[203] *In Matt. hom.* 36.4 (PG 57:417; NPNF 1-10:236).

[204] For a similar, and even more confusing history of the origins of "Hellenism," see Epiphanius, *Pan.* 1.3.

[205] *Comm. in Is.* 2.5 (SC 304:122).

[206] *Or.* 19.314 (LCL 155:452), in *Comm. in Is.* 3.8 (SC 304:186).

elect."[207] The rhetorical scheme of those inside/outside the faith is very common in Chrysostom and in certain cases was applied as a description of the Christians and the Greeks.[208] It is often utilised to demarcate the boundaries of one group (Christians) from another (Jews/Greeks). But sometimes, as in the examples mentioned above, the terminology of those outside the faith is a purely descriptive and not an evaluative term.

When discussing Proverbs 15:1 ("Wrath undoes even the prudent") he claims that even the ἔξωθεν admit so, a cryptic reference that Bady interprets as a signpost to Achilles' wrath in the *Iliad*.[209] In his *Letter to a Young Widow* he mentions a story about the "sophist who taught me", one that exceeded everyone in his reverence towards the gods, and the admiration he expressed about John's mother's widowhood and the fact that women like these exist among the Christians. This reference, besides the fact that it is often used as proof of John's tutelage under Libanius,[210] is also another instance of Chrysostom talking about the ἔξωθεν without directing any praise or criticism towards them. Interestingly, in the beginning of this section Chrysostom indicates that the praise of widowhood is an honorable and admirable thing not only "for us believers, but for the unbelievers as well."[211]

Sometimes he would also cite from classical sources to support his views, which we classify as indifferent here because usually he does not make any value judgements regarding the source itself and often uses it as a way of showing either the antiquity of an idea or its existence in non-Christian circles. Thus, in his second *Exhortation to*

---

[207] Garrett, *An Analysis*, 243.

[208] *In 1 Cor. hom.* 16.2 (PG 61:130): τοὺς ἔσω καὶ τοὺς ἔξω, τοὺς Χριστιανοὺς καὶ τοὺς Ἕλληνας...

[209] *Com. in Prov.* 15.1 (Guillaume Bady, *Le commentaire inédit sur les proverbes attribué à Jean Chrysostome. Introduction, édition critique et traduction*, 2 vols, doctoral dissertation, Université Lyon, 2003, 330).

[210] For a discussion of the issue including assessments of previous scholarship see David G. Hunter, "Libanius and John Chrysostom: New Thoughts on an Old Problem," *Studia Patristica* 22 (Leuven: Peeters, 1989), 129-35.

[211] *Ad. vid. iun.* 2 (SC 138:120). The unbelievers are not necessarily "pagans," as Chrysostom applies the term to the Jews as well (*De Sac.* 4.1, SC 272:236) and, as Malingrey, *Sur Le Sacerdoce*, 236 n. 1, explains, it is applied to the Jews (and consequently to the "pagans") due to their refusal to believe in the divinity of Christ.

Theodore John wants to make the point that nothing is more precious than the soul. To this effect, he cites Euripides' *Alcestis* (which he does not mention as his source) and Homer's *Iliad*.[212] Elsewhere, he makes the poignant observation that the Christians, just like the ἔξωθεν, have developed an infatuation with oratory (λόγων ἔρως), an argument he uses to point out that the Christian preacher should be very well prepared for his sermons.[213] When arguing against the divinization of humans in paganism, he prefaces his statement by citing the philosophers' "comprehensive definition of the human race (for when asked what man was, they answered, he is an animal, rational and mortal),"[214] before attributing the very same divinization to *hoi polloi*. Finally, he will sometimes cite an opinion or a proverb attributed to those "outside" but we have no indication of whom he meant.[215]

iii. How are the Christians supposed to treat the Greeks?

Chrysostom's multiple tirades against the Greeks would inevitably lead some to wonder how they should treat them as Christians. In treating this issue, Chrysostom makes a distinction between the person and their doctrine. A person should never be hated. Their doctrine however, is fair play, as is wicked conduct and a corrupted mindset. One is therefore *not* entitled to call a Greek "polluted" (μιαρὸν), at least without an excuse, or otherwise one will be considered an insulter. However, if one is asked regarding the Greeks' doctrine, then one is entitled to respond that it is indeed polluted and impious. Chrysostom is carefully making clear that this should only be the case if someone asks the Christian or forces him/her to speak. Otherwise, if done on

---

[212] *Ad. Theod.* 2 3.67 (SC 117:64): John's οὐδὲν ψυχῆς τιμιώτερον is from Euripides' *Alc.* 301 (LCL 12:182); ψυχῆς γὰρ οὐδὲν ἀντάξιον, καὶ τῶν ἔξωθέν τις ποιητικὸς ἔφη is from Homer, *Ill.* 9.401 (LCL 170:424), where we see John mentioning the saying but not exactly who is the poet he is citing. It is worth mentioning that in the original texts ψυχή means life, whereas John uses it as soul.

[213] *De Sac.* 5.8 (SC 272:302).

[214] *De stat.* 11.2 (49:121; NPNF 1-9:414).

[215] E.g. *Comm. in Iob* 14.4 (SC 346:358) where he talks about the fact that the sea is not subject to the passage of time because of its immortality, something that even "some of those outside" say.

his/her own initiative, it can cause unnecessary hostilities.[216] The analogy that can help

clarify John's point here is martyrdom. Chrysostom, like many other fathers before him,

condemned the concept of voluntary martyrdom, because it could instigate a larger

number of persecutions and was also seen as a form of intentional suicide.[217] Similarly,

a Christian giving his opinion about the Greeks and their doctrines without being asked

might also be the instigator of persecution or at least of sowing division between the

two groups. The difference and distinction between the two categories we mentioned

previously (humans/doctrine) is that whilst humans are God's work, deceit is the

Devil's and one should not mix the two.

As with many other issues, Chrysostom claims to follow the Pauline example here

and particularly his relationship with the Jews.[218] Paul's treatment is also extended to

debates with the Greeks. The aim of these is to "cure" the Greeks from their doctrines

and to persuade them about the truth of Christianity. Chrysostom provided guidelines

related to these debates and the topics that need to be discussed. The conversation

should begin with the argument whether Christ is God, as well as the Son of God, and

whether the gods of the Greeks are demons. After the establishment of these points,

which Chrysostom calls first elements (τὰ πρῶτα στοιχεῖα), others can follow. Even if

the Greek disbelieves things such as the last judgment, he will find that many of his

philosophers have treated this subject, and although they separated the soul from the

body, they still hold to the idea of a tribunal. John claims that almost everyone is aware

of this, including the poets, and therefore the ideas of the tribunal and of the last

---

[216] *In Col. hom.* 11.2 (PG 62:376).

[217] For a collection of numerous references from works before Chrysostom see Geoffrey E. M. De Ste. Croix, "Voluntary Martyrdom in the Early Church," in *Christian Persecution, Martyrdom, and Orthodoxy*, eds. Geoffrey de Ste. Croix, Michael Whitby, and Joseph Streeter (Oxford: Oxford University Press, 2006), 153-200.

[218] *In 1 Cor. hom.* 33.4 (PG 61:282). Similarly, in *In Col. hom.* 11.3 (PG 62:377), John's advice to Christians not to call the Greeks μιαροὶ is based on Paul's speech in Athens, which did not start with Ὦ μιαροὶ καὶ παμμίαροι but with Ἄνδρες Ἀθηναῖοι, κατὰ πάντα ὡς δεισιδαιμονεστέρους ὑμᾶς θεωρῶ, because Paul knew when it was useful to insult (as in Acts 13:10 against Elymas the Sorcerer) and when it was not.

judgment are not really in dispute. Thus, it would be superfluous for the Christian to debase these issues, especially without setting the foundations of the first elements mentioned previously.[219]

Chrysostom also envisages this conversation in the context of a personal relationship that might lead to a friendship. In this scenario, if a Christian becomes a friend with a Greek then the former should abstain from talking about religious matters until the point where they become really close friends, and even then, only to do so slowly.[220] One would assume that this advice was provided because Chrysostom knew how contentious a subject religion is and therefore saw it as something that should be discussed only when the friendship is solidified. The Christians are also encouraged to pray for the Greeks, and it is God Himself who wills it.[221] John's response to the potential objection of some Christians that they cannot do that is that Christ died even for the Greeks, and the fact that they did not believe was irrelevant since Christ did his part.[222]

Also irrelevant is a person's religious convictions when it comes to the Christian practice of charity and almsgiving. Chrysostom explicitly says that the Christians ought to show kindness when they see a Greek in need, as well as every human that faces exceptional circumstances. What makes this point even more important is the fact that it precedes an accusation against a custom that seems to have prevailed among certain Christians: an overzealous search for monastics and a willingness to do good to them alone, followed by certain excuses when asked why they do not practise charity towards

---

[219] *In Col. hom.* 2.5 (PG 62:316-7). Further below John contrasts the doctrine of judgment with the doctrine of the resurrection and their inherent relation to virtue and vice (ibid., NPNF 1-13:269): "This rule then will hold universally and strictly (κανὼν οὖν οὗτος ἔσται καθολικός). Not one of those who live in virtue wholly disbelieves the doctrine of the Judgment, even though he be a Greek or heretic. None, save a few, of those who live in great wickedness, receives the doctrine of the Resurrection."

[220] *In Col. hom.* 11.2 (PG 62:377).

[221] *In 1 Tim. hom.* 7.2 (PG 62:536). Besides the Greeks the Christians are also encouraged to pray for the heretics, since they are supposed to pray for all men and to refrain from persecuting.

[222] *In 1 Tim. hom.* 7.2 (PG 62:537).

others, such as "unless he be worthy, unless he be righteous, unless he work miracles, I stretch out no hand," an attitude John criticizes for having "taken away the greater part of charity ... and [which] in time will ... utterly destroy the very thing itself."[223] Affliction is an issue that crosses the lines of any earthly division, be it racial, religious, or anything else, and that provides enough justification for Christian aid without the necessity of inquiring about anything related to the afflicted persons' status.

Despite the varied nature of John's recommendations, he has been accused in the past for being not just a vocal but also a practical opponent of Hellenism. As we already indicated in the first chapter, the only actual proof we have, by his own admission but also independently verified by Theodoret, is the mission of the monks to Phoenicia where certain temples were destroyed and violent clashes ensued. However, he has also been accused of another, much greater crime, that is, the ultimate destruction of the Temple of Artemis in Ephesus. John refers to the Temple in his *hypothesis* to his *Homilies on Ephesians*. The initial claim seems to have been made by Clive Foss, who resolutely proclaims that "It [the Temple] was finally despoiled by Patriarch [sic] John Chrysostom during his visit to Ephesus in 401."[224] This claim later also found its way into works by Vasiliki Limberis, Hans Willer Laale and John Freely, who also present the destruction by Chrysostom as a fact.[225] Foss, who is cited by Limberis but not by Laale or Freely, cites a text he claims was previously unnoticed: a forged encomium to the Virgin Mary ascribed to Cyril of Alexandria, where Chrysostom is presented as

---

[223] *In Heb. hom.* 10.4 (PG 63:88; NPNF 1-14:416).

[224] Clive Foss, *Ephesus After Antiquity: A Late Antique, Byzantine and Turkish City* (Cambridge: Cambridge University Press, 1979), 86.

[225] Vasiliki Limberis, "The Council of Ephesos: The Rise of the Cult of the Theotokos and the Demise of the See of Ephesos," in *Ephesos, Metropolis of Asia,* ed. Helmut Koester (Valley Forge: Trinity Press International, 1995), 334: "John Chrysostom, bishop of Constantinople in approximately 400, was instrumental in closing the temple of Artemis..." Hans Willer Laale, *Ephesus (Ephesos): An Abbreviated History from Androclus to Constantine XI* (Bloomington, IN: WestBow, 2011), 305: "What was left of the Temple of Artemis [after its destruction by the Goths in 268 AD] likely was ordered dismantled while Chrysostom was in Ephesus conducting hearings." John Freely, *The Western Shores of Turkey: Discovering the Aegean and Mediterranean Coasts,* 2nd ed. (London: Tauris, 2004), 147-8: "The temple was then destroyed in 401 by a fanatical mob led by the patriarch [sic] John Chrysostom, who saw this as the final triumph of Christianity over paganism."

"destroyer of the demons and overthrower of the Temple of Artemis."[226] Foss admits that "the Homily, however, appears to be a late forgery and thus presents no certain evidence for the destruction of the Temple."[227] Yet Foss contradicts himself elsewhere in the book when he refers to Isidore of Pelusium's *Epistle 55 To Hierax the Clarissimus*[228], which was certainly written after Chrysostom's death and where the Temple of Artemis is mentioned in the context of a reference to Greeks digging up human remains from the Temple in order to revere them.[229] As Frank Trombley indicated, Isidore's epistle provides us with a *terminus ante quem* for the dismantling of the Temple and his reference to its existence in his time should have been enough to dispel that theory.[230] Palladius' Bk 14, concerned with John's visit to Ephesus to deal with issues related to local bishops, makes no mention of this alleged destruction either. Another passage Foss uses to support Chrysostom's involvement is a reference in Proclus' *Oration* 20.3 where, among other achievements it is said that "in Ephesus, he despoiled the art of Midas (In Epheso, artem Midae nudavit)."[231] This sentence could be interpreted in many different ways, but it cannot seriously sustain an argument that Chrysostom and his alleged mob destroyed the Temple. Proclus might have meant that he destroyed objects related to the local cult, or it could simply be a hyperbolic statement that contrasts the presence of a saintly bishop to an urban context that was famous for its devotion to Artemis and consequently, to paganism. This is just one example of certain persistent myths about Chrysostom, but one that through its spread on the internet is now often found cited as an undisputed fact. The question must be

---

[226] PG 77:1032 (trans. Foss, *Ephesus*, 86).

[227] Foss, *Ephesus*, 86.

[228] PG 78:217.

[229] Foss, *Ephesus*, 32.

[230] Trombley, *Hellenic Religion and Christianization v. 2*, 242.

[231] PG 65:832, surviving text in Latin only.

asked again, even if it becomes repetitious: could examples like this be the reason for Chrysostom's reputation as the archenemy of Hellenism?

iv. The heritage of Hellenism

A slightly different point is that Chrysostom sometimes shows that he inherits concepts from Hellenism, which he then adapts to a Christian frame. As we will argue in the chapter on Cynicism, there are certain ideas and concepts that John has directly inherited from Greek sources, with little trace of any biblical influence. While our focus in that chapter is the common basis between Cynic and Christian social ethics, there are other ideas that he seems to have received directly from his Greco-Roman educational background.

One example of this is his belief in the evil eye, or βασκανία as it is called in ancient Greek. The belief in the evil or malevolent eye is shared among many different authors from Greco-Roman antiquity, and it seems that the core of the idea remained popular among the Christians. However, one feature that some Christians could certainly not accept (although this does not imply that it was not used) was the use of amulets and other apotropaic devices as sources of protection from the evil eye. We have already seen John forcefully arguing against these and it seems that their use was condemned in most patristic writings. However, this condemnation did not lead to a wholesale rejection of the concept. Thus, John's references to βασκανία follow the path of previous Christian writers and the concept becomes synonymous with envy whilst also used to describe a series of societal evils: "because of this disease the law courts are thronged with cases. From it come vainglory and avarice. From it come ambition and pride. Because of it, the roads are beset by brutal robbers, and the sea is infested with pirates. Inspired by it, murders are committed throughout the world. By its influence our race is torn apart."[232] Thus, in this specific case John adapts previous Christian and Greco-Roman tradition by extending the arguments against the evil eye to the society as a whole and the consequences it causes. Certain customs could not be Christianized, and John reserved his harshest judgment for them.

e. A man of contradictions

John's ambivalent stance towards Hellenism should not be surprising to anyone who has read his works extensively. Contradictory opinions on the very same matter are present in many places within his corpus, and include examples of seeing him "vehemently condemn[ing] the swearing of any oaths or the use of cosmetics ..." but elsewhere "we find him recommending certain types of oaths or suggesting ways in which beauty may be enhanced."[233] However, this chapter has shown that one can move beyond a simple acknowledgment of his contradictory views on certain practices and try to contextualize these views properly, looking into the argument the views appear in and what he is trying to achieve in each case. If one were to summarize what Hellenism meant for Chrysostom, calling it a way of life would be the most apt description. At the same time, this way of life was certainly different from the Christian way, and in both cases John makes a connection between life and doctrine.[234] In an analogy that brings both elements together, a good way of life is compared to a robe "woven together from

---

[232] *In Ioh. hom.* 64.4 (PG 59:359; trans. Goggin, *Commentary on Saint John vol. 2*, 204-5). For references to βασκανία before Chrysostom see G. W. H. Lampe, *A Patristic Greek Lexicon* (Oxford: Oxford University Press, 1969), 293.

[233] Leyerle, *Theatrical Shows*, 183.

[234] A connection that is elsewhere ascribed to the Greeks as well, this time in the context of the behavior of a Christian slave: "But if they [the Greeks] see their slave, who has been taught the philosophy of displaying more self-command than their own philosophers, and serving with all meekness and good will, he will in every way admire the power of the Gospel. For the Greeks judge not of doctrines by the doctrine itself, but they make the life and conduct the test of the doctrines." The servants (and the women) are then exhorted to be instructors of the Greek through conversation, and the former are also implored to show the untruthfulness of stereotypes about them, which Chrysostom hesitantly admits but, instead of explaining them as natural and inherent, lays the blame decidedly to their masters who care for nothing but to be served. See *In Tit. hom.* 4.4 (PG 62:685; NPNF 1-13:533). The same connection is made in a Chrysostomic definition of virtue: "[virtue is] the preciseness of true doctrines and correctness in life," *Quod nem. laed.* 3 (SC 103:70).

good moral conduct and correct doctrine."[235] Hellenism did not uphold correct doctrine and was thus unable to procure examples of good moral conduct. Even when Chrysostom begrudgingly admits that certain Hellenes led admirable lives, he is quick to dismiss their motivation for doing so. Generally speaking, his polemic against Hellenism is not as frequent or as intense as it has been claimed in the past. Despite the fact that it was a popular subject that pleased his congregation (alongside his arguments against the Manicheans and the Marcionites), he recognized that sometimes "this sort of discourse is out of season", and preferred to put his emphasis on teaching the Christian basic truths such as that being covetous is evil, since a lot of them were not intellectually mature enough to listen to polemic.[236] This is stated unambiguously in two of his most direct statements on Hellenism: "when the life is corrupt, it engenders a doctrine congenial to it, and from this circumstance many are seen to fall into a depth of evil, and to turn aside into Hellenism."[237] But what exactly do these many do when they turn to Hellenism? According to Chrysostom, some, because of their fear of the last judgment, persuade themselves that what the Christians preach are lies. Others turn their faith aside because they try to understand everything through reasonings (*logismoi*). What they forget is that in this case, faith is a safe ship and reasonings a shipwreck. This is because, as we have shown, Chrysostom considers searching into the divine mysteries through reasonings to be blasphemy.[238] Despite Hellenism's many achievements and great ideals, this is where it ultimately fails. It is a rationalizing way of trying to understand God, and, precisely because of that, is to be rejected.

---

[235] *De Christ. div.* 12.5 (SC 396; trans. Harkins, *On the Incomprehensible Nature of God*, 305).

[236] *In Heb. hom.* 9.1 (PG 63:76; NPNF 1-14:409).

[237] *In 1 Tim. hom.* 5.1 (PG 62:527; NPNF 1-13:424, with minor changes): Ὅταν γὰρ ᾖ βίος ἀπεγνωσμένος, καὶ δόγμα τίκτεται τοιοῦτον· καὶ ἔστιν ἰδεῖν πολλοὺς ἐκ τούτου καταπεσόντας εἰς βυθὸν κακῶν, καὶ εἰς Ἑλληνισμὸν ἐκτραπέντας. The other reference is from John's *Commentary on Job* 1.1 (SC 346:86; *St. John Chrysostom, Commentaries on the Sages vol. 1: Commentary on Job*, trans. Robert Charles Hill, Brookline, MA: Holy Cross Orthodox Press, 2006, 16): "A good life, you see, makes one recognize God, just as a bad one does the opposite; knowledge of God is arrived at through one's life…. And so paganism (*Hellenismos*) comes from no other source than an impure life."

[238] *In 1 Tim. hom.* 5.2 (PG 62:527).

3. *Of what fatherland are you*: The dialectics of identity through comparisons

In the previous chapter we extensively analysed Chrysostom's multifaceted approach to Hellenism. We primarily focused on positive, negative and even neutral engagements with Hellenism, primarily through analysing what Chrysostom said about Greek practices, ideas, and customs. These were often reflected in the sayings or attitudes of famous philosophers as well as common everyday people, and it is often the case that John will treat these sayings and attitudes in a paradigmatic and axiomatic way. A lot of the ideas we first encountered in the previous chapter will resurface again, albeit in a different context: in this chapter, we will be looking into John's practice of synkrisis between Greeks and Christians. More specifically, the personifications of what John considers Christian and Greek ideals and virtues as they appear in numerous comparisons between Greeks and Christians in his work. Some of these comparisons have been the subject of scholarly scrutiny before, as in Margaret Mitchell's masterful study of Pauline portraits within Chrysostom's exegesis and Pak-Wah Lai's doctoral dissertation on the hermeneutics of exemplar figures in Chrysostom's works and how they were informed both by Greco-Roman traditions of *paideia* and virtue ethics as well as the Christian tradition. The difference between these works and the present study is that we will be working with more examples than Mitchell and Lai, who primarily focused on Paul (the former) and David (the latter). Our focus is also different, as we are primarily concerned with exemplar figures only in the context of comparisons between Greeks and Christians, and attempt to relate them to the framework of John's reception of Hellenism as discussed in the previous chapter. The task here is to see John's *method and contents* of comparison as we look into yet another aspect of his reception of Hellenism. First, we will examine how, in his rhetoric, John uses the category of martyrs to draw a sharp contrast between Christianity and Hellenism. Then we will look into specific comparisons he draws between Christians and Greeks, starting from major ones between Peter, Paul and John on the one hand, and Plato, Socrates and Pythagoras, on the other. We will then proceed to look into some minor comparisons where we see some small variations on points of emphasis, and then conclude this chapter with a discussion of a seminal text for our purposes, the *Discourse on Babylas*.

a. The martyrs in Chrysostom's rhetoric

In his panegyric to the martyr Lucian, John narrates a striking story from the martyr's trial:

> he [the executioner] escorted him [Lucian] back into court and tortured him and applied incessant questions. But to each question he replied only: "I am a Christian." And when the executioner said: "What country are you from?" said: "I am a Christian." "What's your occupation?" "I am a Christian." "Who are your parents?" To everything he said: "I am a Christian." ... For the person who says, "I am a Christian" has revealed both their country and family history and occupation. Let me explain how. The Christian does not have a city on earth, but the Jerusalem in heaven... The Christian doesn't have an earthly occupation, but arrives at the heavenly way of life... The Christian has as relatives and fellow citizens all the saints.[1]

Regardless of the historicity of the trial, if Chrysostom's account of the conversation were taken at face value it would imply and validate the suspicions of some scholars that one of the aims of Christianity was to create an exclusive religious identity that would make any other affiliation, be it ethnic or societal, irrelevant. Margaret Mitchell has argued against such an interpretation, calling the episode "a legend which dares to imagine an overturned social order through the enthusiastic vision of a single martyr."[2] But Chrysostom made similar arguments elsewhere, without the need to use the martyr's voice: "If you're a Christian, you don't have a city on earth. It's God who's *the builder and maker* (Hebrews 11:10) of our city. Even were we to gain possession of the whole world, we are *strangers and pilgrims* in it all. We're enrolled in heaven; it's there

---

[1] *In. Lucian.* 3 (PG 50:524-5; trans. Mayer, *Cult of the Saints*, 71-2).

[2] Mitchell, *The Heavenly Trumpet*, 234.

that we're citizens."[3] Is Chrysostom's rhetoric a call to arms for Christians to abandon their homelands? Or is it simply an exhortation to Christians that their religious identity trumps every other earthly one *exactly* because he thinks of it as not of this earth?

This is a complicated passage that can easily be considered problematic. However, the danger of taking everything at face value is to neglect the paradigmatic function of sermons as building blocks in identity formation, and as such, prone to hyperbolic statements made in order to strengthen the sense of community. Returning to this passage again, we see that, despite the fact that Lucian had received education ἔξωθεν, he is portrayed as understanding perfectly that there is no need for rhetorical embellishments in this contest. On the surface Chrysostom's statement against rhetorical superfluities seems peculiar: they are very much present in John's rhetoric and there is also something rhetorical about Lucian's statements. And yet even though Lucian was educated, he is portrayed as understanding that in contests such as these faith is more than enough.[4] Chrysostom's point about the lack of *patris* on Lucian's behalf is thus perfectly complementary to his rhetorical use of an apparent lack of rhetoric: both are, in a way, superfluous elements that are already transcended in this present life if a Christian has his/her eye to the *politeia* above.

As we will see, the martyrs and the saints play a prominent role in Chrysostom's reception of Hellenism, serving both as role models and as living proofs of the emergent and victorious Christianity. A brief tour d' horizon will enable us to see both cases in practice, and we will begin with the rhetoric of the power of the martyrs, which in Chrysostom's words "catches in its net not just private persons, but those who wear the diadems" [i.e. the emperors].[5] This same power is a "source of shame for the Greeks"

---

³ *De stat.* 17.12 (PG 49:178; trans. Mayer and Allen, *John Chrysostom*, 114). Sandwell, "John Chrysostom's Audiences," 527, does not consider this passage to be "a simple rhetorical statement of loyalty to God" and thinks that it was intended "to transform every aspect of the life of the Christian."

⁴ *In Lucian.* 3 (PG 50:524).

⁵ *De Phoca* 1 (PG 50:699; trans. Mayer, *Cult of the Saints*, 78).

and "the censure of their error".[6] One might wonder why John thought the Greeks needed to feel shame for the persecutions that the Romans were responsible for. The answer to this is that John thinks of the Roman Emperors as Greeks, and actually calls them so. This can be explained as a statement reflective of the common background of Greco-Roman paganism, or more probably due to a Christian (and Chrysostomic) tendency to categorize anyone who was not a Jew or a Christian as Greek, regardless of their actual ethnicity. One of the texts where he does this is *Demonstration against the Pagans That Christ is God*:

> The emperors were pagans (Ἕλληνες). Augustus, Tiberius, Gaius, Nero, Vespasian, Titus and all his successors were pagans, down to the time of the blessed Emperor Constantine. All the pagan emperors waged war against the Church. Some were less harsh, others were more severe, but all waged their wars against it. Some emperors, it seemed, did leave the Church undisturbed. But they were emperors and obviously pagans and ungodly men. These very facts caused a constant threat of war since other men would ingratiate themselves with the emperors and prove their loyalty by a war against the Church. Yes, men did plot against the Church ... Still, these plots did produce many martyrs. But they left the Church treasures that will never perish, columns that will always stand, towers that no force can take by storm. In death as in life, these martyrs have become a source of strength and assistance to those of a later age.[7]

John's insistence that "yes, men did plot against the church" implies that some members of his audience would find it difficult to believe that something like that could ever have happened. It seems that a series of Christian emperors (whether they were orthodox or not) made the persecutions a long distant memory, and part of Chrysostom's efforts both as a priest and bishop would have been to remind people about the constant possibility of martyrdom.

Such examples show that in the rhetoric of Chrysostom, martyrdom becomes a very significant point of divergence from Hellenism, precisely because, according to John, the Hellenes cannot claim any martyrs for their religion. In another instance

---

[6] Ibid.

[7] *C. Iud. et. gent.* 15.1-2 (PG 47:833; trans. Harkins, *Apologist*, 249). John himself uses the word Ἕλληνες only once, even though Harkins mentions "pagans" three times in his translation, which is completely unnecessary in the third sentence.

Chrysostom compares the martyrs to the disciples of Socrates and their attitude after his death. It is clearly implied that their exile was self-imposed, and that "they appeared more cowardly than frogs" while the martyrs "didn't just despise death but also countless tortures which were crueller than any death." W. Mayer argues that John's allusion might be in reference to Critias, Charmides and Alcibiades, who were all exiled after Socrates' death. However, as we shall see later, when Chrysostom mentions the flight of Socrates' disciples in other writings he has different people in mind.[8] Regardless of their identity though, the important point is the contrast between Socrates' disciples and Christian martyrs and the lack of the former's philosophical convictions whilst facing the prospect of death.[9] Yet John's effort might have been in vain if his aim was to appeal to pagans since people like Libanius would claim that Hellenism did not really need martyrs.[10]

However, we can argue that this was not his intended audience. The martyrs primarily serve as role models for the Christian community, and one thing John always seems to emphasize is their humanity. This is for two reasons: partly because he does not want the believers to consider them as something extraordinary that they could never be, which would mark a departure from many representations of martyrs, and partly because he wants to emphasize their common bond with his audience and the potential they have to emulate them. Chrysostom wanted to avoid giving the impression that the apostles or the saints were of a different nature than that shared by all humans, even when he wanted to make a point about them transcending this very nature, as in

---

[8] *In mart. omn.* 7 (trans. Mayer, *Cult of the Saints*, 245).

[9] Chrysostom extended the concept of exhibiting philosophy through martyrdom to Jewish martyrs as well. Thus, the Maccabean martyrs also provide evidence of their philosophy through their martyrdom and Chrysostom urges the believers to give "evidence of the same philosophical virtue in the battle against the irrational passions, in particular rage, the longing for money, (physical) love, and vainglory." Gerard Rouwhorst, "The Emergence of the Cult of the Maccabean Martyrs in Late Antique Christianity," in *More than a Memory: The Discourse of Martyrdom and the Construction of Christian Identity in the History of Christianity*, ed. Johan Leemans (Leuven: Peeters, 2005), 91. It is also important to note that Chrysostom's exhortation is extended to all Christians, "whether they live in the cities or in the desert, whether they are virgins or whether they conduct a holy married life" (ibid., 92).

[10] Cribiore, *Libanius the Sophist*, 160.

the second homily *In Praise of St Paul*: "Paul did not obtain another nature, nor share a different soul, nor inhabit another world, but, having been reared on the same earth, and land, and laws, and customs, he exceeded all human beings who have existed from the time there have been human beings."[11] Nevertheless, not all persecutions are equal to Paul's.

In addition to his emphasis on the humanity of martyrs, another interesting aspect of John's homilies is his constant effort to avoid the phenomenon of divinizing natural elements. In some cases, he would use the occasion of speaking about a saintly Christian figure in order to argue against such phenomena. Thus, in his *Homily on St Phocas* John argues that "God made the heavens so that we might see the work and adore the Creator, but the Greeks made the work a god,"[12] obviously referring to Uranus in Greek mythology. In another example, he describes Apollo's temple in Daphne as a battleground between Apollo and the martyr Babylas. Here John is evidently celebrating the victory of the martyr after the burning of the temple and teases those who worshipped the sun as a God: ποῦ νῦν εἰσιν οἱ τὸ καλὸν τοῦ Θεοῦ δημιούργημα καὶ πρὸς ὑπηρεσίαν ἡμετέραν γεγονὸς τὸν ἥλιον ἐνυβρίζοντες καὶ τῷ δαίμονι τὸ ἄστρον ἐπιφημίζοντες καὶ τοῦτο ἐκεῖνον εἶναι λέγοντες;[13] What is also evident from this passage, as has already been observed by Schatkin and Mitchell, is the implicit criticism of Julian, who was a self-confessed devotee of Helios.[14] As we can already see, the

---

[11] *De Laud. Paul. hom.* 2.1 (SC 30:144; trans. Mitchell, *The Heavenly Trumpet*, 448).

[12] *De Phoca* 3 (PG 50:703; trans. Mayer, *Cult of the Saints*, 84).

[13] *De Bab. c. Iul. et gent.* 83 (SC 362:204). For a similar sentiment cf. *In Gen. serm.* 1.1 (SC 433:144; *St. John Chrysostom: Eight Sermons on the Book of Genesis*, trans. Robert Charles Hill, Brookline, MA: Holy Cross Orthodox Press, 2004, 24): "If Greeks knew how to exercise their mind properly about creation, they would not have strayed from the truth ... The sky is beautiful, but the reason it was made was for you to adore its maker; the sun is brilliant, but it is for you to worship its creator. If, on the contrary, you are bent on stopping at the wonder of creation, and becoming attached to the beauty of the works, light has become darkness for you- or, rather, you have turned light into darkness."

[14] Mitchell, *The Heavenly Trumpet*, 239, citing Schatkin's introduction to the critical edition of the *Panegyric on Babylas*. In other works, John was not afraid to criticize Julian directly and refer to him by name, as he does e.g. when discussing his plan to rebuild the temple in Jerusalem in his homilies *Against the Jews*, where Julian's brief tenure is described as a period where τὰ Ἑλληνικὰ ἤνθει and Julian himself is described as ἀνδρὸς ἀσεβοῦς καὶ Ἕλληνος, *Adv. Iud. or.* 5.11 (PG 48:901).

martyrs can be used for multiple purposes in John's battle against Hellenism: they, like the apostles, had no earthly homeland and their family and compatriots were the saints, not their earthly family or fellow citizens. They were not afraid of death and the fact that they shared a common human nature with us is proof enough that they can be emulated. And yet, unlike the Greeks who were keen to personify and divinize natural elements like the sun and the sky, the martyrs were not to be divinized. Certain attributes of the martyrs were therefore points of contention, which were only enlarged when they were compared to personalities from the Greek world, as we will see in the next section.

b. Major Comparisons

The comparison method was by no means systematic, and can be found scattered throughout many of Chrysostom's works. As we already mentioned, Margaret Mitchell has firmly established the importance of Chrysostom's use of exemplar portraits (particularly those of Paul) and their central position in his exegetical practice.[15] Pak-Wah Lai has brought attention to the fact that Chrysostom's portrayals are often of an *ad hoc* nature and thus it would be difficult to attempt an ideological interpretation.[16] Mitchell has also made a similar argument: "although several emphases do emerge, both by volume and extent- such as Paul the prisoner for the gospel, Paul the teacher of the world, or Paul the man of sufferings... Chrysostom's portraits of Paul do not constitute a single composite portrait, nor a search for the single most accurate portrait, but rather an extensive portrait series."[17] As we have already seen, a similar case can be made for many of Chrysostom's portraits, even those of non-Christians. In the previous chapter we saw instances where Plato is described as a humble ascetic content with a

---

[15] Mitchell, *The Heavenly Trumpet*, 69-377.

[16] Pak-Wah Lai, "Exemplar Portraits and the Interpretation of John Chrysostom's Doctrine of Recapitulation," in *(Re)Visioning John Chrysostom: New Theories and Approaches*, ed. Wendy Mayer and Chris de Wet (Leiden: Brill, forthcoming).

[17] Mitchell, *The Heavenly Trumpet*, 383.

simple life, while in another he is the arrogant philosopher who failed to establish his

ideal republic on earth. Keeping these caveats in mind, what we are aiming to do here is

to collect and analyse this material, while at the same time trying to contextualize it

within the broader context of John's reception of Hellenism. There will be some

recurrent themes that we will note as we go through the different comparisons, which

we will also summarise in the conclusion to this chapter.

i. Plato, Socrates, Peter, and Paul

The technique that John usually uses to elevate the Christian saints and martyrs over

and against pagan personalities is called *synkrisis*. In ancient literature *synkrisis* (or

comparison) "refers to the comparative juxtaposition of people and things", and when

used in a rhetorical context also includes praise or blame.[18] Time and again Chrysostom

compares figures such as Paul, John or Babylas with pagan figures and uses those

comparisons to extract different lessons for his audience.[19] We will begin our analysis

of these comparisons with a rather long passage that contains a dialogue between a

Christian and a Hellene as reported by John, which compares the eloquence of Paul and

Plato:

> So, prove to me this - that Peter and Paul were eloquent. But you cannot. For
> they were "unskilled" and "unlettered" (Acts 4:13) ... Therefore, when the
> Greeks accuse the disciples of being unskilled, we should accuse them [i.e. the
> apostles] of it even more. Don't let anyone say that Paul was wise, but instead

---

[18] H. A. Gärtner, "Synkrisis", *Brill's New Pauly*. Antiquity volumes edited by Hubert Cancik and
Helmuth Schneider, English Edition by: Christine F. Salazar, Classical Tradition volumes edited by:
Manfred Landfester, English Edition by: Francis G. Gentry. Accessed on 21 November 2017,
http://dx.doi.org/10.1163/1574-9347_bnp_e1127330. Plutarch's *Parallel Lives* are a classic example of
the genre. Definitions and discussions of the technique were a standard staple in the surviving
progymnasmata handbooks of Aelius Theon, ps-Hermogenes, Aphthonius, Nicolaus the Sophist, and
Libanius, which also included practical exercises showcasing each of the rhetorical methods mentioned,
including synkrisis.

[19] Pak-Wah Lai, *John Chrysostom and the Hermeneutics of Exemplar Portraits* (PhD diss., Durham
University, 2010), 257, points out that sometimes martyrs can also be compared to other saints, as in the
synkrisis between Bernike, Prosdoke and Domnina who are presented as greater than Moses and the
Patriarchs. Some of the comparisons we will be discussing go beyond Lai's assertion that in "synkrisis ...
the exemplar concerned is compared with another similar exemplar or even a villainous figure, in order to
highlight the *aretai* and superiority of the exemplar concerned." Sometimes the exemplar is compared to
a figure that is neither saintly nor villainous, at least in the sense Lai uses the term (e.g. Antiochus
Epiphanes' persecution of the Maccabees).

let's exalt for wisdom the famous men among the Greeks, and marvel at their facility in speech, but let's say that all the Christian figures were unskilled. For in this respect we shall overthrow them in no small way; for thus the victories will be magnificent! Now the reason I have said these things is that I once heard a Christian debating in a ridiculous fashion with a Greek, and both of them were demolishing their own case in the battle against the other. For the Greek was saying the things the Christian should have said; and the Christian was proposing the things the Greek customarily should have said. For the dispute was about Paul and Plato, with the Greek trying to prove that Paul was uneducated and unskilled, while the Christian, due to simplicity, was zealously making the case that Paul was more eloquent than Plato. Thus, the victory belonged to the Greek, as this argument prevailed. For if Paul were more eloquent than Plato, likely many would argue back that it was not by grace, but by persuasive speech that he prevailed. Therefore, what the Christian said worked to the advantage of the Greek; and what the Greek was saying to that of the Christian. For if Paul were uneducated, but he prevailed over Plato, as I was saying, the victory was magnificent. For the uneducated man [Paul], taking Plato's disciples, persuaded them all and led them to himself. Whence it is clear that it was not by human wisdom that the gospel prevailed, but by the grace of God. Therefore, so that we might not suffer these things, nor be ridiculed when we are debating with Greeks, since Paul was the one who led them to us, let's accuse the Apostles of being uneducated. For this accusation is an encomium.[20]

In what M. Mitchell calls *"a deliberate rhetorical strategy,"*[21] John argues that it is wrong for a Christian to claim that Paul was more eloquent than Plato. In fact, when a Greek accuses the apostles of being illiterate, the Christian should not only admit to that accusation but push it even further! Mitchell has called this argument "illiteracy by association", and sees it as an effort to harmonize Paul with the other apostles, although Chrysostom usually tries to set him apart in other matters.[22] On the other hand, those on the Greeks' side who were wise and eloquent should be admired by the Christians for their wisdom and eloquence, a statement that is definitely semi-ironic considering the value John sometimes attributed to secular wisdom and eloquence.[23] But exactly the absence of these virtues in connection to the apostles proclaims their victory.

---

[20] *In 1 Cor. hom.* 3.8 (PG 61:27; trans. Mitchell, *The Heavenly Trumpet*, 243-4).

[21] Mitchell, *The Heavenly Trumpet*, 243, emphasis in the original.

[22] Ibid., 278, n. 372.

[23] But see his *In Rom. hom.* 3.3 (PG 60:413-4; NPNF 1-11:353): "And this is why they stood against one another and Aristotle rose up against Plato, and the Stoics blustered against him, and one has become hostile to one, another to another. So that one should not so much marvel at them for their wisdom, as turn away from them indignant and hate them, because through this very thing they have become fools. For had they not trusted what they have to reasonings, and syllogisms, and sophistries, they would not have suffered what they did suffer." The admiration towards the philosophers turns into hatred in this

John's remarks arise out of a dialogue he observed once between a Christian and a Greek. Whether the dialogue was real or imaginary will not concern us here. What does matter is the conclusion he draws from that dialogue, namely that the fact that Paul was uneducated should be a matter of praise. Although Plato was wise and eloquent (in an ironic kind of way), and therefore more illustrious than Paul in regard to these qualities, his followers ended up on Paul's side. The reason John makes this point is very specific- and obvious: the success of the Gospel is not to be attributed to human wisdom or persuasive rhetoric, but to the grace of God. In other words, John's purpose was to "diminish the rhetorical competence of Paul" and by doing that reverses "the encomiastic *topoi* by insisting that Paul was ἀπαίδευτος."[24]

Before there were ever monks, there was Paul, and Paul was stronger than all of the philosophers, and more effective at that.[25] According to Chrysostom, Paul was even stronger than Plato, "who is thought more reverend than the rest of them"[26] and was also considered "the chief of their philosophers"; but Chrysostom also describes him as a pimp, in relation to his view that in the ideal Republic women will be shared in common (*Republic* V).[27] But why is Plato singled out among the many Greek philosophers, not only in John's *Homilies on Titus*, but in many of his other works as

---

passage, and instead of wise they are called fools. However, one cannot avoid thinking that one of the reasons John emphasized the divisions of the philosophical schools must have been the underlying implication that the Church is not divided and her members do not fight each other like the followers of the different schools.

[24] Mitchell, *The Heavenly Trumpet*, 244. Wah, "Exemplar Portraits": "I would argue that Chrysostom's rhetorical strategy is both theologically and pastorally motivated. Theologically speaking, by drawing attention to the lowliness of Paul's origins and upbringing, Chrysostom would be able to demonstrate anew the transforming power of the Spirit. From a pastoral perspective, the same rhetoric also becomes, for Chrysostom, a means of encouraging his listeners to pursue their calling more fervently."

[25] *In Tit. hom.* 2.2 (PG 62:273; NPNF 1-13:525): "Do you not see that Paul put to flight the whole world, that he was more powerful than Plato and all the rest?" M. Mitchell translates the first part of the sentence as "don't you see that Paul turned around the whole world" (ibid., 274), which I think is closer to the meaning of the Greek original.

[26] *In Rom. hom.* 3.3 (PG 60:414; NPNF 1-12:353).

[27] "Another, the chief of their philosophers, approves of their going out to the war, and of their being common, as if he were a pimp and pander to their lusts," *In Tit. hom.* 5.4 (PG 62:694; NPNF 1-13:538). Plato's views on the ideal state were already criticized by Aristotle in the second book of his *Politics*.

well? For Margaret Mitchell, it is because Plato "often serves as a metonym for all of Greek philosophy and learning."[28] One could also argue that this was because of the enduring influence of Platonism in many Christian authors and the status of Plato for educated elites more generally. By focusing on Paul's victory over Plato, John can claim a complete victory of Christianity over philosophy, or, as Mitchell puts it, "the dissolution of the entire enterprise."[29] A. Hartney has also pointed out that in Chrysostom's homilies on the Pauline epistles "it is Plato who appears most often as a figure of comparison", with Aristotle being the second, and speculates that the reason for this choice was because Chrysostom might have felt that "his audience's familiarity with Plato was a direct threat to the status of his beloved Paul."[30] While a direct threat is difficult to establish, John's multiple references to Plato indicate that at a minimum certain Platonic ideas had to be combatted.

The comparison between Plato and Paul has been aptly summarized and analysed by Margaret Mitchell, and we will only make a brief note of it here. The main points are: a) that Plato was incapable of even converting the tyrant of Sicily, while Paul managed to convert the whole world, b) Paul's victory becomes more significant by the fact that he lacked Plato's advanced education, and c) that even without formal training, it was Paul's letters and rhetoric that won the victory over philosophy.[31] Mitchell's third point demands a bit of elaboration. Mitchell herself claims that Paul's lack of *paideia* ensures that he could not have technically been a rhetorician.[32] She also claims that Paul's lack

---

[28] *The Heavenly Trumpet*, 274. In contrast, Paul's persona is often "an apostolic metonym of the morally superior and victorious philosophy" (ibid., 380).

[29] Ibid., 274.

[30] Hartney, *John Chrysostom and the Transformation of the City*, 82. Hartney also mentions that in the whole of John's corpus, Josephus is the second most frequently mentioned writer, after Plato of course (ibid.).

[31] Mitchell, *The Heavenly Trumpet*, 275, with appropriate references to Chrysostom's works.

[32] Ibid., 278. John also interprets Paul's dictum in 1 Corinthians 1:22 ("For Jews demand signs and Greeks desire wisdom") as the Greeks demanding "a rhetorical style, and the acuteness of sophistry" (ῥητορείαν λόγων καὶ δεινότητα σοφισμάτων), *In 1 Cor. hom.* 4.3 (PG 61:33; NPNF 1-12:18). The Christians' preaching of the Cross is actually the exact opposite of this demand, which nevertheless still

of any formal rhetorical training enabled Christianity to appropriate the classical debate between rhetoric and philosophy and to place Paul on the side of philosophy.[33] Mitchell is correct to point out that this portrait of Paul would be hard to sustain however, considering Chrysostom's constant references to his persuasive abilities, which would be considered the hallmark of any good rhetorician. To solve this apparent inconsistency, Mitchell argues, Chrysostom specifies that Paul's rhetoric "defies the elitism of ancient *paideia* (as did its proponents), for it is accessible to all manner of people because it bases its appeal, not on deductive arguments [συλλογισμοί], but on faith [πίστις]."[34]

In that sense, Paul deserves even more praise because his natural aptitudes (and divine grace) were so great that he had no need for formal or technical training. Paul's persuasive abilities were not a result of any special training, and for this reason he was more eloquent than any of the Greek rhetoricians. Compared to them, his speech qualities might have been poorer, but much more powerful and effective, even compared to the rest of the Apostles.[35] We will demonstrate that the argument for the simplicity of the evangelical message and the contrast between faith and reasonings (or syllogisms) reappears in other comparisons as well, which we examine further below. John rejects the sophists and their clever syllogisms for the same reasons.

---

persuades those who would rather hear otherwise. The Cross becomes σοφίας ἀπόδειξις, and, instead of being considered a scandal and an offence, manages to attract people.

[33] Ibid.

[34] Ibid., 279, citing Chrysostom's *In Rom. hom.* 2.5 (PG 60:407): "For this reason, the Athenians themselves now laugh at those philosophers of old, whereas even the barbarians and ignorant and untrained attend to Paul. For his preaching is laid out common to all. He recognizes no difference in status, nor superiority of any nation, or any other such thing. For it requires faith alone, not syllogisms. Hence this proclamation is especially worthy of admiration, not only because of its utility and salvific power, but because it is simple and easy, and readily grasped by all, which is especially a work of God's providence, for he lays out all his gifts in common to all."

[35] "Now if I were demanding the polish of Isocrates and the grandeur of Demosthenes and the dignity of Thucydides and the sublimity of Plato, it would be right to confront me with the testimony of Paul. But in fact, I pass over all those qualities and the superfluous embellishments of pagan (ἔξωθεν) writers. I take no account of diction or style. Let a man's diction be beggarly and his verbal composition simple and artless, but do not let him be inexpert in the knowledge and careful statement of doctrine." *De Sac.* 4.6 (SC 272:268-70; St John Chrysostom, *Six Books on the Priesthood*, trans. Graham Neville, Crestwood, NY: St Vladimir's Seminary Press, 1977, 121-2).

One factor which Mitchell does not pay attention to is the way in which Plato was singled out for comparison because of the perception (on John's part) that he was "the most important —and the most dangerous— of the ancient rebels against the God-given sexual hierarchy."[36] Elizabeth Clark usefully points out John's many references to Bk 5 of the *Republic* and his relevant criticisms against it: women being shared in common, performing activities appropriate to men only, and, most shockingly, the "requirement of physical training for girls."[37] As far as Chrysostom's direct references to the classics go, this is one of the most frequent engagements with one of them, and the most common one outside of work of anti-Christian polemic. Another criticism Chrysostom directs against Plato is his plan for women to receive military instruction, which he deemed as unnatural and linked it with other practices he considered as such, namely homosexuality and infanticide.[38] Finally, the last critical point in connection to John's criticisms against Plato's views on female sexuality was his objection against Plato's advocacy not only of a community of women but also of communal childbearing. Again, these practices are considered as being against the natural order of things, while at the same time he accuses Plato of hypocrisy as he did not practise what he preached regarding the community of women and sarcastically admits that no legislator decided to implement Plato's ideal republic.[39]

Clark argues that John was not against the community of goods *in principle*. On the contrary, he espoused it and very often praised the early members of the Christian community for practising it. She also believes that it was Plato's position on the community of women in particular and not communal living in general that offended John and enabled him to attack Plato's *politeia*. The textual evidence is very much in

---

[36] Elizabeth Clark, *Jerome, Chrysostom, and Friends: Essays and Translations* (Lewiston, NY: Edwin Mellen Press, 1979), 11.

[37] Ibid.

[38] Clark, *Jerome, Chrysostom, and Friends*, 12.

[39] Ibid., 13, where Clark provides ample documentation of John's views from many different texts.

support of Clark's argument, as we shall also see later in this chapter (section C, i), and it seems that one more reason for Chrysostom's choice of Plato as the archetypal villain is his utopian plan to eradicate sexual differences from human society, something that Chrysostom believed would only be achieved in the afterlife, as with every distinction on earth (ethnic, racial, social, etc.).[40]

Finally, we cannot exclude the possibility that the major focus of John's criticisms was to undermine a philosopher whose works were still so highly regarded. This is why John claims that Plato lost not by means of another philosopher but through an unlearned fisherman.[41] In this example, Plato is the ultimate expression of the wisdom shown to be foolish, just as Paul is the epitome of true wisdom despite his lack of learning.

Besides Paul, Plato is also compared to Peter, and, as with Paul, the apostle emerges victorious. The relevant passage begins with a triumphalist statement:

> Where now is Greece with her big pretentions? Where the name of Athens? Where the ravings of the philosophers? He of Galilee, he of Bethsaida, he, the uncouth rustic, has overcome them all. Are you not ashamed —confess it— at the very name of the country of him who has defeated you? But if you hear his own name too, and learn that he was called Cephas, much more will you hide your faces.[42]

This passage from Chrysostom's *Homilies on the Acts* bears striking similarities with Tertullian's famous contrast between Athens and Jerusalem, and we can even say that it is even more triumphant than Tertullian's. At first sight, we might easily dismiss it as a poor effort at bragging on Chrysostom's part. Nevertheless, the rest of the homily contains some very interesting criticisms of Plato's philosophy, and Chrysostom's boasts should not prevent us from analysing it. If, however, one needs to justify the boasting, s/he would have to look no further that Julian's use of Galileans as a

---

[40] Ibid., 14.

[41] *In 1 Cor. hom.* 4.2 (PG 61:33).

[42] *In Act. apost. hom.* 4.3 (PG 60:47; NPNF 11:29).

derogatory term. If seen through this lens, what Chrysostom does here is simply re-appropriation. He reclaims the term Galilean, and embraces it to prove his point.

Moving on from this, John attempts to answer the question as to why Christ did not influence Plato and Pythagoras but chose Peter instead. His response is that this happened because his mind (or soul) was more philosophical than theirs (πολλῷ φιλοσοφωτέρα ἦν ἡ Πέτρου ψυχὴ τῶν ψυχῶν ἐκείνων)![43] It would definitely be problematic if John made this assertion and ended it there. But this is just a prelude to a full-frontal attack that comes out as a result of his comparison between Plato and Peter. The intent of the comparison initially is to describe the habits and pursuits of each. In this description, Plato is someone who wasted his time with foolish and useless doctrines.[44] Chrysostom very much doubts the usefulness (ὄφελος) of Plato's doctrines, particularly his doctrine of metempsychosis, which he ridicules by mentioning Plato's reference to the soul as a fly and saying that since he believed that, his soul might just be a fly! Plato's character also receives a harsh treatment: the man was "full of irony, and of jealous feelings against everyone else,"[45] and exactly because of these character traits it seemed as if he did not want to introduce anything useful to humanity, either when he borrowed ideas from others, as was the case with reincarnation, or when he introduced ideas of his own. Plato's own idea is, of course, his suggestion in the *Republic* that the women will be shared by everyone in his ideal state. But in his *Homilies on Acts* John criticizes other ideas suggested by Plato for his model republic.[46] These include the idea that virgins should be naked, that they should take part in wrestling competitions, and that the children will be common just like the women. John justifies his preference for Plato over examining the doctrines of the Greek poets, lest

---

[43] *In Act. apost. hom.* 4.4 (PG 60:47; NPNF 1-11:30). Paul was also called "more philosophical than philosophers, more eloquent than rhetoricians (ὁ φιλοσόφων φιλοσοφώτερος, ὁ ῥητόρων εὐγλωττότερος)", *De Laz. conc.* 6.9 (PG 48:1041).

[44] *In Act. apost. hom.* 4.4 (PG 60:48).

[45] *In Act. apost. hom.* 4.4 (PG 60:47; NPNF 1-11:30).

[46] Ibid.

someone accuse him of "ripping up fables", the implication being that the works of the poets are hardly worthy of attention because of the myths they contain, whereas John takes the *Republic* as a kind of constitution for the society Plato wanted to establish. Another factor might be the disregard shown to the poets by none other than Plato himself.[47]

Plato is not the only philosopher who is compared with Paul, Peter, or any of the other apostles: John also uses Socrates for this purpose. John's choice of Socrates is not random. Besides the fact that, as Mitchell notes, Libanius uses Socrates as the "zenith and metonym of Greek culture against Christians,"[48] Socrates was also the one philosophical figure that all philosophical schools admired, and thus, by attacking him, the implication is that all those who admire him might be considered guilty by association.[49] References to Socrates from both Christians and pagans were almost always meant to be ideologically charged. For example, in Libanius' works Socrates represents "the intellectual tradition of Hellenism, specifically in opposition to Christianity", and thus works such as the *Comparison between a King and a Monk* can be seen under the lens of John's response to Libanius' polemic against Christianity. John applies Libanius' depictions of Socrates and Julian as ascetics to the monks, and, instead of presenting their virtues as "an argument on behalf of Greek paideia," claims them for the Christian monks, who are the true philosophers.[50]

Chrysostom presents Peter and Paul as victors, but who did the apostles fight against? The answer John provides is against very many people and without the

---

[47] Yet another reason could be the fact that "prose and poetry were inescapably filled with allusions to polytheism, and many of its aspects were far from edifying." Laistner, *Christianity and Pagan Culture*, 49. For Chrysostom's references to Greek poets see P. R. Coleman Norton, "St. Chrysostom's Use of the Greek Poets," *Classical Philology* 28:3 (1932), 213-21. As we saw in the previous chapter Chrysostom had no trouble calling the works of the poets' nonsense.

[48] Mitchell, *The Heavenly Trumpet*, 274.

[49] For a positive reference to Socrates see *In 1 Cor. hom.* 4.5 (PG 61:37; NPNF 1-12:20): "the great Socrates ... who surpassed in philosophy all among them..."

[50] For the previous references above and further discussion of the figure of Socrates in John's *Comparatio* see Hunter, *A Comparison*, 28-9.

supposedly necessary weapons too: "without experience, without skill of the tongue, and in the condition of quite ordinary men, matched against juggling conjurors, against impostors, against the whole throng of sophists, of rhetoricians, of philosophers grown mouldy in the Academy and the walks of the Peripatetics, against all these they fought the battle out."[51] If we could group together under one term all the apostolic attributes that Chrysostom included in his different comparisons, that term would be simplicity, and despite the fact that it is used in contrast to the rhetoricians and the philosophers, it has been recognized as a rhetorical tool itself.[52] Hartney argues that John's praise of Paul and Peter "as simple and untutored men, who nevertheless won a huge following" served as "part of the ongoing 'Christianisation' of discourse, whereby traditional heroes of pagan culture are replaced by their simpler, and by extension more sincere, Christian counterparts."[53] Hartney also considers John's Christianization of discourse as a project that entails a demonstration of Plato's achievements as insignificant failures, thereby establishing Paul's message in their place, and thus "rewriting the cultural heritage of his new Christian citizens."[54]

My objection to this thesis is primarily due to the fact that we know John did not object to the standards of education of his day, which included the literature and philosophy associated with the Greco-Roman cultural heritage. Since that is the case, the role of Paul's texts would not be part of a rewriting of the cultural heritage but rather expanding it to include Christian texts, which would be primarily taught at home and in the church. The connection between simplicity of thought and expression as marks of sincerity on the one hand, and complexity of thought and expression as marks

---

[51] *In Act. apost. hom.* 4.4 (PG 60:47; NPNF 1-11:29).

[52] Hartney, *John Chrysostom and the Transformation of the City*, 81. Cf. Amirav, *Rhetoric and Tradition*, 25: "There is nothing surprising in the fact that the propagation of ideals which centre around rusticity, simplicity, and even idealistic illiteracy depends on the literary skills of their authors. In this sense, Christianity is like any other culture, immortalising the mute and illiterate by means of its urbanity and literacy."

[53] Hartney, *John Chrysostom and the Transformation of the City*, 81.

[54] Ibid., 82.

of insincerity, on the other, is one that John makes in various texts and it can also be considered a rhetorical tool. In fact, it has long been recognized as such, and Chrysostom was not unique in employing it.[55]

And yet, despite his apparent lack of education, Paul was also singlehandedly responsible for the demolition of paganism, according to Chrysostom. In the second *Homily on Eutropius* John describes the religious and social status quo under paganism:

> Formerly there was lamentation, there were altars everywhere, everywhere the smoke and fumes of sacrifice, everywhere unclean rites and mysteries, and sacrifices, everywhere demons holding their orgies, everywhere a citadel of the devil, everywhere fornication decked with wreaths of honour; and Paul stood alone. How did he escape being overwhelmed or torn in pieces? How could he open his mouth?[56]

M. Mitchell has analysed the similarity of the terminology and concepts in the second *Homily on Eutropius* with Libanius' *Oration* 18, where John's teacher is describing in very similar terms the restoration of pagan worship that took place under Julian, and argues that what Chrysostom achieves here is an antithesis between Paul and Julian.[57] In this antithetical scheme, and keeping in mind that Chrysostom's implicit target is probably Julian, Paul represents a solitary figure that stands against what the Emperor tried to resurrect in Chrysostom's time. Many a time in Chrysostom's rhetoric Paul represents the archetypal Christian hero, while Julian and Plato often serve as the

---

[55] "At times it was useful to emphasize the difference, to stress the "simplicity" of Christian literature over the conceit and trickery of rhetoric, or to insist on the irrational, the leap of faith, contrasted with the implied rationality of worldly learning." Cameron, *Christianity and the Rhetoric of Empire*, 85. Even more explicitly, although Cameron refers to Jerome: "Sometimes the claim to simplicity was obviously bogus, juxtaposed as it was with full utilization of the rhetorical repertoire." Ibid., 112. Or, in general on the Fathers: "It is impossible to make any seasoned system out of the utterances of the Fathers. All denounce the folly of contemporary orators and all on occasion avail themselves of their tools." Hubbell, "Chrysostom and Rhetoric," 266.

[56] *De capt. Eutr.* 14 (PG 52.409; NPNF 1-9:261). Referring to pre-Christian times, in his first *Homily on the Cross and the Thief* John explains that the concentration of Jewish worship and sacrifices in Jerusalem was a necessary response to the uncleanliness of the rest of the earth, brought upon it by Hellenic sacrifices: *De cruc. et latr. hom.* 1 1 (PG 49:400). Cf. *De cruc. et latr. hom.* 2 1 (PG 49:409) for the same argument and the additional point that it was Christ who cleansed the earth.

[57] Mitchell, *The Heavenly Trumpet*, 271. Cf. Libanius, *Or.* 18.126 (LCL 451:361). "First of all then, as I have said, he restored piety, as it were, from exile. Some temples he built, others he restored, while he furnished others with statues...Everywhere there were altars, fire, blood offerings, fat and smoke: the mystic ritual was performed, seers were freed from fear, and on the mountain tops were pipings and processions, and the same ox served as worship for the gods and a feast for men."

archetypal pagan villains. It is because of this that Hubbell describes the seven homilies in praise of St. Paul as "not an encomium on Paul but an apology for Christianity, and a proof of its divine origin, using the greatness of Paul as one of the proofs."[58]

As we discussed more extensively in the previous chapter, for Chrysostom pagan worship did not exist in a vacuum. This is particularly important since both Libanius and Julian, as representatives of the Hellenic tradition in Chrysostom's time, are being attacked for their religious views. However, "the particular mode of Chrysostom's argument involves an ethical dimension: the pagans are criticized for maintaining beliefs and forms of worship that contribute to moral decadence." It is an apologetic argument that fits within Chrysostom's efforts to prove the moral superiority of Christianity.[59] Time and again he explicitly connects religion with Greek philosophy, which he considers the element that "provided the logic and justification for the worship of idols."[60] To support this argument Mitchell mentions the *Homilies on Romans*, where John refers to Socrates' command to his followers to sacrifice a rooster to Asclepius.[61] What John is doing is effectively creating a chain of philosophers who are treated as enablers of paganism, starting from Socrates through Plato and down to Julian and Libanius in his own day. Despite his lack of learning, and in contrast to all these men considered wise, Paul is the epitome of true faith because unlike them, he teaches the correct doctrine.

ii. The beloved disciple, Plato and Pythagoras

The argument about the effectiveness of the apostolic teaching reappears in John's *Homilies on John*, in a detailed comparison between the Apostle John, Plato and Pythagoras. John was of no native land, but of an inglorious village of a place little

---

[58] Hubbell, "Chrysostom and Rhetoric," 271.

[59] For further discussion and the aforementioned quotation see Hunter, *A Comparison*, 54.

[60] Mitchell, *The Heavenly Trumpet*, 274.

[61] *In Rom. hom.* 3.3 (PG 60:414)

esteemed,[62] a topos that John has already used in connection to the trial of the martyr Lucian. As for παιδείας τῆς ἔξωθεν, "he had none whatsoever."[63] To put it succinctly, John was not just ἰδιώτης, but also ἀγράμματος. Chrysostom insists that this remained the case both before and after he met and accompanied Christ, but this fact did not affect John's works. Now John being the fisherman that he was, one would expect to hear things about fishing or rivers from him. But, Chrysostom says, "we shall hear none of these, but heavenly things, which no one ever before has learned ... sublime teachings, and a virtuous way and philosophy of life."[64] This statement is followed by a Chrysostomic tirade of rhetorical questions on who is entitled to speak about things like these: "Tell me, are these the words of a fisherman? Of an accomplished orator? Of a sophist or a philosopher? Of someone educated in profane learning? Not at all." Humans cannot philosophize about "that incorrupt and blessed Nature; about the powers closely associated with It; about immortality and everlasting life; about the nature of mortal bodies and of the immortal beings they will afterwards become; about punishment, about the future judgment, and about the accounts to be rendered; for words, for deeds, for thoughts, and for intentions. And to know why man (ἄνθρωπος) exists ... what vice is, and what virtue."[65]

This is the point where Plato and Pythagoras enter the discussion, precisely because they inquired into these matters. Chrysostom's reference to these two only is because "we ought not to recall the others at all, so ridiculous have they all become on this subject through their exaggeration."[66] Plato is the first to be accused, starting, as per usual, with the charge that he spent his life trying to make women common to all. His aim was to disturb the lives of people, by corrupting their marriages and to cause a

---

[62] *In Ioh. hom.* 2.1 (PG 59:30; trans. Goggin, *Commentary on Saint John*, 12).

[63] Ibid. 2.1 (PG 59:30; trans. Goggin, *Commentary on Saint John*, 13).

[64] Ibid. (trans. Goggin, *Commentary on Saint John*, 13-4).

[65] Ibid. (PG 59:30; trans. Goggin, *Commentary on Saint John*, 14).

[66] *In Ioh. hom.* 2.2 (PG 59:30; trans. Goggin, *Commentary on Saint John*, 14).

general upheaval. The second accusation is about the fate of the soul after death, which is an issue we have noted before in relation to comparisons with Plato, with the difference that Chrysostom's reference here is based on a quote by Empedocles: "And with regard to their teachings about the soul, they have omitted nothing at all that is excessively shameful, saying that the souls of men become flies and gnats, and shrubs, declaring that God Himself is a soul..."[67] However, he asserts that the main difference between them and the apostle is this: while they "make all their statements from obscure and undependable reasoning [*logismoi* being the preferred word again here]", John "speaks all things with assurance and, as one founded on a rock, he never wavers."[68]

John's rock-steadiness is contrasted to the Greeks' ever-changing opinion ("always changing their minds about the same matters"), and his lack of education and humility of origin, at which the Greeks poke fun, becomes a source of pride for the Christians. Chrysostom goes as far as to say that no matter how barbarous and distant from Hellenic *paideia* John's "nation" seems to the Greeks, "so much the brighter do our claims appear."[69] Essentially the barbarian and ἀμαθὴς apostle teaches things that no one before him ever knew. There is no need of greater proof of the claim that his sayings are "God-inspired" than the fact that "all his hearers through all time believe."[70] In other words, the argument from conviction reappears in John's case, as it already did with Paul and Peter.

---

[67] Ibid., 2.2 (PG 59:31; trans. Goggin, *Commentary on Saint John*, 15). The passage is from Empedocles 9.569 (ed. Beckby, *Anthologia Graeca* 3.346): Ἤδη γάρ ποτ' ἐγὼ γενόμην κοῦρός τε κόρη τε θάμνος τ' οἰωνός τε καὶ ἐξ ἁλὸς ἔμπυρος ἰχθύς.

[68] Ibid.

[69] Ibid: ὅσῳ γὰρ ἂν τὸ ἔθνος αὐτοῖς βάρβαρον φαίνηται καὶ τῆς Ἑλληνικῆς ἀπέχον παιδεύσεως, τοσούτῳ λαμπρότερα τὰ ἡμέτερα φανεῖται! When we see Chrysostom attacking Greek paideia, we should never forget the fact that he is primarily arguing against views like Julian's, who saw it as "a gift of the gods to mankind" which leads humans to achievements such as the advancement of scientific knowledge or the establishment of different types of political constitutions. See *Contr. Gal.* 229C (LCL 157:387). As Vasiliki Limberis, ""Religion" as the Cipher for Identity: The Cases of Emperor Julian, Libanius, and Gregory Nazianzus," *Harvard Theological Review* 93:4 (2000), 387 points out, "*paideia* becomes something of a religion itself."

[70] *In Ioh. hom.* 2.2 (PG 59:30; trans. Goggin, *Commentary on Saint John*, 16).

The strongest proof of John's divine inspiration, according to Chrysostom, is that he laid no laws of his own, since he was a disciple of Christ's law,[71] and by writing his Gospel he occupies the whole world, in a spiritual sense. But even in the bodily sense, Chrysostom argues, John lived in "the middle of Asia, where of old all those of Greek persuasion used to teach philosophy, and there he is fearful to the demons; shining in the midst of his enemies, dispersing their darkness..."[72] This is obviously a reference to the tradition that John resided in Ephesus for a period of his life, but this is not the most significant part of this passage. The first element that stands out is Chrysostom's reference to the Ionian school of philosophers, whom he calls οἱ τῆς Ἑλληνικῆς συμμορίας ἅπαντες, literally "those of the Greek gang!" The other significant element is the mention of John as dispersing the philosophers' darkness, which serves as a rather subtle allusion to the obscurity of some of the Ionians' writings (e.g. Heraclitus).[73] This is not the only time John refers to the Ionian philosophers.

These comments can be further contextualized by reference to Chrysostom's *hypothesis* on his *Homilies on the Ephesians*: here he dedicates about half of his space to talk about the cult of Artemis in Ephesus and the philosophers who were known as residents in the city in the past. He begins with the cult of the goddess, observing that she was honored as a great god and that the superstition of those who worshipped her was so great that they refused to reveal the name of the one who burnt her temple. This is in reference to the second temple, which was destroyed by Herostratus, and John correctly refers to the fact that the Ephesians forbade anyone from mentioning his name. After indicating that Ephesus was also the place where John the Evangelist died, he

---

[71] Unlike Plato. John's frequent references to Plato's failure in establishing his ideal republic is also better understood within this context.

[72] Ibid.

[73] See Diogenes Laertius *Vit. phil.* 9.1 (LCL 185:408-25). This is not the only instance where John points to the obscurity of the Greeks' writings. In *De Laz. conc.* 3.3 (PG 48:994) he makes the case that the philosophers, orators, and writers of those "outside" not only did not strive for the common good, but even when they had something useful to say they hid it in obscurity, as in a cloud.

goes on to mention the philosophers based there: Pythagoras was said to come from there, perhaps because Samos was also traditionally thought of as part of Ionia, as well as disciples of Parmenides, Zeno and Democritus. The reference to philosophers closes with the observation that one can see a number of them even in Chrysostom's day.[74] Ephesus is then a double apostolic battleground: John (with his presence) and Paul (with his letter) are able to fight and prevail against both a strong philosophical current that goes all the way back to the pre-Socratics *and* a powerful local cult that could not have easily been uprooted.

Nonetheless, the end result of this battle between John and the philosophers should be obvious by now: "the teachings of Pythagoras have fallen silent, as well as those of Plato, which at one time seemed authoritative - and many do not even know them by name."[75] This reference to the two philosophers is followed by a direct criticism of Pythagoras and a very vague reference to Plato's trip to Sicily. The interesting part in the critique of Pythagoras is the reference to his apparent dialogue with oxen, which Chrysostom sees as something that "in no way helped the human race, but even has done it the greatest harm."[76] It seems that the theme of usefulness is a standard trope every time Greek philosophy is mentioned.[77] But John's tirade against Pythagoras does not stop there:

> He did not cause irrational nature to exercise the power of reason (since this is impossible for a man to do), but he deceived the ignorant by tricks. Refraining from teaching man anything useful, he taught that to eat beans was the same as to eat the heads of one's ancestors, and persuaded his followers that the soul of their teacher once was a shrub, then a maiden, then a fish.[78]

---

[74] *In Eph. hom. Arg.* (PG:62.9-10).

[75] *In Ioh. hom.* 2.2 (PG 59:31; trans. Goggin, *Commentary on Saint John*, 16).

[76] Ibid. (trans. Goggin, *Commentary on Saint John*, 16-7).

[77] When receiving the Gospel, the wise do not profit at all by their wisdom and the unlearned are not hurt by their ignorance. In this respect, ignorance is even preferable since it represses "all doubting thoughts" and thus proves wisdom to be useful for nothing. In the end, faith and simplicity are always prioritized over the wisdom from without, which they destroyed. See *In 1 Cor. hom.* 4.1 (PG 61:33; NPNF 1-12:18).

[78] *In Ioh. hom.* 2.2 (PG 59:31; trans. Goggin, *Commentary on Saint John*, 17).

The main criticisms against Pythagoras can be summed up as follows: a) he deceived the foolish with his magic tricks, b) he did not teach anything useful to humans, c) he convinced those who followed him (in this case, Empedocles) to believe in reincarnation. *Au contraire*, John did not bother with the "foolishness about the nature of brute beasts", and "he strove for one single object: that the whole world might learn something that would be both useful to it and capable of conducting it from earth to heaven."[79] It is because John wanted his teachings to be *useful* that he decided to avoid the Pythagoreans' obscurity and teaching practices, such as the five years of silence and the motionless sitting. Chrysostom commends John's rejection of what he calls the "mythology" that the universe consisted of numbers; he also praises the simplicity of his teaching, which was understood not only by men, but also by women and youths. Chrysostom anticipates the question as to why John would want to be understood by all, to which he provides the following response: "he believed that they [his teachings] were both true and useful for all his hearers."[80] Consequently, true philosophy is primarily practical.

After the contrast between Pythagoras and John, Chrysostom returns to the comparison between Plato and John. His focus now is the excessive rhetorical embellishment of Plato, along with a brief criticism of his doctrine of the soul. What we observe in the evangelist's writings are "not ... noise of words or pomposity of style, or careful ordering and artificial, foolish arrangement of nouns and verbs (for these things are far removed from all philosophy), but invincible and divine strength, irresistible power of authentic doctrines, and a wealth of good things without number...."[81] This passage has some similarities to the aforementioned comparison between Plato and Paul, whose eloquence was not a result of technical training, but of divine grace and

---

[79] *In Ioh. hom.* 2.3 (PG 59:32; trans. Goggin, *Commentary on Saint John*, 17).

[80] Ibid. (trans. Goggin, *Commentary on Saint John*, 18).

[81] Ibid. (trans. Goggin, *Commentary on Saint John*, 18).

Paul's natural aptitude for learning. What John assumes here is that Plato did have the writing style he is criticized for, but the difference between this comparison and the one we mentioned earlier between Paul and Plato is that John's focus here is the style of writing whereas earlier it was rhetoric. Even in his writing Paul was much simpler than Plato: but at the same time, his thought (just like his speech) had the strength of true doctrine behind it, and was thus more convincing.

Excessiveness on matters of expression, Chrysostom argues, is not even worthy of the sophists: at this point he introduces the beginning of Plato's *Apology*, where Socrates claims that he is ashamed of this art and tells the judges that "they will hear from him utterances made simply and extemporaneously, not adorned with elaborate expressions or decked out with artificially chosen nouns and verbs. 'It would not, of course, be befitting my age, gentlemen,' he says, 'for me to come in to you like a lad inventing speeches'."[82] Chrysostom uses the example of Socrates in order to accuse Plato of betraying the exact principles that his teacher promoted.

His final attack, which concludes the comparison between John and the philosophers, is an analogy between whitened graves that are filled with stench and rotten bones and Plato's doctrines, especially his doctrine of the soul, "since he both honors it and desecrates it immoderately."[83] On the one hand, Plato is disproportionately honouring the soul when he says that it is of the divine substance. On the other hand, he dishonours and insults it even more when he is "bringing it into swine, asses, and animals even less esteemed than these."[84] John ends his comparison abruptly, since he feels that "if it were possible to learn something useful from this review, it would be necessary to spend even more time on it. But, if the object is only to observe how great unseemliness and absurdity these things possess, then we have

---

[82] *In Ioh. hom.* 2.3 (PG 59.32-3; trans. Goggin, *Commentary on Saint John*, 18-19). Cf. Plato, *Apol. Soc.* 1b-c (LCL 36:106-8).

[83] Ibid., 2.3 (PG 59.33; trans. Goggin, *Commentary on Saint John*, 19).

[84] Ibid.

carried on the discussion further than necessary."[85] It is a fitting end that brings the issue of usefulness full circle, and dismisses Greek philosophy as a collection of absurd fables, precisely because Chrysostom finds no use in it.

c. Minor comparisons

i. The Evangelists and the Philosophers

Chrysostom's very first homily on Matthew, before his actual commentary on the Gospel, serves as an introduction to the work and deals with various issues, such as the occasion of the writing of the gospels as well as their harmony. He makes a point that he will be trying to prove their fundamental agreement with each other throughout the work and says that those who think they disagree only say so because they expected them to use the "same words and forms of speech."[86] This point provides an opportunity for Chrysostom to compare the evangelists with the Greek philosophers. The latter are the ones who "glory greatly in rhetoric and philosophy." Now despite the fact that these (as yet unnamed) men have written many books about the same things, they not only "expressed themselves differently, but have even spoken in opposition to another (οὐ μόνον ἁπλῶς διεφώνησαν, ἀλλὰ καὶ ἐναντίως ἀλλήλοις εἶπον)." The disagreements of the philosophers are a common Chrysostomic trope. Sometimes he is even more specific about it, as in his *Homilies on Romans* where Aristotle rebels against Plato and the Stoics rebel against Aristotle.[87] But in his *Commentary on Galatians* he also recognizes that the Christians are also suffering from their own divisions (probably a reference to the schisms in Antioch), and they thus become a laughing stock for Jews and Greeks.[88] This is yet another instance of Chrysostom using disagreements among

---

[85] *In Ioh. hom.* 2.3 (PG 59.33; trans. Goggin, *Commentary on Saint John*, 19).

[86] *In Matt. hom.* 1.4-5 (PG 57:18-20; NPNF 1-10:4-6). The following analysis and all of Chrysostom's passages within are from this passage.

[87] *In Rom. hom.* 2.3 (PG 60:414).

[88] *In Gal. comm.* 1.6 (PG 61:623).

philosophers and turning them against them, even if he does not provide concrete examples.

After describing the success of the gospel writings Chrysostom makes another point: what the evangelists wrote was "concerning the things in heaven", all the while introducing a unique way of life where things like wealth and poverty or freedom and slavery all radically acquire a new meaning. He then compares the heavenly philosophy to the earthly philosophy of the Greeks, specifically Plato and Zeno (who are both targeted for having written works entitled *Politeia*), as well as anyone who has written a similarly titled work (Diogenes the Cynic allegedly wrote one, and one would think that Aristotle is also included here) or any laws. Chrysostom targets them elsewhere, for the exact same reasons, and many of the arguments are repeated.[89] These writings, Chrysostom argues, manifest an evil spirit that has set its eyes to turning everything upside down. His proof for this claim? The fact that the philosophers want to make the women common to all and to establish illegal marriages, and that virgins are to fight naked in the wrestling school where anyone can gaze at them.

The philosophers also failed in other respects: they did not even know the word virginity, or the concepts of voluntary poverty and fasting. On the contrary, the evangelists, among other things, have "filled the whole earth with the plant of virginity." The knowledge that the evangelists spread with their writings had not even been mentally conceived before them, Chrysostom claims, and how could it be conceived by those "who made for gods images of beasts." The inevitable conclusion, and one that has also been repeated elsewhere, is that the evangelical writings were not only accepted and believed but are still flourishing to this day, whilst the philosophical writings have perished and disappeared.

---

[89] *Adv. Iud. or.* 5.3 (PG 48:886).

But Chrysostom is not done with Plato's *Politeia*. The next comparison is between respective writing circumstances: the philosophers were able to write "not amidst persecutions, nor dangers, nor fightings, but in all security and freedom." On the contrary, the "doctrines of the fishermen" are of men who were themselves chased, men who were "scourged and in jeopardy." His next point regards the length of the work. After the accusation that the philosopher has spent a vast number of lines just to show what justice is (τί ποτέ ἐστι τὸ δίκαιον), he is also accused of being obtuse; even if his writing did contain something profitable, this would be useless for human life. Chrysostom assumes that people like smiths, builders and farmers, indeed manual laborers in general, would not be able to leave behind their art and honest toil for years just to learn what justice is. Before they even get a chance to learn, hunger will destroy them and they will perish without even learning anything useful! This is then contrasted not with the Apostles but with Christ, whose whole teaching is contained in a few simple words: here Chrysostom quotes Matthew 22:40 ("On these two commandments hang all the law and the prophets") and 7:12 ("In everything do to others as you would have them do to you; for this is the law and the prophets"). Everyone, whether a laborer, a servant, a widow, and even a child can comprehend and easily learn these things. But for Chrysostom it is not only just about how easily these respective teachings can be understood. It is also about how easily they can be emulated in all manner of circumstances, regardless of one's location or social status, and in this respect Christ's teaching is yet again victorious.

Chrysostom's initial targeting of the authors comes full circle when he makes his point clear. The fishermen also wrote a *politeia*. But unlike the philosophical *politeia*, with its rules that it has to be taught from childhood or the "law that the virtuous man must be so many years old," the evangelical one is addressed to everyone of any age; where the former resembles children's toys, the latter manifests the truth of things. The place of the Christian *politeia* is in Heaven, and God is its lawgiver. The rewards of this heavenly *politeia* are also different: instead of bay leaves or olives, or eating in public, it provides us with life everlasting with Christ. The guides of the heavenly *politeia* are publicans, fishermen and tent-makers, a point that Chrysostom brings up to show that they were doing good not only whilst they were alive but also now after their death. Finally, this *politeia* is at war not with other humans but with the devil and other incorporeal powers. Its general is God Himself and its armor is not made of steel or skins but of "righteousness, and faith, and all true love of wisdom (*philosophia*)." Chrysostom's conclusion to this introductory homily is that this *politeia* is indeed the subject of Matthew's Gospel and the topic he will be speaking of throughout, and his aim is to enroll those who have yet not become its citizens.

As with other comparisons, certain themes seem to reappear, while others are new. As an example of the latter, Chrysostom here takes the argument regarding the number of the Gospels and turns it against Greek philosophy by emphasizing philosophical disagreements- the implication being that the variety of the Gospels did not have the same outcome. He repeats the claim that the evangelical writings are primarily concerned with the heavenly *politeia* but at the same time emphasizes that the application of their teaching also led to a radical departure from old ways of thinking that have caused a virtuous revolution in society. In contrast, the writings of the philosophers promoted perverse teachings, were ignorant of important things, and have subsequently vanished- even if John's reference to them could be taken to indicate otherwise. Also new is the point about the respective writing conditions of each, but also the brevity of their writings. Chrysostom happily points out that the average philosophical writing could probably never be read by the common man (we use the masculine intentionally here due to Chrysostom referring to male handymen), due to its length, and, one would also assume, complexity. His solution to that is to not even point to the evangelical writings, presumably because one could still claim that these need

sufficient time and dedication to be read. Instead, he deflects the issue by bringing up

Jesus and the Golden Rule, which he considers sufficient and easy enough for everyone

to learn and apply to his/her life.

ii. The Apostles and the Great Men of Greece

Comparisons between the Apostles and of certain famous men among the Greeks

abound in Chrysostom's works. Usually the Apostles are treated as a single entity, with

the exceptions being Paul, Peter, and John, whereas the Greeks are often criticized

individually. In his thirty-third *Homily on Matthew* the targets of the attack initially

seem to be Plato, Pythagoras and the Stoics.[90] However, after mentioning Plato's sale as

a slave and failure to convert even one tyrant, despite the great honor he enjoyed

beforehand,[91] he turns his attention to the Cynics, who, besides their usual

characterization as scum, are also said to have passed by "like a dream and a shadow."[92]

These men were considered glorious for their philosophy, spent their time at leisure,

and profited handsomely. Chrysostom then proceeds to give more examples. The first is

Aristippus of Cyrene, who is accused of purchasing costly whores, something that John

could have easily known from certain anecdotes in Diogenes Laertius.[93] The next two

targets are anonymous: one is a philosopher who made his will without leaving any

inheritance and the other is one who used his disciples as a bridge and walked on them.

The final target is Diogenes the Cynic, and his public exhibitions in the market place.

These examples are used in order to draw a clear line (in his terms) between 'them' (the

---

[90] *In Matt. hom.* 33.4 (PG 57:393; NPNF 1-10:217-8).

[91] This is a very common trope in Chrysostom's works. It usually appears in comparisons between
Paul and Plato and its aim is to show the success of the former against the failure of the latter. For other
references see *In Rom. hom.* 2.5 (PG 60:407); *In Tit. hom.* 2.2 (PG 62:673): Paul more powerful than
Plato not just due to miracles but also by his teaching.

[92] *In Matt. hom.* 33.4 (PG 57:393; NPNF 1-10:217).

[93] E.g. Diogenes Laertius, *Vit. phil.* 2.69 (LCL 184:199): "One day, as he entered the house of a
courtesan, one of the lads with him blushed, whereupon he remarked, "It is not going in that is dangerous,
but being unable to go out.""

Greek philosophers) and 'us' (the Christians). These are the things they do, John claims. On the contrary, there are no such things on the Christian side, and what is there is σωφροσύνη καὶ κοσμιότης and a war against the entire world in defense of truth and piety.[94] But the Greeks did not just have philosophers. They also had men exceedingly skilled in warfare, and the examples used here are Pericles and Themistocles. Compared to the achievements of the fishermen, their achievements look like children's toys. Chrysostom is not particularly impressed with Themistocles' persuasive abilities when he convinced the Athenians to lure Xerxes' fleet into the straits of Salamis. In the Apostles' case, it is not just Xerxes marching onto Greece but the devil and his innumerable demons fighting against the Apostles not just once, but throughout their lives. Even the method of their prevalence was exemplary, since they did not have to slay their adversaries, and converted them instead.[95] In this example we have two significant diversions from previous comparisons. Besides the usual suspects (Plato, Pythagoras), John is willing to widen the net and include people like Aristippus of Cyrene and even anecdotes about anonymous philosophers in order to demarcate the boundaries between the philosophers and the Christians. Furthermore, the repertoire is also expanded with the addition of personalities famous for their involvement with Greek politics and warfare. In this case John downplays their achievement by saying that the apostles exceeded them since their opponent was not human but the devil himself, whilst also bringing back the conviction argument and comparing it to the slaughters any warfare inevitably brings with it.

iii. The flight of the philosophers, the fight over science, and faith against reasonings

In John's *Homilies on Colossians* Paul's bonds are compared to those of Socrates, and while the similarity of their imprisonment is mentioned, the emphasis is on the

---

[94] *In Matt. hom.* 33.4 (PG 57:393; NPNF 1-10:217).

[95] *In Matt. hom.* 33.4 (PG 57:393; NPNF 1-10:217-8).

reaction of their respective disciples. Socrates' students fled to Megara, while Paul's became more confident because they saw that even though Paul was in chains the preaching could not be hindered.[96] The theme of the flight of Socrates' students reappears in Chrysostom's fourth homily *In praise of St. Paul*, but this time in order to make a contrast between present day Greeks (who are called εὐτελεῖς and εὐκαταφρόνητοι) and the legendary Greeks of the past (who are called θαυμαστοί and ἐπὶ φιλοσοφίᾳ βεβοημένοι).[97] John mentions Plato, Diagoras, Anaxagoras and Zeno and talks about their flight to Megara after Socrates' death and their subsequent deprivations of their native lands as well as their failures to win any converts. It is also recalled that although these philosophers lacked nothing, and that they were in fact proficient speakers as well as wealthy and citizens of a celebrated land, they in fact had no power at all. Chrysostom ends this passage triumphantly, by observing that "such is the case with deception, that even when no one troubles it, it falls in ruins; such with the truth that, even when many battle against it, it is promoted."[98]

We call this theme "the flight of the philosophers", since the disciples of Socrates are not the only ones it is applied to. It also appears when John contrasts the attitude of the monks with the attitude of the philosophers during the statues riots in Antioch.[99] In this case the ascetics manifest themselves as the real lovers of wisdom through their actions and their life in virtue, and are contrasted with a caricature of the contemporary philosophers in Antioch. In F. G. Downing's opinion Chrysostom is "showing that it is

---

[96] *In Col. hom.* 10.4 (PG 62:370).

[97] See n. 98 below for the full reference to John's text.

[98] *De Laud. Paul. hom.* 4.19 (SC 300:224-6; trans. Mitchell, *The Heavenly Trumpet*, 466): Καὶ τί λέγω τοὺς παρόντας Ἕλληνας νῦν, τοὺς εὐτελεῖς καὶ εὐκαταφρονήτους; Τοὺς τότε θαυμαστοὺς παραγάγωμεν εἰς μέσον, τοὺς ἐπὶ φιλοσοφίᾳ βεβοημένους, τὸν Πλάτωνα, τὸν Διαγόραν, τὸν Κλαζομένιον, καὶ ἑτέρους πολλοὺς τοιούτους, καὶ ὄψει τότε τοῦ κηρύγματος τὴν ἰσχύν. Μετὰ γὰρ τὸ κώνειον τοῦ Σωκράτους, οἱ μὲν εἰς Μέγαρα ἀπῆλθον, δεδοικότες μὴ τὰ αὐτὰ πάθωσιν· οἱ δὲ καὶ τῆς πατρίδος καὶ τῆς ἐλευθερίας ἐξέπεσον, καὶ πλέον μιᾶς γυναικός, οὐδενὸς ἑτέρου περιεγένοντο· ὁ δὲ Κιτιεὺς ἐν τοῖς γράμμασιν ἀφεὶς τὴν πολιτείαν, οὕτω κατέλυσε. Καίτοι οὐδὲν ἦν τότε τὸ ἐμποδίζον, οὐ κίνδυνος, οὐκ ἰδιωτεία, ἀλλὰ καὶ δεινοὶ λέγειν ἦσαν, καὶ χρημάτων εὐπόρουν, καὶ τῆς παρὰ πᾶσι βοωμένης πατρίδος ἐτύγχανον ὄντες· ἀλλ' οὐδὲν ἴσχυσαν. Τοιοῦτον γὰρ ἡ πλάνη, καὶ μηδενὸς ἐνοχλοῦντος, καταρρεῖ· τοιοῦτον ἡ ἀλήθεια, καὶ πολλῶν πολεμούντων, διεγείρεται.

[99] *De stat.* 17.2 (PG 49:173-4).

the penniless Christian monks ... who in reality display the Cynic virtues, live up to the Cynic ideals."[100] The manifestation of the philosophical ideal by the monks is something that Chrysostom would do time and time again and was another weapon used as a proof of concept in his use of the theme of usefulness and how each side benefits humanity either in critical events such as the riots or in their everyday lives.[101]

In the final analysis, according to Chrysostom, faith is what really makes people philosophers and allows the Christians to differentiate from the Greeks, who base their beliefs on their reasonings (*logismoi*) rather than faith. The distinction between *logismoi/syllogismoi* and *pistis*, which were already mentioned in connection to Paul's eloquence and his superiority over Plato, become metonyms that come to represent the mind-sets of the Greeks and the Christians respectively, as well as their respective writings: "secular writings ... are full of questions and sophistry (syllogisms)."[102] Additionally, Chrysostom argues in regard to his own time, "not even now persuade we by argumentation (συλλογισμῶν); but from the Divine Scriptures, and from the miracles done at that time, we produce the proof of what we say." At the same time, he admits that even the Apostles didn't persuade just by signs, but also through discourse (διαλεγόμενοι), even though their words were powerful not due to their shrewdness (δεινότης) but primarily because of the signs and the witness of the OT.[103] The dialectic relationship between faith and reasonings is a constant feature in Chrysostom's works but here we will limit ourselves only to the extent that it relates to the concepts being

---

[100] F. Gerald Downing, *Cynics and Christian Origins* (Edinburgh: T&T Clark,1992), 287.

[101] Cf. J. H. W. G. Liebeschuetz, *Antioch: City and Imperial Administration in the Later Roman Empire* (Oxford: Oxford University Press, 1972), 235-6: "The writings of John Chrysostom show how a man who had fully absorbed classical education could nevertheless describe the quite un-Hellenic phenomenon of monasticism in terms that were long familiar as descriptions of the philosopher-sage."

[102] *Com. in Prov.* 8.9 (Bady, *Le Commentaire*, 258; *St. John Chrysostom, Commentary on the Sages vol. 2: Commentary on Proverbs-Commentary on Ecclesiastes*, trans. Robert Charles Hill; Brookline, MA: Holy Cross Orthodox Press, 2006, 98). The comparison here is between the Proverbs of the OT, which provide knowledge, and secular writings, which obviously do not.

[103] *In 1 Cor. hom.* 6.2 (PG 61:50-1; NPNF 1-12:31).

considered as representative of Christianity and Hellenism. In this respect, John contrasts the two attitudes through the prism of education and knowledge:

> Let us, then, have faith, and let us not entrust our own affairs altogether to reason. Why is it, may I ask, that the Greeks were able to discover nothing of God? Did they not know all the pagan wisdom? How is it, then, that they were unable to get the better of fishermen and tent-makers, and unlettered men? Was it not because the Greeks trusted everything to reason, while the latter placed all their confidence in faith? That is why these prevailed over Plato and Pythagoras and, in a word, over all who were in error: those familiar with astrology, and mathematics, and geometry, and arithmetic. They surpassed all who had had a thorough and complete education, and became as far superior to them as true philosophers to those who are actually dull and witless by nature. Notice that [those of the Christian faith] assert that the soul is immortal, or, rather, they have not only asserted this, but have even argued in favour of this fact. The others, on the contrary, at first did not even know what in the world a soul is. But when they did discover it and had distinguished it from the body, they once more fell into error, some maintaining that it is incorporeal, others that it is a material body and fused with the body itself. Once more, regarding heaven, some said it was animated by a soul and was a god, while the fishermen both taught and argued that it is a work of God and part of His creation. However, it is not at all strange that the Greeks make use of reason, but it is a lamentable thing when those who seem to be of the faith are discovered to be concerned only with this life.[104]

In the passage above, John is prepared to admit that the Greeks were well educated in all of the ἔξωθεν wisdom. With that being the case, how could they not prevail against the fishermen and the tent-makers? In Chrysostom's mind, it was because the Greeks chose to trust their λογισμοί and not faith, as the apostles did. It is precisely *because* of their faith that the apostles were able to prevail over Plato and Pythagoras, and everyone whose life was devoted to astrology, mathematics, arithmetic, geometry and every other branch of learning. Chrysostom's choice of the sciences is interesting. If we rule out mathematics as a science that encompasses both arithmetic and geometry, what he refers to here are three out of the four sciences that comprised the ancient Greek quadrivium, except for music. It should be noted that the medieval quadrivium had significant differences to Plato's version, including the intensity and seriousness of mathematical studies. Chrysostom's diatribe against these sciences is exactly because

---

[104] *In Ioh. hom.* 63.3 (PG 59:352; trans. Goggin, *Commentary on Saint John vol. 2*, 186).

"Plato emphasized the sovereign importance of mathematics for all higher study" and "firmly believed that mathematics was the true and proper propaedeutic to philosophy."[105] If for Plato mathematics were τῷ ὄντι ἀναγκαῖον ... μάθημα, ἐπειδὴ φαίνεταί γε προσαναγκάζον αὐτῇ τῇ νοήσει χρῆσθαι τὴν ψυχὴν ἐπ' αὐτὴν τὴν ἀλήθειαν,[106] this was definitely not the case for Chrysostom and it seems that his choice of sciences is related to Plato's very high estimation of them.

This is not the only instance of John detailing Plato's preoccupation with geometry and numbers in general: "What great labours did Plato endure, and his followers, discoursing to us about a line, and an angle, and a point, and about numbers even and odd, and equal unto one another and unequal, and such-like spiderwebs; ... and without doing good to any one great or small by their means..." Even Plato's endeavour to prove that the soul is immortal failed to persuade people, whereas the Cross was able to persuade even through unlearned men, "and of all men it made philosophers: the very rustics, the utterly unlearned."[107] Chrysostom's comments here are clearly targeting one of the fundamental principles of Platonism, as expressed above the door of the Academy: ἀγεωμέτρητος μηδεὶς εἰσίτω expresses an elitism that John strongly argues against, and counters it with an assertion that all humans are philosophers, regardless of profession or knowledge.

Another reason why John focuses on maths and the sciences in general might have been because these were technical subjects that had to be taught. Again, John seems to be responding to Hellenic criticisms that the fishermen were illiterate with the counterpoint that there is a kind of wisdom that does not need tuition. He would also employ a similar analogy when comparing rural Christians, whose wisdom was not based on their education but on their simplicity and were thus superior to both urban

---

[105] Ernest Baker, *Greek Political Theory: Plato and his Predecessors* (1918; repr., London: Routledge, 2010, 230-1).

[106] Plato, *Rep.* VII.526a-b.

[107] *In 1 Cor hom.* 4.3 (PG 61:34; NPNF 1-12:19).

Christians as well as educated Greeks.[108] On the contrary, he believes that these views

did not lead to the truth in other matters of importance, such as the immortality of the

soul or the nature of the sky.[109] Whereas in these matters the apostles held firm views,

arguing for the immortality of the soul and that the sun was God's creation, and

managed to convince others about their views as well, the Greeks cannot come to an

agreement and hold divided opinions. John did not hesitate to make much of Greek

disagreements, as we have already seen.

Besides faith, the other crucial element that proves the apostolic victory over Plato

and Pythagoras is the fact that the apostles did not just say and teach things, but were

also able to convince others and convert them to their beliefs, and this is proven by the

use of ἔπεισαν twice in the passage above. When it comes down to the effectiveness of

teaching, the apostles *convinced* humans with their faith (and teachings), whereas the

reasonings of the Greeks did not.[110] This is a recurring motif in Chrysostom's works. In

his *Homilies on Romans* he uses it to compare the effectiveness of Paul versus Plato:

"All Greece and all barbarian lands has the tentmaker converted. But Plato, who is so

cried up and carried about among them (Ὁ δὲ παρ' αὐτοῖς ἀγόμενος καὶ περιφερόμενος

Πλάτων), coming a third time to Sicily with the bombast of those words of his, with his

brilliant reputation (ὑπολήψεως), did not even get the better of a single king, but came

off so wretchedly, as even to have lost his liberty. But this tentmaker ran over not Sicily

alone or Italy, but the whole world."[111] The success of the Christian preaching is also

attributed to the power of faith against reasonings: "For his preaching is set forth to all

---

[108] For relevant references see Christine Shepardson, *Controlling Contested Places: Late Antique Antioch and the Spatial Politics of Religious Controversy* (Berkeley: University of California Press, 2014), 142-3. Shepardson argues that the aim of these references was a challenge from John to his audience, who wanted to demonstrate the superiority of rural Christians through the trope of actions being more powerful (and preferable) than words.

[109] *In Ioh. hom.* 63.3 (PG 59:352).

[110] Cf. *De Laud. Paul. hom.* 2.4 (SC 300:148; trans. Mitchell, *The Heavenly Trumpet*, 449): "Don't speak to me of cities and nations and kings and legions and weapons and possessions and provinces and power, for he [Paul] did not consider these things equal to a cobweb."

[111] *In Rom. hom.* 2.5 (PG 60:407; NPNF 1-11:347).

alike, it knows no distinction of rank, no preeminence of nation, no other thing of the sort; for faith alone does it require, and not reasonings."[112]

Could it be that Chrysostom's aversion to the idea of the pre-eminence of any nation led some to call him "the champion of anti-Hellenism?" It is certainly possible. His insistence on faith over against reasonings, which he believes allows the Christian preaching to be comprehensible to all, is a very flexible apologetic trope that Chrysostom can apply to any number of situations. From the apostolic times to his own day, it can be used to explain such a variety of themes like why Paul was victorious against Plato and Pythagoras to why knowledge of geometry or any other science is irrelevant to salvation. These ideas are not necessarily linked. His aversion to the pre-eminence of any nation would include all nations of his time, not just the Greeks. But the faith versus reasonings debate is a core idea explicitly connected with Hellenism and is related to the production of knowledge. Chrysostom does not doubt that philosophy can produce knowledge from a strictly secular point of view. Nevertheless, he very much doubts its usefulness- another core theme that appears repeatedly in the process of *synkrisis*. Finally, the proof that faith is stronger than reasonings and that the apostolic teaching is more useful to humans than the philosophic one is related to the third core theme we have seen so far: the success of the apostles versus the failure of the philosophers. Even though during his time Chrysostom could still not claim that the Empire has been wholeheartedly Christianised, the signs were obvious that this would soon be the reality.

d. Babylas and the Greeks

As we demonstrated in chapter 2, some scholars have argued that Chrysostom was an impassioned enemy of Hellenism. Before we turn to a detailed analysis of the *Discourse on Blessed Babylas and Against the Greeks*, we must begin with an example

---

[112] *In Rom. hom.* 2.5 (PG 60:407; NPNF 1-11:348).

that shows how certain myths have managed to prevail in scholarship despite evidence to the contrary, just like the alleged destruction of the Temple of Artemis by Chrysostom. We will contrast an extract from *Babylas* with one of the letters of Julian the Emperor.

In an interesting turn of phrase, the Emperor Julian asks Ecdicius, the Prefect of Egypt, to seek out and acquire the personal library of George of Cappadocia, Arian Bishop of Alexandria during Athanasius' third exile, who was now dead.

> For there were in his house many [books] on philosophy, and many on rhetoric; many also on the teachings of the impious Galileans. These latter I should wish to be utterly annihilated, but for fear that along with them more useful works may be destroyed by mistake, let all these also be sought for with the greatest care.[113]

Julian would wish that the Christian books were annihilated, but in this case, he cannot order their immediate destruction because other more useful works might be destroyed as well, whilst he could also use them in his anti-Christian polemic.[114] Another implication of that statement is that Julian thinks he could distinguish between the "useful" and the Christian books, but he is clearly not confident that those he sent to seek out the books would be able to. We can compare this attitude to Chrysostom's reference to Christians preserving pagan books in his *Discourse on Blessed Babylas and against the Greeks*:

> The philosophers and talented orators had a great reputation with the public on account of their dignity and ability to speak. After the battle against us they became ridiculous and seemed no different from foolish children. From so many nations and peoples, they were not able to change anyone, wise, ignorant, male, female, or even a small child. The estimation of what they wrote is so low that their books dissapeared a long time ago, and mostly perished when they first appeared. If anything at all is found preserved, one finds it being preserved by Christians.[115]

---

[113] Julian, *Letter* 23 (LCL 157:73-5).

[114] David Hunt, "The Christian context of Julian's *Against the Galileans*," in *Emperor and Author: The Writings of Julian the Apostate*, ed. Nicholas Baker-Brian and Shaun Tougher (Swansea: Classical Press of Wales, 2012), 255.

[115] *De Bab. c. Iul. et gent.* 11 (SC 362:106; trans. Schatkin, *Apologist*, 82).

Chrysostom thinks these books are of little value, since they could not even convince a child, and were usually a cause of laughter, which presumably led to the demise of a lot of them. However, the ones that are still extant, he claims, are to be found among the Christians. If we limit ourselves to Chrysostom's time, his claim is most probably true, considering that even one of Libanius' texts (the *Monody on the Shrine at Daphne*) survives in its refutation by Chrysostom.

The attitudes of both Julian and John in these examples are indicative of the ineffectiveness of certain stereotypes that are by and large standard in scholarship: that of Julian as the enlightened Emperor that tried vainly to restore the ancient glory of the Empire,[116] and that of John as a pathological enemy of the Hellenic cultural heritage. In Julian's letter, his attitude towards Christian books is far from open-minded, although both he and John share the idea that one can distinguish between useful and non-useful books. On the other hand, John's attitude towards Greek literature, even if motivated by apologetic reasons, is far more tolerant, despite its scornful assessment regarding its value. It seems then that for Julian Christian books are either useless or dangerous, while for John there are both useful and useless books within classical literature.

Therefore, by examining a small treatise of Chrysostom (which, as we shall see, might or might have not been written as a partial response to some of Julian's writings), we have identified two contrasting attitudes which help us to grasp the basic tenets that characterize Chrysostom's understanding of Hellenism and its legacy.

The text we are going to analyze in some detail is the small apologetic treatise *Discourse on Blessed Babylas and against the Greeks*.[117] It was written between 363

---

[116] See e.g. Athanassiadi-Fowden, *Julian and Hellenism.*

[117] The text we will be citing from is published in *Saint John Chrysostom: Apologist.* Along with this translation we will be citing the *Sources chrétiennes* critical edition of the text, edited by Schatkin as well and used as the basis for her English translation. To avoid repetition, the numbers in parentheses at the end of or within sentences are to the translation. It should be noted that this treatise is different from a *Homily on Babylas*, delivered on the feast of the martyr and published together with it in the aforementioned critical edition. Schatkin also eliminates the reference to Julian in the title of the work as it is not frequently attested in the manuscript tradition of the text.

and 379-380, most probably in 378.[118] M. Schatkin argues that specific issues and tensions between pagans and Christians provided the occasion of the writing of the *Discourse* (16-17). The first of them is probably the writings of Porphyry, a Neoplatonic philosopher and one of the most energetic opponents of Christianity in late antiquity. The fact that Chrysostom was aware of Porphyry (and Celsus) is indicated when he refers to both as witnesses to the antiquity of the books of the NT.[119] In another possible reference to the same two authors he mentions "the book of a certain foul pagan philosopher written against us, and also that of that other old one", with the express intention, as he says to the Christians, "to arouse you and draw you out of your excessive apathy."[120]

The context in the latter case is the Christians' unwillingness to put forward a defence of their faith in response to legitimate questions that might come from the Greeks, such as how the doctrine of the Trinity differs from polytheism. Schatkin argues that the *Discourse* is a general response to Porphyry's *Philosophy from Oracles*[121] (17) and perhaps another of Porphyry's works, his fifteen books *Against Christians*.[122] In this respect, Chrysostom follows a long line of previous Christian writers who wrote against Porphyry, including Methodius, Apollinarius of Laodicea, Gregory of Nazianzus and even his own teacher, Diodore of Tarsus (18-19). Schatkin also argues that Chrysostom was probably in possession of a copy of *Against Christians*, as he claims that Christians were the ones responsible for the preservation of

---

[118] Schatkin, *Apologist*, 16. Christine Shepardson has narrowed the date between spring 379 and spring 380, arguing that there is a possibility the text was written for St. Babylas's feast day on January 24, 380: Christine Shepardson, "Rewriting Julian's Legacy: John Chrysostom's *On Babylas* and Libanius' *Oration* 24," *Journal of Late Antiquity* 2.1 (2009), 99-115.

[119] *In 1 Cor. hom.* 6.3 (PG 61:52).

[120] *In Ioh. hom.* 17.4 (PG 59:113; trans. Goggin, *Commentary on Saint John*, 171-2).

[121] Written before the persecutions of Christians under Diocletian and Galerius.

[122] Written during Porphyry's retirement in Sicily from 268 AD onwards. For John's knowledge of *Contra Christianos* and the inclusion of fragments from the work in his homilies see Michael Bland Simmons, *Universal Salvation in Late Antiquity: Porphyry of Tyre and the Pagan-Christian Debate* (Oxford: Oxford University Press, 2015), 68-9.

anti-Christian writings (23). It is also possible that certain of the arguments Chrysostom used were directed against Hierocles and his anti-Christian *Philalethes*, but most of them can also be found in Eusebius' *Against Hierocles* (27), in which case Chrysostom is probably repeating Eusebius' arguments and does not deal directly with Hierocles' text.

The second important focus of tension between pagans and Christians is possibly the Emperor Julian and his three books *Against Christians* (or Galileans).[123] In this work we meet some arguments against Christianity that have already been used by Porphyry and Hierocles, but some new ones as well, particularly the charge that Christians have resorted to violence against pagans and heretics, something that is directly opposed to Jesus' teachings. Julian also attacked the practice of almsgiving, and accused the Christians of worshipping a corpse (29). Chrysostom's responses to these charges can be considered an indication that he was acquainted with Julian's work (29).

The writings of Gregory of Nazianzus and Ephraim the Syrian, composed after the death of Julian, are characterized by "exultation at the defeat of one of God's enemies." In stark contrast, John's discourse on Babylas "does not have the same bitter tone", according to Schatkin (36). In fact, Schatkin argues that "Chrysostom uses the principles of Greek ethical theory to demonstrate that the Hellenic ideal of virtue is realized only among Christians."[124] Paul Harkins offers a different view, calling the *Discourse on Babylas* "an encomium on the triumph of Christianity and the downfall of paganism" (p. 181), while according to J.N.D. Kelly, "its theme, developed with bravura and sometimes tedious repetitiveness, is the assertion that the source of Christianity's victory over paganism is the power of Christ, which is just as visible

---

[123] Dated 362-3.

[124] In different parts of the treatise: *De Bab. c. Iul. et gent.* 34-36, 45ff, 47, 49 (*Apologist*, 42).

today as when he was alive on earth."[125] Wilken's assessment echoes both Harkins and Kelly: "Here he presents the strife between Christianity and Hellenism as a conflict over the role of divine power in history. Whose power is greatest-that of the gods of the Greeks and Romans, reflected in the fortunes of the empire, or that of Christ, reflected in the fortunes of the Church?"[126] It is clear, then, that while Kelly, Harkins and Wilken emphasize the apologetic and triumphant nature of the work, and therefore make it sound strikingly similar to Gregory's and Ephraim's writings against Julian, Schatkin resists that effort and emphasizes John's appropriation of the Hellenic ideal of virtue.

Other scholars have emphasised a more contextual understanding, stressing the particular setting, rather than the general contrast between Christian and Greek. Shepardson, for example, has suggested that *On Babylas* might have been written after encouragement by Meletius of Antioch and was thus "one more propaganda effort by Meletius to appropriate the authority of Babylas for his Antiochene community."[127] Sandwell stresses the literary context, arguing that both the *Demonstration* and the *Discourse* can be something more than merely apologetic texts: they could also be "a form of edification for Christian audiences, or as education in how to argue against Greeks."[128]

Hunter makes the valid point that "Chrysostom does not simply attack an abstract "Hellenism" as it was represented in the figures of the ancient philosophers or in the myth of Daphne and Apollo [but] also attacks specific contemporary pagans, the emperor Julian and the sophist Libanius."[129] These attacks are related to specific incidents of his time: on the one hand, in Julian's case what provoked John was his

---

[125] J. N. D. Kelly, *Golden Mouth: The Story of John Chrysostom, Ascetic, Preacher, Bishop* (London: Duckworth, 1995), 41. Cf. Liebeschuetz, *Ambrose and John Chrysostom*, 148: "the treatise *De sancto Babyla* is Chrysostom's fullest statement of the Christian case against the pagans."

[126] Wilken, *John Chrysostom and the Jews*, 131.

[127] Shepardson, "Rewriting Julian's Legacy," 113.

[128] Sandwell, *Religious Identity in Late Antiquity*, 76.

[129] Hunter, *A Comparison*, 52.

decision for the removal of St. Babylas' relics from Daphne and his failed attempt to rebuild the Jewish Temple in Jerusalem.[130] On the other hand, Libanius is specifically attacked "for his oratorical efforts on behalf of Julian and the cult of Apollo."[131] This is the reason the *Discourse* includes passages from Libanius' *Oration 60* (*Monody on the Shrine at Daphne*), where Libanius laments the burning of the shrine of Apollo.[132]

However, Hunter continues his argument about Libanius and Julian by claiming that they both fulfilled the archetypal pair of philosophers and orators in John's work: "It is significant that Chrysostom portrays the evil which must be overcome in terms of the inherited values of a culture, passed down by previous generations and confirmed by pagan education; philosophers and orators."[133] References to the philosophers and orators abound both in the *Demonstration* and the *Discourse on Babylas*. It is very likely that Chrysostom had Julian and Libanius in mind. The former was well-known as a philosopher, the latter famed as an orator. The argument of the *Demonstration*, therefore, is not simply that the spread of the Christian movement has fulfilled prophecy. Chrysostom also argues that the teachings of Christ and the apostles provide superior moral pedagogy. The apostles replaced the old familial and cultural values with a "new habit" (καινὴ συνήθεια): fasting instead of luxury, poverty instead of love of money, temperance instead of immorality, meekness instead of anger, kindness instead of envy. Moreover, unlike the "philosophers and orators," who merely confirmed the

---

[130] For an analysis of the relationship between John's apologetics against Hellenism and Julian's effort to rebuild the temple see Wilken, *John Chrysostom and the Jews*, 148-60.

[131] Ibid. Simon Swain provides another interpretation regarding the attack on Libanius, which he originally found incomprehensible since John seems to go out of his way to do it. He speculates that this might be due to Libanius' *Or. 24 On Avenging Julian*, which was addressed to the new emperor, Theodosius, and called on him to follow and avenge Julian. See Simon Swain, "Sophists and Emperors: The Case of Libanius," in *Approaching Late Antiquity: The Transformation from Early to Late Empire*, eds. Simon Swain and Mark Edwards (Oxford: Oxford University Press, 2004), 400. On the other hand, Ameringer relates the attack to Chrysostom's abhorrence of pagan worship, "of which the sophists were the official champions and defenders." See *The Stylistic Influence*, 27.

[132] One of the only two direct references to Libanius (although in both cases he calls him the sophist), the other being his reference to the latter's tribute to Chrysostom's mother, included in his letter *To a Young Widow* 2 (SC 138:120).

[133] Hunter, *A Comparison*, 49.

accepted values, the apostles achieved their notable moral results without the supposed benefits of Greek culture.

John's text certainly seems to take its starting point from the continuing power associated with the remains of Babylas, bishop of Antioch and martyr c. 250. When translated from the old city cemetery to the suburb of Daphne, they had first caused mischiefs to stop there. They then reduced the nearby oracle of Apollo to silence,[134] and finally, when returned by the outraged emperor Julian to their former resting place, had struck back by making Apollo's famous temple go up in flames.[135] In what folllows, our aim will be twofold: on the one hand, we are going to analyse the text briefly and see if it fits the competing claims about its nature that we mentioned earlier. On the other hand, we will also attempt to assess John's attitude towards Hellenism through that text and as part of the larger picture that will emerge through the study of his corpus, of which this work is particularly important for our evaluation of Chrysostom's reception of Hellenism.

John begins the treatise by admitting that there have been many teachers before Christ, who also had disciples and were able to perform wonders. He attributes that claim to the Greeks (par. 1; p. 75; pp. 90-2).[136] He is willing to admit that although Jesus is admired as a wonderworker, everyone should worship him as God not only based on his miracles but also on his precepts. Indeed, Chrysostom is generally prone to emphasise faith over signs. Elsewhere he mentions a hypothetical scenario regarding the second coming of Christ and the effects it would produce on the Greeks, which would

---

[134] An argument that Downing, *Cynics and Christian Origins*, 294, claims comes from Oenomaus of Gadara. Shepardson, *Controlling Contested Places*, 73: "In Chrysostom's view, not only the Christian God, Christianity itself, and Christians, but even the relics of Christian saints have the ability to overwhelm the gods and their clients."

[135] Kelly, *Golden Mouth*, 41.

[136] Καίτοι πολλοὶ ἕτεροι διδάσκαλοί τε ἐγένοντο καὶ μαθητὰς ἔσχον καὶ θαύματα ἐπεδείξαντο καθὼς Ἑλλήνων παῖδες κομπάζουσι, ἀλλ' ὅμως οὐδεὶς οὐδέποτε ἐκείνων τοιοῦτον οὐδὲν οὔτε εἰς νοῦν ἐβάλετο οὔτε εἰπεῖν ἐτόλμησεν. Again, to avoid repetition we will be inserting references to the text at the end of sentences. The first reference will be to the paragraph and page of Schatkin's translation and the second to the pages in the critical edition.

presumably include their confession of His divinity and worship. But in Chrysostom's eyes this would not be faith (ὅτι τοῦτο πίστις οὐκ ἔστιν), but a result of necessity and of things seen, as it would be not a result of *prohairesis* but of the "vastness of the spectacle." He concludes by claiming that the more overpowering an event like this is, the more the faith is abridged, and this is why signs are not happening anymore (διὰ τοῦτο σημεῖα νῦν οὐ γίνεται).[137]

In the *Discourse on Babylas* John sees the Incarnation as the final blow to the sacrificial system, and amazingly Jesus does not only rescue Christians, but also the Greeks who blaspheme (βλασφημοῦντας) against him, particularly from their position of being tyrannised by sacrifices to demons (as John thinks; 6; p. 78; p. 98). Chrysostom spends quite some time describing sacrifices as an integral part of Greek religion, something that might initially seem odd since in other texts he presents Greek religion as something that is practically dead. It seems that this conflicting attitude can be explained by the difference between the ultimate aim of each reference: when addressing Greeks, Chrysostom is not very eager to present Greek religion as something alive since he does not want it to appear as an option for them. But when he compares Christianity to Greek religion and its practices, his emphasis on blood sacrifice functions on a deeper symbolic level: that of a distinguishing feature that defines and separates the two religions.[138] The emphasis on sacrifice is also an indirect attack on

---

[137] *In 1 Cor. hom.* 6.2 (PG 61:51; NPNF 1-12:31). The Library of the Fathers translated the last sentence as miracles instead of signs, which I think is incorrect because elsewhere Chrysostom clearly mentions the miracles of the saints in his own time, thus reserving the signs as manifestations of Christ's power in Apostolic times. The difference is in the phraseology, and the use of the word θαύματα instead of σημεία. However, he is willing to admit that signs still exist in his times, although of a different kind, which include the conversion of the *oikoumene*, the spread of "philosophy" (i.e. faith) among the barbarians, the taming of wild customs and the intensification of piety.

[138] For this tension in Chrysostom's thought see Sandwell, *Religious Identity in Late Antiquity*, 77. C. Shepardson also notes Chrysostom's "emphasis ... on bloody sacrifice, the relation of which to the violent murder of the saint himself would not have been lost on Chrysostom's audience." See Shepardson, *Controlling Contested Places*, 76.

Julian and "the grotesqueness of ritual practices that Chrysostom associates with Julian."[139]

Chrysostom then goes on to make the accusation that the pagans' doctrine has never been persecuted, because it is not in the character of Christians to "eradicate error by constraint and force, but to save humanity by persuasion and reason and gentleness (πειθοῖ καὶ λόγῳ καὶ προσηνείᾳ)" (13; p. 83; pp. 106-8). Therefore, no Christian emperor has persecuted them, unlike pagan emperors who were constantly contriving against the Christians. These references might seem strange to a modern reader, considering that John's career largely coincided with that of Theodosius, but if we consider the date of the work then we see that Theodosius has not enacted his ban on paganism just yet.[140] More important is the fact that Chrysostom uses the Socratic king-tyrant distinction to make his point: it is a striking example of the practice of Christians using techniques they acquired in "pagan" schools against paganism itself.[141]

Chrysostom next attributes the collapse of the ancient Greek religion not to external factors, but to causes coming from within. It might not have been obliterated yet, but it is easy to see that it will be in the near future (13; p. 83; p. 108). Despite the universal character of the ancient religion, it was destroyed by Christ's power, a statement that seems to be at odds with what John mentioned before as the reason for its collapse (15; p. 84; p. 110).[142] Christ's power (*dynamis*) here (15) is to be associated with the means

---

[139] Shepardson, ibid.

[140] The most comprehensive law of Theodosius against paganism was *CTh* 16.10.12, which was issued on 8 November 392. While not the first, this was his last law for that matter. For more information on anti-pagan legislation under Theodosius and after his death, and the distinction between ritual paganism (which was prohibited) and cultural paganism (which was widely tolerated) see Liebeschuetz, *Barbarians and Bishops*, 150. Nevertheless, even the issuing of this law was not enough for Chrysostom to use in his arguments against paganism: "His recriminations against pagan idolatry and sacrifice are, for example, never backed up by reference to imperial laws against these." Isabella Sandwell, "Christian Self-Definition in the Fourth Century AD: John Chrysostom on Christianity, Imperial Rule and the City," in *Culture and Society in Later Roman Antioch*, ed. Sandwell and Huskinson, 42.

[141] See Robert E. Carter, "Saint John Chrysostom's Rhetorical Use of the Socratic Distinction between Kingship and Tyranny," *Tradition* 14 (1958), 367-71.

[142] "The religion of the Greeks [Hellenism] had been spread all over the earth and controlled the souls of all humanity; only later, after gaining so much strength, was it destroyed by Christ's power." Schatkin (84) situates this argument within a tradition of apologetics that goes back to Eusebius. *In Vid.*

that he used to save humanity (persuasion, reason, gentleness), and not physical might. Either way, in the first case John seems to attribute the demise of the ancient religion to internal factors, while in the second it seems that Christianity (or divine will) becomes the reason for its collapse.

Using an image that was meant to showcase the impossible, John compares the Greeks who attempt to contradict the Christians with those who try to drain the ocean by emptying it with their bare hands. He believes that the proper response to that is to laugh and weep for the Greeks, because what they are attempting is more difficult than trying to drain the ocean (21; p. 87; p. 116)! John uses here the poetic device of the *adynaton*, or impossibility, to emphasize his point and make sure that his audience understands the improbability of such an enterprise.

John's subject, the bishop and martyr Babylas, becomes an example of someone who "was instructed by the divine teaching that all worldly activities are a shadow, and a dream ..." (34; p. 95; p. 134).[143] Then, the unbelievers realize, to their amazement, that Christ has imbued his disciples with great courage, and upon this finding "they derided their own servility, bondage, and humiliation, and saw the great distance between the nobility of the Christians and the degradation of the Greeks" (40-41; p. 98; pp. 140-2).

John also accuses the pagan priests of performing the rituals due to fear of the emperors (ibid.). He contrasts this attitude with the situation of a Christian ascending the imperial throne and makes the interesting observation that when this happens Christianity deteriorates (42; p. 99; pp. 142-4). What he probably has in mind here is the series of Arian Emperors that succeeded Constantine to the throne. Chrysostom seems

---

dom. hom. 4.3 (SC 277:152; trans. Hill, *St. John Chrysostom Old Testament Homilies vol. 2*, 85) it is Peter who is undoing Greek religion like a spider's web: "What of Peter ... unskilled in the word and overwhelming orator, unlettered yet stopping the mouths of the philosophers, undoing the pagan religion like a spider web..."

[143] A common topos in the Hellenic tradition: cf. Pindar, *Pyth.* 8.99f., Aeschylus, *Ag.* 1327f., Sophocles, *Aj.* 125f., Euripides, *Med.* 1224.

to appreciate more the situation when an "impious man" is ruling and persecutes the Christians, because this allows the Christian message to spread and provides the Christians with the opportunity to win a martyr's crown (ibid.).[144]

To summarize what we have been discussing so far: a number of themes seem to emerge from our examination of Chrysostom's text. First, John is systematically disparaging the Greeks for a number of different reasons: especially the fact that they have not been persecuted, their own persecution of the Christians, and the decline of their religion. The emphasis is usually on their immorality and inexperience of humiliation in the past. At the same time, John uses these arguments to emphasize the moral superiority and power of Christianity, which seems to be on a mission to convert the former followers of paganism. The apologetic nature of the text justifies this latter statement, especially in light of its alleged status as a response to a number of pagan texts.

Despite the fact that Chrysostom is anxious to downplay the continued presence of paganism in the cities of the Empire, as it stands "the treatise provides indirect evidence of the strength of the pagan minority in Antioch in the late 370s."[145] His description of idol-worship might show an awareness of certain pagan rituals that were taking place in Antioch at the time: "daily and nocturnal feasts, the flutes and kettle-drums, the licence to use obscene language and to act even more obscenely, gluttony to the point of bursting, delirium from intoxication, degeneration into most shameful madness" (43; p.

---

[144] Cf.: "Our cause is not the same as the cause of the Greeks; it is not dependent upon the disposition of a ruler, but it rests on its own internal strength, and shines forth with greater luster, the more vehemently it is assailed," *Adv. opp. vit. mon.* 2.9 (PG 47:344; trans. Schatkin, *Apologist*, 99). "For now indeed that we are in the enjoyment of peace, we are become supine and lax, and have filled the Church with countless evils; but when we were persecuted, we were more sober-minded, and kinder, and more earnest, and readier as to these assemblies and as to hearing. For what fire is to gold, that is affliction unto souls; wiping away filth, rendering men clean, making them bright and shining," *In 2 Cor. hom.* 26.4 (PG 61:580; NPNF 1-12:401). Another theme that can be inferred from the passage is the danger that exists when times of peace are combined with luxury. For Chrysostom's idea of imperial rule in contrast to the Eusebeian model, which is often assumed to have been universally accepted by all Christian writers after Constantine, see Sandwell, "Christian Self-Definition," *passim* and especially 42.

[145] Kelly, *Golden Mouth*, 41.

99; p. 144). However, we must not exclude the possibility that these might be just generic descriptions of what a Christian of the time thought the pagan rituals consisted of.

But John does not limit himself to criticism of non-Christian religious rituals. He also criticizes the phenomenon and the abuses of parasitism and contrasts it with the Christian attitude towards idle individuals, who are encouraged to find a job and to contribute to the wellbeing of themselves and the community at large (43-4; p. 100; pp. 144-6). Parasitism is also explicitly connected with both the debauchery that follows the pagan rituals and the system of patronage and its implications for society (ibid.). To further advance the contrast, John uses the figure of Babylas again. This time Babylas is contrasted with the philosophers, who are characterized by "vainglory, impudence, and puerility" (45; pp. 100-1; p. 146). He is also explicitly compared with Diogenes of Sinope, although Babylas did not live in a wine cask and did not go to the market wearing rags. Though John does admire Diogenes' actions since they seem to "involve much labor and extreme pain, [they] nevertheless are deprived of all praise ... [because] useless labor is deprived of every encomium" (ibid.).[146] The point John is trying to make here is a contrast between Greek parasitism and Christian usefulness. This statement demands an elaboration: for society at large, an individual's contributions to it are measured by the usefulness of his/her actions. In this case, Chrysostom's thesis appears to be that all philosophers are ultimately useless. Even Diogenes, who at least expended labour in his efforts to teach, was useless, because he was expending useless labour. Thus, although Diogenes was not a parasite, he still was not labouring for a purpose. If John can prove that even Diogenes, a figure admired by many of the philosophical schools, was useless, the implication would be that all philosophers are

---

[146] And not just actions either. John was an ardent believer of the principle that "however much a person may say, if it does not issue in something advantageous, he speaks to no purpose." *In Act. apost. hom.* 6.2 (PG 60:59; NPNF 1-11:40).

useless. He will therefore attempt to prove just that and we will try to systematically examine his thoughts as we proceed.

In an imaginary dialogue with an admirer of Diogenes, John brings forth the admirer's argument that Diogenes addressed Alexander with great παρρησία. He goes on to recount the story of their meeting, when Alexander asked Diogenes what he needed and his reply was that he needed nothing except for the king not to cast his shadow upon him. John is of the opinion that Diogenes' reply should not be a matter of pride for his admirers but should bring them to shame, since he could have asked for something useful instead of sunbathing like an infant (46; pp. 101-2; pp. 148-50). It is not παρρησία that characterized Diogenes, John says, but pure eccentricity. The ἀγαθὸς ἀνήρ is called as such only when all his actions aim for the common welfare and strive to improve the lot of humanity (πρὸς τὸ κοινωφελὲς ἅπαντα πράττειν χρὴ καὶ τὸν τῶν ἄλλων βίον κατορθοῦν). Diogenes' request to not be put in the shade was of no benefit (διέσωσεν) to any city, household, man or woman. "Tell the fruit of his liberty (or freedom of speech)" (εἰπὲ τῆς παρρησίας τὸ κέρδος), John concludes, with a certain hint towards Diogenes' useless' existence (47; p. 102; p. 150). It is now clear that for Chrysostom freedom of speech and frankness are not virtues unless they bear fruits, an idea that he will expand in other works, when he calls things such as chastity and fasting as neither good nor evil in and of themselves, but characterizes them as such only according to the purpose they serve.

The example of Diogenes is used in this case as a prelude to, and a comparison with, Babylas' attitude towards the emperor (Decius) and the different scope of his actions. John refers to an incident when Babylas chased the emperor out of the church, a fact that proves that John "was not boasting when I said that he [Babylas] demonstrated the childishness (παιδικῆς ἔργα διανοίας) of your philosopher's marvellous deeds" (48; p. 102; p. 152). Babylas' attitude towards the emperor is used here as an example to show that Diogenes is childish because he a) asks for something useless, and b) because the very act of making a request proves his servility towards the emperor. In contrast, Babylas not only does not ask for anything, but also shows that he has power over the emperor. The imaginary dialogue with Diogenes' fan continues. This time he supposedly argues that Diogenes was temperate and lived in abstinence, even refusing to get married. John's response to that is that his opponent is partially concealing the truth by not mentioning Diogenes' foul and shameful sexual actions in public (48; pp. 102-103; p. 152).[147] Chrysostom's comment on Diogenes' sexuality concludes his diatribe against him, and is immediately followed by a frontal attack on Aristotle, Epicurus, Plato and Socrates.

The accusations are different, but they are all related to sexual matters and opinions. He censures Aristotle about his alleged habit of eating human semen. He wonders if there is any profit (ὄφελος) if someone has intercourse with mothers and sisters, as promulgated by Epicurus.[148] He closes this section by mentioning the founders of the Platonic Academy, Socrates and Plato, whom he reproaches of hiding their preference for pederasty under a veil of allegory and thereby considering it as something respectable and a part of philosophy.[149] John seems to imply here that their alleged preference for pederasty is not only contrary to Christian morals, but also useless, because they bear no physical progeny. But since he does not make a concrete reference to a Platonic source, due to the already lengthy nature of his work (as he himself points out) our assumption about the text he is referring to must be speculative. I would argue that the most probable text that underlies John's response is *Symposium* 209a-e, of which we will cite just a selection:

---

[147] Cf. Diogenes Laertius, *Vit. phil.* 6.69.

[148] Cf. SVF 3:185. See also Schatkin's comment on this last accusation: "a retortion of the slander of "Oedipodean intercourse," i.e., incest, made against the early church," 104, n. 98.

[149] "…one suspects that rhetorical excess has colored Chrysostom's attack on pederasty. Furthermore, pederasty in Chrysostom's mind was a vice intimately associated with Greek paideia and, therefore, this polemic is part of his more general attack on Greek culture." Hunter, *A Comparison*, 140, n. 45.

Now those who are teeming in body betake them rather to women, and are amorous on this wise: by getting children they acquire an immortality, a memorial, and a state of bliss, which in their imagining they "for all succeeding time procure." But pregnancy of soul—for there are persons,' she declared,' who in their souls still more than in their bodies conceive those things which are proper for soul to conceive and bring forth; and what are those things? Prudence, and virtue in general ... when a man's soul is so far divine that it is made pregnant with these from his youth, and on attaining manhood immediately desires to bring forth and beget, he too, I imagine, goes about seeking the beautiful object whereon he may do his begetting since he will never beget upon the ugly. Hence it is the beautiful rather than the ugly bodies that he welcomes in his pregnancy, and if he chances also on a soul that is fair and noble and well-endowed, he gladly cherishes the two combined in one ...Equally too with him he shares the nurturing of what is begotten, so that men in this condition enjoy a far fuller community with each other than that which comes with children, and a far surer friendship, since the children of their union are fairer and more deathless. Everyone would choose to have got children such as these rather than the human sort...[150]

John seems to be justified in his criticism, at least concerning the distinction between physical/spiritual offspring. Plato (via Diotima) certainly considers the second as significantly more important than the first, an argument he supports by mentioning the works of Homer, Hesiod, Lycurgus and Solon, which he characterizes as their very own immortal offspring. We can also see how John could infer an endorsement of pederasty and homosexuality from Plato, an interpretation that is also in line with modern exegesis of the same text. To summarize our argument regarding the platonic text: although at first sight Plato seems to imply that philosophy (or poetry, or law making) lead to better progeny than sexual intercourse, it is not something that he leaves outside his field of vision. He just includes it within the context of a lover instilling his wisdom in a young boy, a relationship that involves a carnal and spiritual

---

[150] Plato, *Symp.* 209a-e (LCL 166:198-201). If our speculation about the platonic text that John is responding to is correct, then he would not be the only one that sees pederasty as one of the underlying themes of this passage. Modern commentators of Plato have interpreted it along the same lines. See for example C. D. C. Reeve, Introduction to *Plato on Love: Lysis, Symposium, Phaedrus, Alcibiades, with Selections from Republic and Laws* (Indianapolis, IN: Hackett, 2006), xxv: "...like spermatozoa the embryology that the *Symposium* implicitly embraces when it portrays forth *the lover* (italics in the original) as pregnant and as seeking a beautiful boy in which to beget an offspring– need only be ejaculated into the right receptacle in order to grow into their mature forms. Sex can lead to virtue, in other words, without the need for hard work. As soon as the illusion is enjoyed, therefore, it gives birth not to a realistic attempt to acquire virtue but to the sexual seduction fantasy mentioned earlier. The origins of this fantasy -though, no doubt, partly personal- are predominantly social. It is the complex ideology of Athenian *paiderasteia*..."

paideusis and can only lead to spiritual offspring. If our hypothesis is correct, it is in line with both modern exegesis as well as Chrysostom's interpretation of the same passage.

John concludes and brings his argument full circle by mentioning the example of Diogenes again: if he, "who prevails in courage and temperance, according to the seemingly more austere branch of philosophy, appears so disgraceful, eccentric and unbalanced –he even said it is indifferent to eat human beings[151] –what argument against the others is left us, if one who eclipsed the rest at the acme of the profession is convicted of absurdity, puerility, and stupidity in the eyes of all" (49; p. 103; p. 154).

Chrysostom's next targets are the Olympian gods themselves. He accuses Apollo of using excuses to escape from difficulties when the people consulted his oracles, as in Delphi, and mocks him for his weakness and inability to perform by claiming that it was the presence of a corpse (i.e. Babylas's relics) that prevented him from doing so (84; pp. 204-6). Chrysostom further claims that Apollo's oracles are purposefully obscure in order to make people visit again, looking for a solution (88; p. 126-7; p. 210). His next object of ridicule is none other than Zeus himself. But in the process of ridiculing the father of the gods, John also attacks his former teacher Libanius "and derisively tears to pieces the lament which Libanius (a sincere pagan who felt genuinely shattered by the event) had composed for the destruction of the temple [of Apollo]."[152] The way Chrysostom does that is by selecting certain passages from Libanius' lament, echoing them but reversing their meaning, and mocking him for feeling sadness over the destruction of Apollo's temple. Kelly believes that only the tension between the pagans and the Christians in Antioch can explain John's intemperate onslaught on Libanius, who was still alive and in the city. This is a reasonable assumption, but we cannot

---

[151] Diogenes Laertius, *Vit. phil.* 6.73. See Schatkin's comment: "In effect, a retortion of the slander of "Thyestean feasts" (cannibalism) made against the early Christians," 104, n. 104.

[152] Kelly, *Golden Mouth*, 41.

exclude the personal aspect of the attack, considering that, for John, Libanius must have personified many of the evils he saw in the surviving remnants of paganism. It is fair to say, though, that paganism was far from dead, especially after Julian's brief tenure, and that that must have been a cause of anxiety for John, no matter how much he tried to downplay it.[153] John's references to Julian's sacrifices at the shrine of Apollo at Daphne further validate this point (80, 100, 103; pp. 200, 228-30, 232).

However, although we often mention Julian and Libanius together, we must not overlook their differences as personalities and the ideas they espoused. For example, as D. Hunter argues, Libanius, unlike Julian, had no interest in philosophy *per se*, and his writings and orations show no trace of Neoplatonic influence.[154] Their attitudes towards traditional religion and piety were also significant – and disputed by scholars. On the one hand, Athanassiadi argues that Libanius, "unlike Julian, worshipped Culture and stopped there."[155] On the other hand, Hunter would very much disagree with this statement, considering the strong connection between λόγοι and ἱερά, or education and religion, in Libanius's works: Libanius would also agree with Julian that *paideia* was a pagan possession and utilized Julian's conversion to prove just that. The second way Libanius utilized Julian as a symbol of Hellenism was by promoting him as a figure of a higher moral status, and an ascetic who abstained from many of life's vices. Hunter further argues that "the crucial difference in Libanius' presentation is that the formation of Julian's virtue and nobility of character is credited to Greek paideia. Homer, the orators, historians, and especially the philosophers are held responsible for Julian's humanity (φιλανθρωπία) and clemency (ἡμερότης)."[156] These together with the fact that

---

[153] Kelly, *Golden Mouth*, 42.

[154] Hunter, *A Comparison*, 54.

[155] Athanassiadi-Fowden, *Julian and Hellenism*, 207.

[156] Hunter, *A Comparison*, 54.

they shared an antipathy towards Christianity were the main reasons John often argued against them as a duo.

One might think that Chrysostom's treatise should have ended by now, since he has described Babylas' life up until his death. But for Chrysostom this is a Greek way of thinking, "since Greeks … have limited their hope to the present life." However, for the Christians the end of this life is just the beginning of another, brighter existence (64; p. 111; p. 172). However, John only finishes his treatise after referring to the things Babylas achieved after his death: "he put an end to the strength of the demon; utterly refuted the deceit of the Greeks; exposed the nonsense of divination, shattered its mask, and displayed all its hypocrisy laid bare, having silenced and defeated by main force the one who seemed to be its master [Apollo]."[157] The power (ἰσχύς) of the saints is great and fearsome, not only for the demons or the devil, but even for the emperor himself (127; p. 152; p. 274)! In the words of J.N.D. Kelly, "the message hammered home is that pagans should be persuaded, by the contrast between the laughable ineffectiveness of the old gods and the extraordinary miracles which Christ continues to work through his saints, to transfer their allegiance to him."[158]

Two key themes emerge from our reading of the text. First, Chrysostom personifies his arguments against paganism by comparing the lives of individuals from both the Christian and the pagan sides. In this small treatise, the bishop Babylas exemplifies the ideal Christian. His life and attitude are compared with the lives and ideas of a number of Greek philosophers, mainly Diogenes, but also Plato, Aristotle, Epicurus, and even the Olympian gods, who are all found wanting. He is also powerful after his death,

---

[157] In his *Homily on Martyr Babylas*, delivered in Antioch on the martyr's feast day on January 24, John observes that "where there is recollection of martyrs, the shaming of the Greeks occurs there too" (SC 362:302; trans. Wendy Mayer, '*Let us Die That We May Live*,' 145) before moving to an outburst against Apollo and his request for Babylas' body to be moved.

[158] Kelly, *Golden Mouth*, 41.

particularly through the translation of his relics from Daphne, where the narrative functions as a way of "shaping a new collective Christian identity."[159]

Secondly, the theme of usefulness plays a prominent role in his criticism, and one of his major arguments against the most eminent philosophers of Hellenism is that their lives (in some cases) and theories (in other cases) were ultimately worthless, because they either served no purpose at all or plainly failed. In the *Discourse on Babylas* his main focus of criticism are the lives of the philosophers, although this is just one aspect of his critique of Hellenism.

With regard to the debate on the nature of the text, we think that a combination of the different interpretations as outlined above is applicable. As per Schatkin's comment, the text does talk about Greek ethical theory and tries to prove that Babylas was a much better practitioner than those who initially conceived this theory, so that he is a prime example of the vindication of Christian philosophy. But the *Discourse on Babylas* is also a triumphal witness to an emergent and victorious Christianity and its subversion of paganism, as per Harkins' and Kelly's views. There are strong references to power, victory and domination that John emphasizes against the weakness and subservience of the Greeks.

Both sides of the debate seem to assume a certain mode of discourse to the exclusion of others: thus, Kelly and Harkins tend to highlight the rhetorical nature of the text as the dominant mode and see it as a primary example of the *psogos* genre, in which a speaker tries to insult and/or degrade someone or something. On the other hand, Schatkin seems to assume that the dominant mode is philosophical, primarily through an emphasis on ethical theory. Our analysis above, however, has shown that both modes are to be found in the text, especially given what Chrysostom has to say about Christianity's victory being won through both power and persuasion. Babylas is a *better*

---

[159] Shepardson, *Controlling Contested Places*, 73.

philosopher than the Greeks because his actions are actually useful, whilst his power remains strong even after death, when his relics make the false gods leave their abodes. This is what he claims Babylas (and all the saints) did, and John's best homage to the former bishop of Antioch is a homily that is powerfully persuasive through rhetoric and philosophy.

e. Conclusion

In this chapter, we have highlighted the following themes as they appear in many comparisons between Christians and Greeks: first, simplicity versus *paideia*, where *paideia* is sometimes construed in terms of philosophy and sometimes in terms of rhetoric. In the Christians' case, it was persuasive even when not taught, and despite the simplicity of its message. Second, faith versus reasonings/*logismoi*. Whilst the latter does not originally have a negative connotation, since it is a God-given gift to humanity, excessive dependence on reason is a characteristic of the Greeks and one of the original reasons for their downfall. Third, unity versus division. Although this theme appears a few times, John does not press it as hard as he could, especially considering that there were precedents within Hellenic tradition that emphasized philosophical disagreements. However, it seems that the fragile situation of Nicene Christianity and the divisions in Antioch did not enable him to make as much use of it as he could. Fourth, the theme of useful versus useless philosophy, particularly as a way of transmission of a way of life. Even when Chrysostom gives in and admits that there could be some admirable elements to a pagan philosopher, he ultimately denies them on the basis that they would be useless for the other humans. On the other hand, the Christians' lives are not just paradigmatic and useful, but can also be emulated. Finally, the theme of success versus failure. This was more obvious in John's later career rather than earlier, but even during his time in Antioch he could point to a future that looked decidedly Christian in a lot of ways. Where the philosophers failed, the Apostles succeeded, and with them they converted what John understood as the whole world.

Moreover, John sometimes employs the contrast in a philosophical mode (e.g. Christian virtue is identifiable by Greeks as virtue, but Christians do it better) and sometimes in a rhetorical mode, as when he triumphantly proclaims the victory of Christianity over Hellenism. The works of Mitchell and Lai we mentioned in the beginning already made the point that these comparisons are not very systematic and are often of an *ad hoc* manner. I would argue that the two exceptions to this rule are the *Discourse on Babylas* and the introduction to the *Homilies on Matthew*. They are too well crafted to not have been prepared in advance and they respond to specific texts, sometimes verbatim in the *Discourse's* case. Therefore, the comparisons might not be very systematic but there is a certain consistency in John's strategy. By using *synkrisis*, Chrysostom grapples with the similarities and differences in such a way that certain themes emerge (such as the ones listed previously), and these themes are addressed sometimes in a philosophical and sometimes in a rhetorical mode.

Many of these themes are Pauline in nature, but often John extends Paul's thought to its logical conclusion by framing it in the context of his own time. For example, when discussing 1 Corinthians 1:17 ("For Christ did not send me to baptize but to proclaim the gospel, and not with eloquent wisdom, so that the cross of Christ might not be emptied of its power") Chrysostom argues that this wisdom is explicitly at war with the Cross and the Gospel, and therefore one "should not boast about it, but ... retire with shame."[160] It is precisely because of this that the Apostles were unwise. It was not any weakness on their part, but a preventative measure so that the Gospel wouldn't suffer any harm. While in the hands of the unwise Apostles the Word is established, in the

---

[160] *In 1 Cor. hom.* 3.3 (PG 61:26; NPNF 1-12:13).

hands of the wise it is defamed.[161] This cosmic battle is always described as a case of the weak overcoming the strong, or the twelve versus the world.[162] Chrysostom's polemic against Hellenism is then an extension of this mission. Peter, Paul, and the others might have set the stage for the initial battle, but Chrysostom sees it continued through martyrs of later times, such as Babylas, and the responsibility he must have felt to continue in this tradition.

If we refer our conclusion to the title of this chapter and the issue of identity, we would argue that Chrysostom expresses a collective Christian identity through these *synkriseis* by establishing the apostles and the saints as protagonists in a cosmic battleground where the trophies are the souls of men and women. John would argue that the philosophers cannot offer any kind of salvation and to prove his point he would constantly refer back to their failures, which were then compared implicitly or explicitly with the successes of Christianity. In this respect, both the philosophers and the apostles, the generals and the saints, are carriers of identity. Despite the fact that, as we saw in chapter 2, Chrysostom could sometimes praise certain famous or anonymous Greeks, one would not expect him to do so when comparing them to Christians. Yet he would sometimes do that, but always on the level of discourse about everyday attitudes exhibited by anonymous Greeks and Christians. On the level of each group's heroic figures, Plato could never hope to beat Paul.

---

[161] *In 1 Cor. hom.* 3.3 (PG 61:26; NPNF 1-12:13).

[162] Ibid., 3.4 (PG 61:28).

4. "Dogs priced at three obols"[1]: The reception of Cynicism in John Chrysostom[2]

Christianity and its doctrines have often been analysed or compared with the philosophical schools of antiquity, primarily Platonism and Stoicism. However, despite a renaissance of studies on Cynicism as a legitimate philosophical school, the number of studies on Christianity and Cynicism is still limited. As we shall show, Cynicism is a particularly interesting focal point for a comparison between Christianity and Hellenism because both Christians and their enemies saw certain similarities between them. If we were to sum up the interaction between philosophical schools and Christianity in the view of modern scholarship, it has been construed as a relationship of opposition/appropriation,[3] synthesis,[4] transformation,[5] and symbiosis.[6] If we take the

---

[1] This phrase was used by Chrysostom to characterize the Cynics, their philosophy, and Greek philosophy overall, in his *In Eph. hom.* 21.2 (PG 62:153): Εἰ γὰρ Ἕλληνες ἄνδρες τριωβολιμαῖοί τινες καὶ κύνες, φιλοσοφίαν τοιαύτην ἀναδεξάμενοι τριωβολιμαῖον (τοιαύτη γὰρ ἡ Ἑλληνικὴ) ... The application of the term to the Cynics is obviously an ironic use of ps-Crates' exhortation in *Epistle 22 To Metrocles* (trans. Ronald F. Hock in *The Cynic Epistles: A Study Edition*, ed. Abraham J. Malherbe, Missoula, MT: Scholars Press,1977, 73): "Do not take from everyone but only from the worthy, and do not take the same amount from everyone, but accept three obols from the prudent and a mina from spendthrifts." Cf. *Epistle 27 To the Athenians* (ibid., 77): "Diogenes the Cynic used to say that all things belong to God and that friends have things in common, so that all things belong to the wise man... do not be angry whenever you are asked for three obols by wise men. For you are giving back not what is yours but what is theirs."

[2] A version of this chapter will appear in *(Re)visioning John Chrysostom: New Perspectives, Theories and Approaches*, eds. Chris L. de Wet and Wendy Mayer (Leiden: Brill, forthcoming). I would like to thank the editors for their careful reading of the text and their insightful comments on it.

[3] As in Siniossoglou, *Plato and Theodoret*. S. Lilla refers to three distinct positions among Christian authors between the first and fifth centuries: "(1) a rejection and total condemnation, (2) a moderate openness, (3) and an enthusiasm, leading even to an impassioned defense of Hellenic thought." S. Lilla, "Hellenism and Christianity," in *Encyclopedia of Ancient Christianity vol. 2*, ed. Angelo di Berardino (Downers Grove, IL: IVP Academic, 2014), 205. While John Chrysostom has often been presented as an advocate of the first position, a more nuanced study of his work will show that he often displays the second attitude as well, but certainly not the third.

[4] As in Jaeger, *Early Christianity and Greek Paideia*. Jaeger's classic examples of this synthesis are Origen and the Cappadocians.

[5] As in Pelikan, *Christianity and Classical Culture*.

[6] The symbiotic position appears to be the most popular in contemporary scholarship, especially since the symbiosis of two organizations can encompass a wide range of relationships within it, including, but not limited to, antagonism, correlation, parallel influences, and negotiation. This can sometimes lead to overly minimalistic positions, such as the claim that "when Constantine made Christianity legal, very little differentiated Christian intellectuals from their non-Christian intellectual neighbours; what separated them were nuances." At the same time, I am sympathetic towards the proposition that "Greek Christians thus did not conquer, adopt, or appropriate *logoi* and *paideia* (that is, Hellenism or pagan culture) because one does not adopt, conquer, or appropriate what one possesses by birth, education, and divine design." Elm, *Sons of Hellenism, Fathers of the Church*, 11.

aforementioned positions as applicable to many, if not most, patristic writers, where does Chrysostom stand? A superficial reading will reveal a deep hostility to philosophy, an "anti-intellectual posturing,"[7] an impression further reinforced in the most detailed collection of his references to Greek philosophers, where it is argued that "to their writings he probably seldom recurred for recreation", and that his opinion of Greek philosophy was "low".[8] As we have seen in chapter 1, more recent works have discarded this position and provided certain nuances, not only in relation to Chrysostom's references to the philosophers, but also to the influence of philosophy in his own thought.[9] It has also been shown that more often than not Chrysostom's arguments on different subjects can be placed within "existing intellectual traditions" that were part of Hellenistic secular *paideia*."[10] Modern scholarship on Chrysostom recognizes "predominantly Stoic and Cynic frameworks, but also ... Platonic, Aristotelian, and Epicurean elements, in the main little different from those of his pagan counterparts who had been educated in the same philosophical schools."[11]

Chrysostom then, as most church Fathers, is representative of a philosophical eclecticism. In terms of his reception of Cynic ideas, there have been studies that examined the influence of Cynic and Stoic ethic as well as elements from other

---

[7] Which is defined as "not the total rejection of philosophy and contemporary oratory that it seems, but a rejection of what misleadingly he represents as the sum total of Greek paideia and secular rhetorical-philosophical pedagogy, namely, epideictic rhetoric or oratory that is showy and aimed at applause and self-promotion." Wendy Mayer, "Shaping the Sick Soul: Reshaping the Identity of John Chrysostom," in *Christians Shaping Identity from the Roman Empire to Byzantium: Studies inspired by Pauline Allen*, eds. Geoffrey D. Dunn and Wendy Mayer (Leiden: Brill, 2015), 150.

[8] P.R. Coleman-Norton, "St. Chrysostom and the Greek Philosophers," 305. The article collects Chrysostom's references to Greek philosophers and his assessment of some of their ideas. Although it often lacks analysis and context, it continues to be a useful resource. Coleman-Norton's opinion is still cited uncritically in modern scholarly works, even though a large number of studies have put Chrysostom's opinion into perspective.

[9] Margaret Mitchell, "John Chrysostom on the Sermon on the Mount: φιλοσοφία as the basis for the Christian πολιτεία," in *The Sermon on the Mount through the Centuries: From the Early Church to John Paul II*, ed. J.P. Greenman, T. Larsen and S.R. Spender (Grand Rapids, MI: Brazos Press, 2007), 19-42.

[10] Wendy Mayer, "A Son of Hellenism."

[11] Pauline Allen and Silke Sitzler, Introduction to *Preaching Poverty in Late Antiquity: Perceptions and Realities*, eds. Pauline Allen, Bronwen Neil, Wendy Mayer (Leipzig: Evangelische Verlagsanstalt, 2009), 24.

philosophical schools, in his teachings on wealth, poverty, and almsgiving.[12] The question of philosophical influences in Chrysostom's thought as well as his reception of philosophical ideas are issues that also touch on religious identity in late antiquity. Isabella Sandwell's work in this area has pioneered a variety of approaches in the subject and our chapter can be considered as a complement to Sandwell who focuses on *praxis* rather than *theoria*. In sum: for a full picture of Chrysostom's understanding of Hellenism and its ideas there needs to be a balance between assessing his opinions of individual philosophers and their ideas and his reception and incorporation of the very same ideas into his own teachings, where we can confidently say that his approach is much subtler and engaged.

Our chapter is also part of a larger discussion on the nature, transformation, and reception of Cynicism in late antiquity.[13] The school curriculum during that period preserves a number of Diogenes traditions, and even from earlier times, such as the first and second century AD, Diogenes had become a stock character and a cultural archetype in a number of literary writings. His sayings (*chreiai*) formed a large part of the common rhetorical education and he figures prominently in rhetorical handbooks, possibly more than any other philosopher. This, more than any other factor, helps to explain the continued relevance of Cynicism not only during late antiquity but also in Byzantium. Other factors include polemical writings and references against them, such as those of Julian the Emperor (who tended to disregard his contemporary Cynics but praise Diogenes, even though a number of them were present at his court) and Christians who self-identified as Cynics (such as Maximus, the archbishop of

---

[12] Giovanni Viansino, "Aspetti dell' opera di Giovanni Crisostomo", *Koinonia* 25 (2001), 137-205, cited in Wendy Mayer, "John Chrysostom on Poverty," in Pauline Allen, Bronwen Neil, Wendy Mayer, ibid., 81.

[13] The following paragraph draws substantially on Derek Krueger, "Diogenes in Late Antiquity," in his *Symeon the Holy Fool: Leontius' Life and the Late Antique City* (Berkeley: University of California Press, 1996), 74-8. In his "Diogenes the Cynic Among the Fourth Century Fathers," 29-30, Krueger observed that Cynicism in Late Antiquity has not yet received serious attention but argued that the reception of Cynic philosophical ideals in Christian philosophy was through the absorption of Cynic ideas in the Stoic tradition of the late-first and second centuries.

Constantinople). Augustine, for instance, indicated their continued existence into the fifth century. It is a historical paradox that sometimes the Cynics would even appear in Christian writings as the representatives of Greek philosophy *par excellence*. Regardless of how the Cynics themselves were presented, or even how late we might think that people who self-identified as Cynics in reality existed, however, it remains a fact that a considerable number of Cynic themes persisted in Christian writings throughout the centuries.[14]

a. Early Christianity and Cynicism: Views Past and Present

Previous scholarship on early Christianity and Cynicism has a tendency to examine a large number of diachronic sources, which is not very helpful for understanding the dynamics of the reception of Cynicism in different historical periods.[15] While useful for the large number of writings of the Church Fathers subject to Cynic influence they have identified, these studies often lack the type of analysis that would facilitate understanding how the two movements differed or resembled each other and the precise influence of Cynicism on Christian writers. This is in stark contrast to studies on Cynicism and Christianity during the New Testament era, where studies abound, despite the controversial conclusions of this particular line of research.[16] In discussing Cynicism and some of its main concepts, we will face an inevitable question: how did certain philosophical concepts, such as *autarkeia* (autarchy or self-sufficiency), contribute to the development of Christian discourse in late antiquity? In other words,

---

[14] For the legacies of Cynicism see the studies of William Desmond, *Cynics* (Ancient Philosophies; Stocksfield: Acumen, 2008); *The Greek Praise of Poverty: Origins of Ancient Cynicism* (Notre Dame, IN: University of Notre Dame Press, 2006).

[15] The definitive study on the subject is still Downing's *Cynics and Christian Origins*. Studies on Cynicism as a philosophical and cultural movement are on the increase but it is still understudied in terms of the reception of its ideals in the Patristic era.

[16] Besides Downing's works, other noteworthy studies include John Dominic Crossan, *The Historical Jesus: The Life of a Mediterranean Jewish Peasant* (San Francisco: Harper San Francisco, 1991), the main proponent (along with Burton Mack and Downing) of the Cynic Jesus hypothesis. See Gregory Boyd, *Cynic Sage or Son of God? Recovering the Real Jesus in an Age of Revisionist Replies* (Wheaton, IL: Victor Books, 1995) for a critique of this thesis.

did *autarkeia* mean the same thing for John Chrysostom as it did for Diogenes and the Cynics in general? By focusing on one specific concept as a case-study, we will be able to focus the question of Chrysostom's attitude to Hellenism as sharply as possible.

Early Christians and Cynics were sometimes grouped together in literary references, as we will see. There are further similarities in the ascetic practices and rhetorical methods of the Christians and Cynics.[17] The two groups were also intertwined in instances of Christians becoming Cynics, such as Peregrinus, or Christian bishops being called Cynics, such as the Bishop Maximus of Constantinople in the fourth century.[18] Sometimes it is difficult to distinguish whether someone like Maximus was called Cynic due to his beliefs, ascetic lifestyle, or even way of dressing. Nevertheless, these similarities, such as the fondness that some Christian authors and the Cynics had for poverty,[19] as well as the differences, such as the reception of Cynic shamelessness, lead us to the topic of this chapter. Besides the obvious common elements between Christianity and Cynicism, can we talk of a deeper ideological alliance that they shared in terms of social ethics? Does the fact that they employed many common terms in similar kinds of ways mean anything more than the assumption that they were often part of the same intellectual climate? We will also examine the reception of Cynics as personalities themselves, both in the writings of John Chrysostom and other Church Fathers, in an attempt to delineate whether their opinion about them is reflective of a consensus on certain themes or not. The most important interaction, and central for the

---

[17] The most common of the latter being the diatribe, "the instrument of the Cynic, preaching virtue on the street corner…" Hubbell, "Chrysostom and Rhetoric," 263.

[18] Although this fact should not be overstated: "Despite partial similarities between ascetic Cynicism and ascetic strains of Christianity, in antiquity the two seem to have occupied very different cultural spaces, too separate for a single person to bridge. The record at least seems to indicate very few who were both Cynics and Christians. By one reckoning. we know of only three such persons, at the most, and they span three centuries: Peregrinus Proteus, Heraclas, and Maximus Hero." Desmond, *Cynics*, 219. Rowland Smith, *Julian's Gods: Religion and Philosophy in the Thought and Action of Julian the Apostate* (London: Routledge, 1995), 87, points out that the designation of Maximus as a Cynic might have denoted a Nicene Christian "who dresses in peculiar costume in illustration of virtues that remain the monopoly of Christians."

[19] For example, both Chrysostom and the Cynics consider poverty to be praiseworthy, which the former allies "to the Christian idea of heavenly wealth." Mayer, "John Chrysostom on Poverty," 101.

argument of this chapter, occurs when the two groups were lumped together by outsiders based on a number of similar characteristics. For example, in the second century AD Aelius Aristides accuses the Cynics of twisting the meaning of words, when they believe

> [t]hat shamelessness is freedom, being hated means they have been speaking frankly, and taking is being generous... They deceive like flatterers, but they are as insolent as if they were of higher rank... behaving like those impious men of Palestine. For the proof of the impiety of those people is that they do not believe in the higher power. And these men in a certain fashion have defected from the Greek race, or rather from all that is higher.[20]

A number of common behavioural traits leads Aristides to the conclusion that the Cynics resemble the Christians, at least in terms of public appearance.[21]

During Chrysostom's time, Julian's *To the Cynic Herakleios* provides a vivid description of contemporary Cynics and makes an interesting comparison with another group, the Christian monks. He wonders what Herakleios has done to earn the staff of Diogenes and his παρρησία and what kind of *askesis* he has practiced. This is followed by a description of the lifestyle of Cynics in the fourth century A.D.: "Do you really think it so great an achievement to carry a staff and let your hair grow, and haunt cities and camps uttering calumnies against the noblest men and flattering the vilest?"[22] Julian aligns these Cynics with the Christian monks (ἀποτακτιστάς, renunciators), as he says the δυσσεβεῖς Γαλιλαῖοι (impious Galileans) call them, because just like them, "by making small sacrifices they gain much or rather everything from all sources."[23] In

---

[20] Aelius Aristides, *Or. 3 To Plato: In Defence of the Four* (ed. Lenz and Behr, 666-671; trans. Behr, 274-5).

[21] For other ancient to late-ancient texts that identify similarities between Christianity and Cynicism see F. Gerald Downing, "Cynics and Early Christianity," in *Le Cynisme Ancien et ses Prolongements*, eds. Marie-Odile Goulet-Cazé and Richard Goulet (Paris: Presses Universitaires de France, 1993), 281-304.

[22] Julian, *Or.* 7.223 (LCL 29:121).

[23] Julian, *Or.* 7.224 (LCL 29: 122-3). It has also been argued that Julian's attack on the Cynics of his time is due to the fact that he viewed them as social revolutionaries who threatened social cohesion as much as the Christians. See Nikolaos M. Skouteropoulos, *Οι Αρχαίοι Κυνικοί: Αποσπάσματα και Μαρτυρίες* [*The Ancient Cynics: Fragments and Testimonies*] (Athens: Gnosi, 2006), 189; and Elm, *Sons of Hellenism*, 110: "False Cynics and Christian renunciators were guilty of a similar mistake, indeed crime: their rejections of the gods and of the laws of society was a willful innovation. It posed a grave

many respects they are the same, except for money-making: the Christian monks collect money and call it ἐλεημοσύνην (almsgiving). As for the rest, "in all other respects your habits and theirs are very much alike", and more importantly, "like them you have abandoned your country".[24] Abandoning one's homeland (or city) is a major accusation Julian raises against both the monks and the Cynics, or, rather, those who falsely claim the name of "Cynics." The latter are also held responsible for making philosophy εὐκαταφρόνητος (lightly esteemed) and for equating Cynicism with the stereotypical attributes Julian never fails to mention: βακτηρία (staff), τρίβων (cloak), κόμη (long hair) ... ἀμαθία, θράσος, ἰταμότης καὶ πάντα ἁπλῶς τὰ τοιαῦτα (impudence, insolence, and in a word everything of the sort).[25] The examples of Aristides and Julian allow us to identify some common accusations that will also be employed later by some Christians: the Cynics (of their time) are shameless, hated for their tendencies to insult people (particularly the rich and prominent), and depend on others for their living. They are also defectors from the Greek race, atheists, and pay more attention to external characteristics than to philosophy.[26] In sum, Julian's strong dislike toward the Cynics of his day can be attributed to their rootlessness, and their ἀπαιδευσία.[27] Others have also

---

danger to the *politeia*, threatening its very foundations, and could not, for that reason, be considered philosophical in the least ... Such excessive rejection marked false Cynics and certain Christians (by using "Galileans," a label denoting a small ethnic group, Julian accused all Christians of marginal status, which the renunciators then pushed to extreme)." G.W. Bowersock's interpretation of Julian's attack on the Cynics of his time includes a claim that Julian's ideal Cynic was the description of a person "remarkably like himself" and his attack on other forms of paganism showed that his character was "of a bigot, and a puritanical one at that." Bowersock, *Julian the Apostate*, 82.

[24] In his *Deipnosophistae* 13.611c (LCL 345:91) Athenaeus also accuses the Cynics of retaining the worst of the dogs' characteristics: "But the creature also has an abusive mouth and is willing to eat anything, and in addition it leads an impoverished existence, stripped of all possessions—and you devote yourselves to both qualities, since you are foul-mouthed gluttons, and on top of that you live without a hearth or a home!"

[25] Julian, *Or.* 7.225 (LCL 29:124-5). Chrysostom uses fairly similar phraseology in one of his criticisms of the philosophers, without making it specific to Cynicism: *Hab. eund. spir. hom.* 1.3 (PG 51:274).

[26] Christian critiques of Cynicism often resembled similar Graeco-Roman arguments against the movement, including an emphasis on certain exterior features that different authors considered problematic, such as appearance (cloak, staff, long beard) and lifestyle (sleeping rough, begging, verbal abuse of others).

[27] Athanassiadi, *Julian and Hellenism*, 128-31.

seen his opposition to them as part of his effort to "forge an Hellenic orthodoxy" which presupposed the "fundamental unity of all Greek philosophy," with the exception of these pseudo-Cynics.[28]

Similarities between Cynics and Christians have also been the subject of study in modern scholarship. F. Gerald Downing, for example, has argued that some early Christians "were at least content to be seen as and even understood as a kind of Cynic" and for that reason they did little to distinguish themselves from genuine Cynics. He refers to some Christians looking at points of similarity, even though other aspects of Cynicism horrified them, and he draws an analogy with the Christian reception of Plato and the Stoics.[29] In reference to the specific case of Diogenes, Derek Krueger has pointed out that we cannot claim a unified Christian stance towards him, and even among individual Christian writers their opinion was not always consistent.[30] Both of these arguments will be exemplified in our discussion on the patristic reception of Cynicism. On the other hand, Rowland Smith has argued that the appeal of the movements might have been comparable on the social level but rejects the possibility of a positive ideological rapport.[31]

In section b, we will argue that early Christian authors found some Cynic ideas easier to accept and others much less acceptable. This caused an interesting tension which runs throughout Christian discourse about the Cynics. The main aim of this section will be to describe and analyse this tension in a selection of general Christian accounts of Cynicism. This necessarily brief account will serve primarily to illuminate both the context in which John Chrysostom discusses Cynicism and his reaction to it. This will be followed by a closer examination of Chrysostom's reception of Cynicism,

---

[28] Arnaldo Marcone, "The forging of an Hellenic orthodoxy: Julian's speeches against the Cynics," in *Emperor and Author*, ed. Baker-Brian and Tougher, 241.

[29] Downing, *Cynics and Christian Origins*, 23. Other studies on the topic will be referenced throughout the chapter.

[30] Krueger, "Diogenes the Cynic," 43.

[31] Smith, *Julian's Gods*, 88.

divided into his opinion of individual Cynics and Cynics in general (section c) and his appropriation of Cynic ideas (section d). As we will argue, some of the concepts in his thought, and particularly the one which will be analysed in section d (*autarkeia*), were very much influenced by Cynicism. *Autarkeia* -and *parrhesia* [outspokenness], *tuphos* [in the sense of vanity], etc.- are not concepts found exclusively in Cynicism, but are nonetheless popularly employed in combination with a number of other catchwords that represent the *spirit* of Cynicism. As Downing explains, "the attitudes and commitments that are expressed in witty sayings, in lively metaphors and parables, and in striking actions, all together articulate the life-style that is lived."[32] What we would identify as the main common theme is an understanding of philosophy primarily as a way of life, an emphasis that can be found in Christianity's appropriation of the word *philosophia* itself as well as Cynicism's exemplification of philosophy through actions narrated in popular anecdotes and witty sayings.

b. Patristic Reception of Cynic Philosophers: Criticism, Praise and Distortion

It has often been noted in scholarship on Cynicism and Christianity that there was a degree of sympathy between them, with different scholars citing various reasons for this.[33] The resemblance of the two movements was already commented upon in

---

[32] Downing, *Cynics and Christian Origins*, 49. For a full list of these words see ibid., 47.

[33] Thus, Donald Dudley, *A History of Cynicism: From Diogenes to the Sixth Century A.D.* (2nd ed.; Bristol: Bristol Classical Press, 1998), 174, proposes that "the Jews, the Cynics, and the Christians were alike hostile to the general standards of Graeco-Roman civilization." Downing, *Cynics and Christian Origins*, 170, posits the following as points of alignment between the two groups: "concentration on practice rather than rational discussion, severe self-discipline, rejection of wealth, fame, pleasure, family, social distinction and even respectable clothing." Earlier, Pierre de Labriolle emphasized attitudes toward traditional religion, social ethics and modes of rhetoric as things that made some Christians sympathetic towards the Cynics: "Cynicism made fun of the established religion and its traditional legends, and declared them immoral, absurd, quite unacceptable. It did not even spare the most hallowed of the mysteries. It stood out forcefully against customs and immoralities which the Christians also condemned – for example, exposing infants, homosexuality, and war, too. Add to this the fact that the Cynic preachers didn't shut themselves away in little rooms on their own with a small select audience-they spoke to the masses, putting their teaching across openly in public...this communication in the open air and this freedom of speech were far from displeasing to the Christians." *La réaction païenne : Étude sur la polémique antichrétienne du Ier au VIe siècle* (Paris: L' artisan du Livre, 1934), 84 (trans. Downing, *Cynics and Christian Origins*, 192). Gilles Dorival, "L'image des Cyniques chez les Pères grecs", in *Le Cynisme Ancien*, ed. Goulet-Cazé and Goulet, 442-3, identifies three different attitudes in terms of the reception of Cynicism in the Greek Fathers: a) an identification of Cynicism with Hellenism, which

antiquity. We have already seen the examples of Aelius Aristides and Julian, and it seems that certain attitudes and appearances created the impression that Cynics and Christians shared a number of similar attitudes.[34] We will start our brief analysis of Christian responses to Cynicism with Diogenes, since most scholars today consider him, and not Antisthenes, as the founder of Cynicism, but also because the stories about his life provided more opportunities for commentary, from both Christians and non-Christians alike.

i. Diogenes[35]

The first major feature of the patristic interpretation of Cynicism is that criticism of the Cynics is often paired with praise; this is hardly unique, since, as we have shown in chapter 2, other personalities and philosophical schools from the Greek world could be praised and criticized at the same time.[36] What is surprising about Cynicism is the

---

corresponds to a desire to mark the radical novelty of Christianity; b) a more sensitive approach to the continuity between Hellenism and Christianity, where some Fathers present a positive image of Cynicism, that they see as either an ally in the battle against paganism or even as a preparatory stage for the Christian life; c) an attitude of hesitation and embarrassment, especially towards the more radical aspects of Cynicism. Finally, William Desmond, *Cynics*, 218-9, refers to admiration by Christian writers who saw the Cynics as predecessors of the Gospel: "Their overall criticisms notwithstanding, Christian writers could also express admiration for some aspects of Cynicism, and often in the very treatises that condemned the Cynics as shameless vainglorious atheists. For although the Cynics were "atheists", at least they did not believe in the pagan gods and with their criticism of pagan customs they helped prepare the way for the Gospel ... Perhaps most enduring here is the admiration of Cynic asceticism as quasi-Christian, as if their renunciation of worldly goods such as wealth and power foreshadowed the holy poverty of Jesus and the Apostles."

[34] Hans Dieter-Betz, *Antike und Christentum: Gesammelte Aufsätze IV* (Tübingen: Mohr Siebeck, 1998), 40, comments that "Pagan attacks against Christianity, however, make use of similarities between Christian and Cynic preachers" and that this type of comparison became "a stereotypical anti-Christian propaganda tool, used then also by the Christians themselves against "heretics" like Marcion, the Encratites, and the so-called Apotactites in fourth-century Asia Minor." Cf. Downing, "Cynics and Early Christianity," 285: "Cynicism as a sect seems to have been for the early Christians both a model and an ally, while also a most important rival, having too much in common with the newer movement to be other than disturbing."

[35] The following references provide a small but representative sample of the contours of Diogenes' image in the Church Fathers. For a more detailed discussion, see Krueger, *Symeon the Holy Fool*, 72-89.

[36] For example, John Chrysostom could as easily mock Plato for his failure to establish his republic, as in *In mart. omn.* 15 (trans. Mayer, *Cult of the Saints*, 252), but at the same time praise him when he compares him with Dionysius, the tyrant of Sicily, as in *Adv. opp. vit. mon.* 2.5 (PG 47:339-40). Cf. Derek Krueger, "The Bawdy and Society: The Shamelessness of Diogenes in Roman Imperial Culture," in *The Cynics: The Cynic movement in Antiquity and its Legacy*, eds. Robert Bracht Branham and Marie-Odile Goulet-Cazé (Berkeley, CA: University of California Press, 1997), 225: "Pagans and Christians alike praised Diogenes for his life of voluntary poverty and condemned him for obscenity." Downing, "Cynics and Early Christianity," 302: "[Greek Christian writers] criticise aspects of Cynicism and in

extent of its influence, particularly in the Eastern Church, with both positive and negative attitudes appearing in many different authors and writings. The reason we called it surprising is because one might have thought Cynicism would be long dead by the time the Cappadocians or Chrysostom engaged with its ideas. However, as we saw earlier, this was hardly true, and Cynicism continued to fascinate Christians and non-Christians alike for many centuries. Their commentary proves that even though the Cynics lacked personalities like Diogenes or Crates by that time, their ideas were as strong and influential as ever, and the polemic from both pagans and Christians shows that Cynic ideas must have had quite an influence in at least some segments of the population. One of the main drivers behind the negative attitudes of the Christians is primarily the fact that non-Christian Cynicism could be (and was) a competitor to late antique Christianity in the same way that all other philosophical schools were. In its attempt at self-definition Christianity had to clarify elements that might have seemed all too common to a third-party observer, such as the emphasis on asceticism and freedom, the frankness of speech, the similarities between Cynic street preachers and Paul's preaching in the *agorai* of ancient cities, etc. While certain anecdotes and opinions from the radical Cynic tradition were clearly hard to swallow, at the same time much of the Cynic ethos had "become indigenous" and Cynic attitudes and sayings are still discussed and analysed in the fifth century and beyond, and for as long as Diogenes' sayings formed a large part of the curriculum in late antiquity and Byzantium.[37]

Thus, Gregory of Nazianzus mixes his criticism of Diogenes with praise. The "dog from Sinope" was "simple and moderate in life … not observing laws from God, and not on account of any hope." He only had one thing in his possession, his stick, and lived in a tub to protect himself from the winds, which for him was much more valuable

---

particular Cynics, while still making full use of *chreiai*, maxims, examples and above all the ascetic ethic drawn from Cynic tradition."

[37] Downing, *Cynics and Christian Origins*, 295.

than rooms with golden ceilings. His food was casual, but made without labour (τροφή τε σχέδιος, οὐ πονουμένη).[38]

The influence of the Cynics is also evident in references on the Latin side. Thus, Lactantius eagerly approves of Diogenes' "strict and superior brand of virtue that subjects everything to scorn", but at the same time criticizes him for making a living out of begging instead of engaging in honest trade.[39] He wonders what kind of society there would be if everyone adopted this lifestyle and proceeds to criticize the Cynic custom of performing sexual acts in public. His conclusion is that there is no real virtue in Cynicism since it lacks a sense of shame.[40]

Augustine repeats the criticism of the alleged Cynic support for sexual acts in public view, an idea he attributes to Diogenes.[41] He proudly declares that our "innate sense of decency triumphed over this wild fancy" and is glad that the Cynic successors to Diogenes did not follow his example. Augustine is of the opinion that Diogenes did not really perform the act, but only pretended to do so, and finishes with the remark that the Cynics of his day refuse to do this in case the mob stones them.[42] Augustine's view of the Cynics of his day is in contrast to the opinion of others, such as Julian the Emperor,

---

[38] Gregory Nazianzus, *Carm. mor.* 1.2.10, ll. 218-27 (PG 37:696; trans. Krueger, *Symeon the Holy Fool*, 86). For a discussion of Gregory's Cynicism see Claudio Moreschini, "Gregory Nazianzen and Philosophy, with Remarks on Gregory's Cynicism", trans. Carol Chiodo, in *Re-Reading Gregory of Nazianzus: Essays on History, Theology and Culture*, ed. Christopher Beeley (Washington, D.C: Catholic University of America Press, 2012), 103-24.

[39] Lactantius, *Epit.* 34.4-6 (ed. Heck and Wlosok, 48; trans. R. Dobbin, *The Cynic Philosophers: From Diogenes to Julian*, London: Penguin Books, 2012, 54).

[40] Lactantius was not the first to indicate that Cynicism has no sense of shame. It seems that his source in this case is Cicero, *De off.* 1.41.148 (LCL 30:151): "But the Cynics' whole system of philosophy must be rejected, for it is inimical to moral sensibility, and without moral sensibility nothing can be upright, nothing morally good."

[41] Augustine's reference is better explained in Diogenes Laertius, *Vit. phil.* 6.69 (LCL 185:71), where the following story is told about Diogenes: "It was his habit to do everything in public, the works of Demeter and of Aphrodite alike. He used to draw out the following arguments. "If to breakfast be not absurd, neither is it absurd in the market-place; but to breakfast is not absurd, therefore it is not absurd to breakfast in the marketplace." Behaving indecently in public, he wished "it were as easy to banish hunger by rubbing the belly'." Diogenes' attitude in this incident is also indirectly criticized by Plutarch, whose original target is Chrysippus and his praise of Diogenes for rejecting pleasure in principle but behaving shamelessly in public for the sake of pleasure: *Stoic. rep.* 1044b (LCL 470:501). The accusation is repeated by John Chrysostom, *In Matt. hom.* 33.5 (PG 57:392).

[42] Augustine, *Civ.* 14.20 (LCL 414:368; trans. Dobbin, *The Cynic Philosophers*, 54-55).

that the Cynics of this period were actually significantly worse than the founders of the movement.

In the context of his discussion of Greek philosophers who subjected themselves to voluntary poverty, Origen mentions Diogenes' life in a tub as an example of extreme poverty and claims that no sane person would say that Diogenes was subjected to evils (due to the fact that he lived in a tub).[43] This is one of the passages that shows a neutral stance towards the famous Cynic, with no evident hints of praise or hostility. Epiphanius also displays a neutral attitude towards Diogenes, claiming that he agreed with Antisthenes on everything and approvingly cites his saying that "the good is natural to every wise man but everything else is simply foolishness."[44]

On the other hand, Jerome's stance is overwhelmingly positive. He believes Diogenes to be stronger than Alexander the Great and to have been a "victor over human nature" (*naturae victor humanae*). Diogenes is also the standard of comparison for Christian ascetics and his example is used in an attempt to shame some of them with an example of a "pagan" philosopher famous for his austerity: "I have cited the example of only one philosopher, so that our fine, erect, muscular athletes … who either know nothing of apostolic poverty and the hardness of the cross, or despise it, may at least imitate Gentile moderation."[45] Jerome seems to be a unique case when he uses the example of Diogenes as a measuring stick for the conduct of Christian ascetics. While other Christian writers were not hesitant to point out certain weaknesses in the personalities or attitudes of Christian ascetics, using a "pagan" to embarrass them would require a level of boldness that not many were ready to exhibit. The use of a pagan

---

[43] Origen, *Cels.* 2.41 (SC 132:380; trans. Chadwick, *Contra Celsum*, 98-9). Other philosophers mentioned in the same passage are Democritus, "who allowed his estate to become a pasture for sheep, and about Crates who set himself free by giving to the Thebans the money which he realized by selling all his possessions."

[44] Epiphanius, *De Fide* (=Pan.) 3.2.9 (trans. Frank Williams, *The Panarion of Epiphanius of Salamis, Books II and III. De Fide*, Leiden: Brill, 2012, 666).

[45] Jerome, *Jov.* 2.14 (PL 23:318; NPNF 2-6:398).

philosopher to shame the Christian ascetics so directly is something very different compared to appropriating or using the example of an OT prophet, who would presumably have been a figure of reverence or authority for most Christian ascetics. There are instances of writers such as John Chrysostom using examples from classical literature in order to shame their audience, but in this case most, if not almost all, of the recipients of the message would be regular church members, not ascetics.[46] Finally, even Diogenes' manner of death meets with approval by Jerome, who praises his virtue (*virtutem*) and continence (*continentiam*) and highlights his ultimate battle with fever, which is resolved by his voluntary death.[47]

Basil of Caesarea also offers a more positive appraisal of Diogenes' personality, particularly his simplicity.[48] The story comes from Diogenes Laertius, as per usual: "One day, observing a child drinking out of his hands, he cast away the cup from his wallet with the words, 'A child has beaten me in plainness of living.'" He also threw away his bowl when in like manner he saw a child who had broken his plate taking up his lentils with the hollow part of a morsel of bread."[49] For Basil, the significant part here is that Diogenes is being taught simplicity from a child, which is a positive example in and of itself. This incident leads to Basil's praise for him through the personification of poverty in his *Letter* 4: "As for Diogenes, Basil never ceased admiring him, the philosopher who was so set upon being content with nothing but the gifts of nature that he even threw away his drinking-cup, after he had learned from a boy how to bend over and drink from the hollow of his hands."[50] Furthermore, Basil

---

[46] For an example, as we saw in chapter 2, when discussing certain wrong (in his view) Christian attitudes to death Chrysostom uses three different examples from Greek history in order to highlight true philosophical behaviour in the face of death and the fact that the Greeks do not behave like women: *In Joh. hom.* 62.4 (PG 59:347).

[47] Jerome, *Jov.* 2.14 (PL 23:318).

[48] Cf. Crates' hymn to simplicity in *Anth. Pal.* 10.104 (LCL 85:55): "Hail! divine lady Simplicity, child of glorious Temperance, beloved by good men. All who practise righteousness venerate thy virtue."

[49] Diogenes Laertius, *Vit. phil.* 6.37 (LCL 185:39).

[50] Basil, *Ep. 4 To Olympius* (LCL 190:31).

approvingly cites Diogenes' opinion that "the care of the hair or of dress, is … the mark of men who are either unfortunate or doing wrong."[51]

Interestingly, some of the most famous stories and anecdotes about Diogenes were distorted by Christian (and sometimes pagan) authors and were given an entirely different meaning from that which the original tale may have had. Thus, the story of Diogenes and the lamp in the daytime, where he says he is looking for an honest man,[52] becomes for Theodoret of Cyrus a story of Diogenes having sex in public. In this story, Diogenes is presented as an advocate of philosophy in words but becomes enslaved to pleasure and has sex with prostitutes in public, providing a bad example to the onlookers. When someone scorns him, and asks what he's doing, Diogenes responds by saying "you scum, I am looking for a man."[53] This is not the first or the last Christian effort to deconstruct the austere and ascetic image of Diogenes, which was even proving alluring for writers like Jerome. Its uniqueness, if one can call it that, is that it bases its negative assessment on a story that was clearly invented, whereas other writers, like Chrysostom, tended to criticize Diogenes based on traditions about Diogenes that were commonly accepted as genuine by both Christians and non-Christians.

To summarize the general patristic consensus on Diogenes: while admired by many for certain aspects of his lifestyle as well as his *parrhesia*, his behaviour is also evaluated negatively, specifically his alleged lewd sexual acts. Interestingly, some aspects of the Diogenes tradition have clearly been altered, intentionally or unintentionally, which leads to certain new interpretations (or, perhaps, misinterpretations), such as the aforementioned example from Theodoret. The

---

[51] Basil, *Address to Young Men on Greek Literature* 9.4 (LCL 270:417). Cf. Dudley, *A History of Cynicism*, 207: "St. Basil expressed admiration for Diogenes, whose way of life he regarded as a heathen exemplar of the poor monk." Krueger, "Diogenes the Cynic," 35-6: "With Basil, Diogenes became firmly rooted in a Christian intellectual tradition… Diogenes was good for the care of the soul because it was possible to illustrate appropriate Christian behaviour from the example of Diogenes."

[52] Diogenes Laertius, *Vit. phil.* 6.2.41 (LCL 185:42).

[53] Theodoret, *Aff.* 12.48-9 (SC 57:434).

considerable number of stories about Diogenes' personality and actions enabled patristic writers to strategically reconstruct his image and utilize it according to their purposes. For example, Jerome lavishly praises him but his aim was to use his example as a way of shaming Christian ascetics that failed to emulate even the example of a pagan, whereas Theodoret -even though he praises Crates on one occasion- and others tend to downplay the significance of Diogenes' actions and add that often he was acting as a pervert or that his motives were just an extension of his vainglorious personality. Others -John Chrysostom among them, as we will see- could be critical or positive in different circumstances. As a result, we cannot speak of a clear consensus among patristic authors in regard to how Diogenes was received. The patristic Diogenes, rather, acts as a "mixed" exemplum, supporting at one moment values of poverty and self-renunciation, at another, going against the virtue of modesty.[54]

ii. Antisthenes

Like Diogenes, Antisthenes,[55] who was considered by many as the founder of Cynicism in antiquity, is praised by Jerome in his *Adversus Jovinianum*. He is credited as a teacher of rhetoric and student of Socrates and commended for selling and dispensing with all his belongings except for a small cloak.[56] Antisthenes is also praised by Gregory of Nazianzus who calls him μέγας (great) because of a story where someone thrashed Antisthenes' face. His response was solely to write the beater's name

---

[54] Krueger, "Diogenes the Cynic," 31: "Christians' manipulation of Diogenes' meaning was part of their synthesis of the cultural legacy of the pagan past."

[55] I am aware that many scholars of Cynicism do not consider Antisthenes as the founder of the movement, crediting Diogenes instead. For the purposes of this chapter I will include Antisthenes among the Cynics because most of the ancient sources I refer to do so as well, including some early Christian sources.

[56] Jerome, *Jov.* 2.14 (PL 23:318). Jerome has clearly mistaken Crates' dispersal of his wealth with Antisthenes. See Diogenes Laertius, *Vit. phil.* 6.87 (LCL 185:90). Among other things, Downing (*Cynics and Christian Origins*, 237) lists the following points as instances of Jerome advocating ideals which were also central in Cynicism: objection to reliance on high birth and desire for fame, the fact that wealth might be ill-gotten, and the fact that "men and women are equally fallible, and we should judge people's virtue not by their sex but by their character."

on his forehead, in order to make plain who was responsible for beating him.[57] Clement of Alexandria[58] and Theodoret of Cyrus[59] both approvingly cite Antisthenes' view that humility is the ultimate end in life.

Origen names Antisthenes together with Crates and Diogenes as part of a Cynic trio in a passage from *Contra Celsum* where he discusses the gift of prophecy among the Prophets of the Old Testament. The Cynics' lives are said to have been "of unexampled courage and freedom ... And reason demands that the prophets of the supreme God should be such people. They make the courage of Antisthenes, Crates, and Diogenes appear as child's play."[60] Again, this is a comment that mixes praise with criticism and it is important that it appears in an apologetic text. Origen does admit that the Cynics were courageous; but when compared to the Prophets, their courage is simply a childish version of the prophetic one.

Theodoret uses the example of the same Cynic trio, but instead of comparing them with the prophets, like Origen, he compares them to the Stoics. Theodoret accuses the Cynics of κενοδοξία and contrasts Antisthenes, Diogenes and Crates' vainglory to the mindset of the Stoics, who do the good for its own sake and not for the sake of their δόξα.[61] This is a rare occurrence where a Christian writer explicitly states his preference for one "pagan" philosophical school over another. The Christian preoccupation with the Cynics' vainglory might be explained by the fact that it also appears as a criticism in non-Christian sources. Thus, Diogenes Laertius tells the story of a crowd where some were giving Diogenes a "thorough drenching" while others took pity on him. Plato was also there, and told those who pitied him that if they really felt

---

[57] Gregory Nazianzen, *Or.* 4.72 (PG 35:596).

[58] Clement, *Strom.* 2.21.130 (GCS 52:184).

[59] Theodoret, *Aff.* 11.8 (SC 57:393–94).

[60] Origen, *Cels.* 7.7 (SC 150:30; trans. Chadwick, *Contra Celsum*, 400).

[61] Theodoret, *Aff.* 12.32 (SC 57:429).

pity for him they should move away, "alluding to his vanity" (ἐνδεικνύμενος φιλοδοξίαν αὐτοῦ). [62]

iii. Crates

We will conclude our section on the Christian reception of the founders of Cynicism with Crates of Thebes, a student of Diogenes and teacher of Zeno of Citium. Crates was famous for dispersing his wealth and being one of the few (to our knowledge) married Cynics. His wife was Ipparchia, daughter of his student Metrocles and a follower of Cynicism in her own right. As we will see, this marriage became the subject of criticism from Christian writers. Yet Crates is particularly praised by Gregory of Nazianzus, who says the following in *Oration* 4: "Crates is a great man with you [the Greeks]; and certainly it was philosophic conduct for a sheep-farmer to have cast away his fortune - conduct quite like that of our own philosophers."[63] Gregory believes that the reason Crates cast away his fortune was because he considered it a maidservant to vice and to bodily needs (κακίας ὑπηρέτιν καὶ σωμάτων).[64] His description of the famous story of Crates giving away his wealth is fascinating and has led some scholars to consider certain parts of Crates' poem as it appears in Gregory's work to be passages from Crates' lost works.[65] Here is how he narrates it: Crates is in Olympia, in a place above the shrine. He stands there and shouts: "Crates from Thebes is freeing Crates (Ἐλευθεροῖ Κράτητα Θηβαῖον Κράτης)." Gregory's interpretation of this action is that Crates did it because he knew well that to be bound by material things is a form of slavery.[66]

---

[62] Diogenes Laertius, *Vit. phil.* 6.41 (LCL 185:42-3).

[63] Gregory Nazianzen, *Or.* 4.72 (PG 35:596; *Julian the Emperor*, trans. Charles William King, London, 1888, 42).

[64] Gregory Nazianzen, *Carm. mor.* 1.2.10, II. 230 (PG 37:697).

[65] For further information, see Skouteropoulos, *Οι Αρχαίοι Κυνικοί*, 501.

[66] Gregory Nazianzen, *Carm. mor.* 1.2.10, II. 228-243 (PG 37:697). As with other Christian writers, Gregory was not hesitant to condemn other aspects of Cynicism he found unacceptable. See Moreschini, "Gregory Nazianzen and Philosophy," 106-107. Furthermore, and in agreement with Julian, he rejected

We should note that although Crates was famous for dispensing with his property, there are different accounts of how he did it. In Gregory's account, he is in a shrine in Olympia while according to Chrysostom, as we will see later, he dumps it in the sea, a difference that can be explained by the use of different literary sources. Either way, our focus in both cases should be the action itself and not the manner in which it happened. Origen praised Crates, similarly to Gregory. Epiphanius also cites with approval Crates' *chreia* that "poverty is liberty."[67]

Crates' abandonment of his wealth was not always seen in a positive light. In the context of his interpretation of Jesus' admonition to the rich young man to sell his possessions, Clement of Alexandria argues that "the renunciation of wealth and the bestowment of it on the poor or needy" was nothing new. On the contrary, "many did so before the Saviour's advent, —some because of the leisure (thereby obtained) for learning, and on account of a dead wisdom; and others for empty fame and vainglory, as the Anaxagorases, the Democriti, and the Crateses."[68] The accusation again seems to be that these were the right actions but performed for the wrong reasons and motives, namely fame and vainglory, and all in service of a dead wisdom.

Moreover, it was Crates' marriage to Ipparchia that seemed to annoy many Christians, particularly because they believed the stories about the couple's public intercourse. Thus, Theodoret accuses Crates of "surrendering to passion" and performing "the Cynic wedding in public" (κυνογάμια, literally a dog's wedding, is probably a euphemism for the Cynics' alleged tendencies for public sex).[69] Nevertheless, Theodoret's attitude towards Crates, as is usually the case with other

---

his contemporary Cynics for not living up to the ideals of the great founders of the movement. See Krueger, "Diogenes the Cynic," 41-2.

[67] ἔλεγεν ἐλευθερίαν εἶναι τὴν ἀκτημοσύνην. Epiphanius, *De Fide* 3.2.9 (GCS 37:507).

[68] Clement, *Quis div.* 11.3-4 (GCS 17:166-7; ANF 2:594).

[69] Theodoret, *Aff.* 12.49 (SC 57:434). Cf. a similar reference to Ipparchia in an extensive catalogue of ancient Greek women philosophers and poets in Clement of Alexandria, *Strom.* 4.19.121 (GCS 17:302). This is yet another example of Theodoret using a real event (the marriage of Crates and Ipparchia) and interpreting it in a way that would appear shameful for the Cynics.

Christian writers and their attitude towards the Cynics, is an ambivalent one. In another instance, he wholeheartedly approves Crates' love for virtue and quotes his dictum "Those, unenslaved and unbended by servile pleasure, love the immortal kingdom and freedom."[70]

iv. Ambivalence and Assimilation

The common fight for the ideals of freedom, poverty, asceticism, as well as a radical critique of traditional religious practices often united Cynics and Christians in an ideological alliance that might have been unthinkable otherwise, considering the different roots of each movement. The fact that the Christians often held an ambivalent position towards the figures of Cynicism and their ideas is significant, not only for understanding the reception (and eclecticism) of Greek moral philosophy in early Christian thought, but also for highlighting the complexity of Christian utilisations of "pagan" exempla. Although this ambivalence to the Cynics is not very different to the attitude shown to other philosophical schools, significantly less scholarship has been devoted to this issue. This is not to suggest that one could be a Cynic and a Christian at the same time, just as one could not *strictly* be a Stoic or Platonist Christian.[71] Despite Christianity's animosity towards split allegiances, one could easily assimilate ideals from the Greek philosophical schools without having to claim to be a disciple of Plato or Diogenes, and, as we have already seen, philosophical eclecticism was the norm among patristic authors.

Modern scholars have also criticized the Cynics for being overly negative reactionaries who principally criticized people for their vices and constantly attacked

---

[70] Theodoret, *Aff.* 12.49 (SC 57:434.13–14). It seems that Theodoret's source for this saying is Clement of Alexandria, *Strom.* 2.20.121, and we cite this translation because the Greek text is identical (GCS 17:179; ANF 2:373).

[71] Downing, *Cynics and Christian Origins*, 177: "One could not 'be' a Stoic, maintaining a Stoic pantheism and be a Christian, or a Platonist, holding to a doctrine of the transmigration of souls, and be a Christian. And, similarly- strictly analogously- one could not be a Cynic in the most rigorous and 'shameless' tradition of Diogenes, and also a Christian."

various political and social institutions.[72] The issue at heart in this appraisal is not the practice of criticising others itself but rather the Cynics' failure to offer positive role models. Even when they did offer positive examples, it was their own exclusive model that was recommended and their way of life that others were directed to follow and nothing else. Diogenes was their hero not because he was their founder but because he was the most radical exponent of their principles. The Christians often shared the sentiment that their way of life was the only one considered worthy. But they also offered a variety of positive role models in their criticisms of people or political institutions -Christ himself, the Apostles, martyrs and saints- as well as models of social experimentation, such as the first Christian community in Jerusalem as described in Acts.

c. John Chrysostom on the Cynics

A substantial number of references to Cynicism occur in Chrysostom's works, and in this section both his criticisms against and his occasional praises of Cynic philosophers will be investigated. Chrysostom does not usually refer to the Cynics by name except for Diogenes. When he mentions Cynics without a reference to Diogenes he is usually referring to contemporary Cynics. In both cases, it is the vainglory of the Cynics that becomes the main subject of criticism.[73]

---

[72] See Margarethe Billerbeck, "Greek Cynicism in Imperial Rome," in *Die Kyniker in der modernen Forschung: Aufsätze mit Einführung und Bibliographie*, ed. Margarethe Billerbeck (Amsterdam: B.R. Grüner, 1991), 150. Others have focused on the fact that later Cynics seemed to adapt the name in order to justify certain behaviours. For this view see Eduard Zeller, *Outlines of the History of Greek Philosophy*, 13th ed., rev. Wilhem Nestle, trans. L.R. Palmer (London: Routledge & Kegan, 1963), 273: "Even in the best of its representatives Cynicism was not free from many excesses and it served not a few as a mere pretext for a life of idleness and parasitism, immorality and the gratification of vanity by an attitude of boastful ostentation." Many of these criticisms have already been pronounced by Chrysostom, as we will see below.

[73] John also included Crates and Diogenes in another list of Greek philosophers that were in his opinion "obsessed (ἐμμανεῖς)" with glory, i.e. attention seekers. The other philosophers named are Epaminondas, Aristides and Socrates: *Ad vid. iun.* 6 (SC 138:146-8). In her translation of *De Bab. c. Iul. et gent.* (*Apologist*, 100), Margaret Schatkin notes: "Chrysostom frequently states that the passion for glory was the motive for all the amazing deeds of the philosophers."

i. Criticism against Diogenes (and Crates): Vainglory, perversion, and uselessness

In Chrysostom's *Homilies on 1 Corinthians*, we find the Cynics contrasted to the Apostles, whose "motive of all they did" was "not vainglory but benevolence" (οὐ διὰ κενοδοξίαν, ἀλλὰ διὰ φιλανθρωπίαν ἅπαντα ἔπραττον).[74] The Cynics are called enemies of our common nature, and certain of their actions are severely criticized. Crates (whom he calls a madman, but does not mention by name) is the first example John adduces, mentioning Crates' act of throwing all of his property in the sea, not for any good reason but because of his φιλοτιμία.[75] This is in contrast to the apostolic attitude of receiving everything that was given to them and then giving it for free to the poor. The key criticism seems to be about why things are done, and not what these things/actions are. Crates squanders his property to no benefit and is thus of no profit to others.

The second example is Diogenes who, clothed in rags and living in a barrel, "astonished many, but profited none (ἐξέπληξε μὲν πολλούς, ὠφέλησε δὲ οὐδένα)."[76] There is nothing to admire in Diogenes, John says, since the way of life he modelled failed to engender virtue in others. This is in contrast to Paul's behaviour, who did not wish for anyone's φιλοτιμία but wore proper, decent clothes and lived in a house like most people. What John stresses here is Paul's conventionality, in contrast to Diogenes' unconventional lifestyle, which did not prevent Paul from living a perfectly virtuous life. Diogenes sneered at such behaviour while at the same time he shamed himself in

---

[74] *In 1 Cor. hom.* 35.4 (PG 61:301; NPNF 1-12:212). Krueger, "Diogenes the Cynic," 39: "For Chrysostom, the notion that Diogenes had been motivated by δόξα was sufficient grounds to condemn him." Chrysostom could have possibly inferred this as fact by looking at the pseudonymous Cynic epistles where ps-Crates (*Epistle 8 To Diogenes*, trans. Ronald F. Hock, *The Cynic Epistles*, 59) admits as much: "We are indeed free from wealth, but fame (δόξα) has up to this point not yet released us from bondage to her..." According to Malherbe, *The Cynic Epistles*, 10, the "Crates letters are to be dated at the earliest in the first or second century A.D." However, in the letters of Ps-Diogenes, which are earlier than the Crates letters, Diogenes proclaims himself "free from popular opinion (δόξα)" and "living not in conformity with popular opinion but according to nature...", *Epistle 7 To Hicetas* (trans. Benjamin Fiore, *The Cynic Epistles*, 99).

[75] *In Act. apost. hom.* 7.1 (PG 60:64) is another reference to the same story, but again without referring to Crates by name. John also mentions other philosophers who gave up their land, and in this case attributes their actions not to real contempt of wealth, but to folly and madness (μωρία καὶ ἄνοια)!

[76] *In 1 Cor. hom.* 35.4 (PG 61:302; NPNF 1-12:212).

public -probably another reference to his public sexual performances- "dragged away by his mad passion for glory" (ὑπὸ τῆς περὶ τὴν δόξαν μανίας συρόμενος). John concludes by saying that the only reason Diogenes lived in a barrel was his κενοδοξία.[77] It appears that the main difference between Christians, such as Paul or the monks, and the Cynics is in this case their relationality to other humans and the outcome of their actions. John is obviously of the opinion that the former's actions had a positive impact on those around them, whereas the Cynics' outrageous actions, even if they initially appear pure and genuine, profited none other than themselves.

Just like Augustine, John also accuses Diogenes of acts of public indecency and of behaviour contrary to nature. In his thirty-third *Homily on Matthew* John refers to the Cynics as mere outcasts (Κυνικὰ καθάρματα) who "have all passed by like a dream and a shadow."[78] This part of the text is preceded by a series of rhetorical questions about Plato, Pythagoras, and the Stoics, indicating how they have ultimately failed in their enterprises. This is followed by an ironic declaration about how these philosophers became glorious. Among the examples mentioned, he refers to the Athenians making a public monument to the epistles of Plato, and to philosophers passing all their time at ease and being wealthy (the example of this being Aristippus who used to purchase costly harlots). Chrysostom saves the final mention for the philosopher "of Sinope" who ... "even behaved himself unseemly in the market place."[79] As is usually the case with Chrysostom's references to Greeks, the reason he mentions all these is to contrast them to opposite Christian attitudes: "but there is no such thing here, but a strict temperance (σωφροσύνη), and a perfect decency (κοσμιότης), and a war against the whole world on behalf of truth and godliness."[80]

---

[77] Ibid. (PG 61:301-2; NPNF 1-12:212).

[78] *In Matt. hom.* 33.4 (PG 57:392; NPNF 1-10:217).

[79] Ibid.

[80] Ibid.

Besides Paul, Diogenes is also compared, in John's *Discourse on Blessed Babylas*, to the bishop and martyr Babylas.[81] What Babylas demonstrated with his life was that "the philosophers, of whom they boast, are characterized by vainglory, impudence, and puerility."[82] The argumentation is very similar to the *synkrisis* between Diogenes and Paul: Babylas did not live in a wine cask, nor was he clothed in rags. John realizes that for some people Diogenes' actions might seem astounding, involving much labor and pain, which he is willing to admit. But what he also admits is that whatever Diogenes did was without praise, since "useless labor is deprived of any encomium."[83] Diogenes, just like Crates, did not benefit the poor through his actions, or anyone else for that matter. The feats of Diogenes are further downplayed when Chrysostom refers to men (i.e. circus performers) who eat pointed and sharpened nails or chew up and devour sandals and says that these phenomena are much more impressive than the wine cask and rags.[84]

We have already mentioned the comparison between Babylas and Diogenes in the previous chapter, and we would argue again that what the examples of Paul and Babylas demonstrate, and the point we believe John is trying to make with this *synkrisis*, is a contrast between Greek parasitism and Christian usefulness. In addition, Diogenes serves rhetorically to condemn all Greek philosophy by the use of an *a fortiori* argument.[85] If Diogenes, who was generally admired by all philosophical schools, was found wanting, then all other philosophers were as well. Whilst Chrysostom calls Plato "the chief of their philosophers", his frequent references to Diogenes show that he was

---

[81] Which Dorival, "L' Image," 423, called "the most vigorous denunciation of Cynicism" in John's corpus.

[82] *De Bab. c. Iul. et gent.* 45.1-3 (SC 362:146; trans. Schatkin, *Apologist*, 100).

[83] *De Bab. c. Iul. et gent.* 45.11 (SC 362:148; trans. Schatkin, *Apologist*, 101).

[84] *De Bab. c. Iul. et gent.* 45.12-18 (SC 362:148).

[85] Krueger, "Diogenes the Cynic," 37: "the value of Diogenes as a model of moral behavior was part of the larger debate between pagans and Christians in the second half of the fourth century over which community was the legitimate heir of Greco-Roman educational and philosophical traditions."

as equally, and even possibly more, admired as Plato, although for different reasons. We also saw the conclusions Chrysostom draws from the story of Diogenes meeting Alexander: Diogenes' request was useless and selfish and his frankness was of benefit to no one.

If we were to summarize John's critique of Cynicism as personified in Diogenes, we could say that it fits all four main categories of patristic Christian criticisms against the Cynics as established by Gilles Dorival: Cynic "indifference, uselessness, hypocrisy and perversion, and vainglory."[86] As we have already seen, similar criticism has already been used by pagan opponents of the Cynics, and thus far Chrysostom is conforming to a common trope. Nevertheless, the fact that, along with Plato, Diogenes was the one philosopher whom Chrysostom repeatedly attempted to discredit by reinterpreting the motivations behind his behaviour might have another explanation: "Chrysostom is specifically interested in discrediting this pagan exemplar who most seems to embody Christian ideals."[87]

ii. Praising Diogenes: A re-evaluation of kingship

However, John praises Diogenes elsewhere as a philosopher who is wealthier than all the kings, despite being clothed with rags, and as someone so important that King Alexander of Macedon abandoned his expedition against the Persians when he saw him and went to ask him if he needed anything, to which Diogenes gave no response.[88] There are two closely connected ideas at play here: wealth and power. Cynics and Christians shared a re-evaluation of the idea of kingship in their various comparisons

---

[86] Dorival, "L'image," 431-2. However, I do not agree with Dorival that Cynicism was the primary Greek adversary for Christians and that when they attack Greek philosophy they primarily attack the Cynics. In John Chrysostom's case, at least, Plato is attacked much more frequently than Diogenes when it comes to philosophers from the Classical period.

[87] Krueger, "Diogenes the Cynic," 39.

[88] *Adv. opp. vit. mon.* 2.5 (PG 47:339).

between the king and the ascetic philosopher/monk respectively.[89] The Cynic idea basically comes down to the point that "only the ascetic philosopher is really a king, since only he is independent and capable of guiding other people."[90] John claims with approval that Alexander the Great was also eager to provide Diogenes with everything in order to be able to touch his (spiritual) wealth. [91] It seems that the reception of Diogenes in John's writings is more faithful to the Diogenes literary tradition than Julian's or Epictetus', who tended to refer to the previous literary tradition and expand it with ideas that could hardly be applicable to the historical Diogenes, and were also keen to emphasize certain features that are not particularly highlighted in literary references to Diogenes as they survive today.[92] It may, of course, be the case that Julian, Epictetus, or even John Chrysostom, had access to a greater range of sources than we have today at our disposal. Without being able to verify this, what appears to be original in John's image of Diogenes is his *interpretation* of Diogenes' attitudes, particularly his discussion of the usefulness of Diogenes' actions. His reconstruction of Diogenes can be either positive or negative, based on the requirements of his argument.

---

[89] Modern scholarship has identified other similarities as well: "The Cynic ascetic was a predecessor of the monk in more than one way, but particularly in his role as a moral educator of humankind, whose moral instruction presupposes a) knowledge of virtue, b) following his moral principles, c) self-education and self-discipline." Billerbeck, "Greek Cynicism," 162.

[90] Billerbeck, "Greek Cynicism," 152. It is not the only idea that has been identified as pronounced by the Cynics and later emphasized in Christian thought. Another example is the total renunciation of material possessions, "and in advancing as a prime motive for doing so the opportunity which it provided for the contemplation of real and lasting values," which could be achieved primarily through the practice of *autarkeia*. See A.R. Hands, *Charities and Social Aid in Greece and Rome* (London: Thames and Hudson, 1968), 76.

[91] *Adv. opp. vit. mon.* 2.4 (PG 47:335; trans. Hunter, *A Comparison*, 103): "How much money do you think Alexander would have given to Diogenes, if Diogenes had wished to accept it? But he did not wish to. But Alexander tried hard and did everything so as to be able to approach the wealth of Diogenes." John used the example of Diogenes here to show that there was a precedent for the monks' contempt of wealth. Cf. Krueger, "Diogenes the Cynic," 38: "Chrysostom's invocation of Diogenes in defence of monasticism needs to be considered in light of the considerable suspicion against asceticism among Christian elites."

[92] For the biases Julian brought to his assessment of the Cynics, see Abraham Malherbe, "Self-Definition among Epicureans and Cynics," in *Jewish and Christian Self-Definition vol. 3: Self-Definition in the Greco-Roman World*, eds. Ben F. Meyer and E.P. Sanders (Philadelphia, PA: Fortress Press, 1983), 58: "His own austerity, susceptibility to religious mysticism, constant seeking for divine guidance, and the polemical nature of his addresses on the Cynics colour his views to an inordinate degree."

While Diogenes seems to have been the only Cynic who was singled out individually, there are other references to the Cynics in John's writings where they are criticized as a group. Thus, when talking about the riots in 387 in Antioch, he draws an unfavourable contrast between the attitudes of what appears to be Cynic philosophers and the monks during the crisis:

> Now where are those wearing threadbare cloaks, sporting a long beard, and carrying a staff in their right hands- the pagan philosophers, canine outcasts who are more miserable than dogs under the table and do everything for the sake of their stomachs? At that time, they all left the city, they all leapt away, and hid in caves. It was only the ones who by their actions had truly demonstrated wisdom who appeared so fearlessly in the market-place, as if no adversity had overtaken the city. While the inhabitants of the cities fled to the mountains and the deserts, the citizens of the desert rushed to the city, showing by their actions what on previous days I haven't stopped talking about, namely that not even a furnace will be able to harm in any way the person who lives a virtuous life.[93]

Here the phrase Κυνικά καθάρματα appears for a second time, but, in this instance, instead of the old Cynics passing as a dream and a shadow, their contemporaries also prove themselves worthless of their title as philosophers. Only the monks manifested themselves as real lovers of wisdom, proper philosophers, who were not afraid to show their virtue with their deeds, when they showed up in the city at the moment when everyone else, including the pagan philosophers, was leaving. The courage the monks displayed, in contradistinction to the cowardice of the so-called philosophers, shows that they are the truly manly philosophers who manifest their love of wisdom in direct correlation with their actions. We cannot be absolutely certain that many or most contemporary philosophers in Antioch John refers to were Cynics. But even if that was not the case, we can hypothesize that he chose to mention them over others due to Cynicism's alleged bravery when confronting rulers -as in the example of Diogenes with Alexander- and the contemporary Cynics' failure to emulate that attitude.

---

[93] *De stat.* 17.5 (PG 49:173; trans. Mayer and Allen, *John Chrysostom*, 108). John explicitly mentions the Cynics, but this is not obvious from the translation.

Another reference to the Cynics occurs in Chrysostom's *Homilies on Matthew*, where all Greek philosophers are accused of wanting to emulate the shamelessness of the Cynics, without understanding that there is no point living in a tub if one is profligate at the same time. This is both an indirect reference to popular stories about Diogenes and also a point against him when compared to John the Baptist, who is the main character of this homily. John's life represents the exact opposite of the Greek philosophers' lifestyle: "showing forth all strictness of self-restraint" (πᾶσαν ἀκριβῆ φιλοσοφίαν ἐπιδεικνύμενος), "being a champion of godliness" (ἀθλητὴς εὐσεβείας ὤν), "and a philosopher of that philosophy which is worthy of the heavens" (καὶ φιλόσοφος τῆς τῶν οὐρανῶν ἀξίας φιλοσοφίας).[94] Chrysostom's point should be clear by now: despite the fact that some might hesitate to call the monks or John the Baptist "philosophers" in the usual sense of the word, their life and deeds prove them to be the only ones worthy of the name - and in fact they demonstrate a *more* precise example of philosophy.

iv. Summing up Chrysostom on the Cynics

These are not the only references to Cynics in John's writings. However, they are representative of John's overall view. What we should keep in mind is that, besides the obvious references, there are also instances where Chrysostom introduces Cynicism (or apparent allusions to Cynicism) in a context which seemingly refers to something else. Thus, Chrysostom's interpretation of the story of the Syro-Phoenician woman (Matthew 15:21-28), particularly in his fifty second *Homily on Matthew*, is filled with a number of common Cynic *topoi*, including *anaideia, parrhesia, and karteria,* and presents the woman as a (Cynic?) philosopher in her own right, which in this case is a title of praise.[95] In many respects, then, John's critique of Cynicism has two aspects. The first

---

[94] *In Matt. hom.* 10.4 (PG 57:188; NPNF 1-10:62).

[95] *In Matt. hom.* 52 (PG 58:518-521). For a fuller discussion of the patristic interpretation of the story and the image of the woman as a Cynic philosopher see Downing, "Cynics and Early Christianity," 302.

is his criticism of the older Cynics, which resembles critiques from the earlier Christian literary tradition. Here his main contribution is a series of comparative portraits where individual Christians such as Paul, Babylas, and John the Baptist are compared to Diogenes. The second is his criticism of contemporary Cynics, which resembles Julian's critique minus the idolizing of Diogenes, and focuses on the Cynics' attitude in the aftermath of the riots. Finally, in terms of his praise of Diogenes, although it was limited compared to Basil or Jerome, it is still an indication that he could find positive attributes in individuals from the pagan world, even if he is harsh in his condemnation of them on other occasions.[96]

d. *Autarkeia* in the Thought of John Chrysostom

From consideration of Chrysostom's reception of the Cynics, we now turn to his reception of Cynic ideas. Before it became one of the most important ideas in the history of Greek philosophy, *autarkeia* (self-sufficiency) was primarily a political ideal related to the life of the *polis* in antiquity.[97] But the concept rose to particular prominence when applied "to the individual life, to the divine and to the cosmos as a whole."[98] Glenn Most has shown that there is a certain degree of continuity from the self-sufficient *oikos* of the Homeric poems to the Aristotelian conception of the self-sufficient *polis* as the ideal society, which concludes with Aristotle's claim that humans,

---

[96] Krueger's explanation of what some might consider as lack of consistency is still unparalleled: "We can make the general observation that Late Ancient Christians cited Diogenes positively to support their arguments in favor of the life of poverty and self-control, and negatively to argue against surrendering to passion and lust. However, Christian lack of consistency with regard to Diogenes should not be surprising. Christians presented a varied picture of Diogenes because they had received a varied picture. The πρόσωπον of Diogenes was a composite of asceticism and shamelessness. The variety of ways in which Christians employed the *chreiai* attributed to Diogenes reflected the diversity within the figure of Diogenes which the chreiai preserved." "Diogenes the Cynic," 44.

[97] Thus, "a state [*polis*] comes into being since each of us is not independent, but actually needs the support of many people," Plato, *Rep.* 2.369b (LCL 237:161). See also Marcus Wheeler, "Self-Sufficiency and the Greek City," *Journal of the History of Ideas* 16.3 (1955), 416-20.

[98] Desmond, *Cynics*, 172. Glenn Most has defined it as "independence of external needs and freedom from external compulsion." Glenn Most, "The Stranger's Stratagem: Self-Disclosure and Self-Sufficiency in Greek Culture," *Journal of Hellenic Studies* 109 (1989), 127.

unlike the gods and the animals, cannot be entirely self-sufficient.[99] On the level of the individual person, *autarkeia* is an ethical ideal, something that one strives for, and its personification in Greek philosophy is the divine itself. Thus, for Diogenes, the richest man is the one who is self-sufficient. Starting with Diogenes,[100] then, self-sufficiency became one of the fundamental principles of Cynicism and an ideal that would later be favourably received in the Christian tradition.

i. Cynic autarkeia

There are three characteristics of *autarkeia* that are of particular significance to the comparison between Cynic and Christian virtues. First, *autarkeia* functions on two levels in Cynicism: one is its physical aspect, where someone is content with "the bare necessities of life." There is also a spiritual aspect: "complete detachment from the world and worldly values."[101] On the physical level, getting rid of superfluous things and reducing needs to an absolute minimum was the proper path to *autarkeia,* while on the spiritual level the possession of virtue was all that was required for happiness. The most rigid form of *autarkeia* recognized no value in the things that the majority seem to value the most, including wealth, pleasure, knowledge, and friendship, which a Cynic sometimes regarded as unnecessary luxuries. In other words, "nothing…that was to be derived from any source external to himself had any value for him or could affect him in any way."[102] Diogenes even gave up sexual intercourse to emulate Pan, thus renouncing what others thought of as most necessary.[103] While the Cynic conception of

---

[99] Most, "The Stranger's Stratagem," 128 with references to numerous ancient texts on *autarkeia.*

[100] Although there are already references to Antisthenes in Xenophon, *Symp.* 4.35-44 (LCL 168.610-14).

[101] Audrey N. M. Rich, "The Cynic Conception of AYTAPKEIA," in *Die Kyniker in der modernen Forschung: Aufsätze mit Einführung und Bibliographie,* ed. Margarethe Billerbeck (Amsterdam: B.R. Grüner, 1991), 233. The description of *autarkeia* in the next two paragraphs is indebted to this article.

[102] Ibid.

[103] Dio Chrysostom, *Tyr.* 17-20 (LCL 257:259-61).

autarkeia would soften over time, the original version was the one considered to be characteristically and genuinely Cynic.

While the phrase "less is more" is first found in Robert Browning's poem "Andrea del Sarto (called 'The Faultless Painter')", the idea behind it has definitive Cynic roots. If you have little, you have little to lose, and if you desire nothing, you cannot be disappointed by anything. Cynicism is by and large a philosophy of zero expectations and just enough possessions to avoid death. Being self-sufficient allows the Cynic to operate on two levels: on the one hand his life resembles that of an animal and its very limited needs, or, in the words of Epictetus, every animal "is sufficient to himself, and lacks neither its own proper food nor that way of life which is appropriate to it and in harmony with nature."[104] However, the Cynic also operates on another, higher level: that of the divinity, who is entirely self-sufficient or as Diogenes put it, "it was the privilege of the gods to need nothing and of god-like men to want but little."[105] This paradox, the fact that the "αὐτάρκης is sub-human in so far as he descends to the animal level, super-human in so far as he approximates to the divine,"[106] was simultaneously a point of pride for the Cynics and a weapon in the hands of their opponents, who would often equate them with irrational animals. Even Diogenes' legendary meeting with Alexander is a paradigmatic case of *autarkeia*: Diogenes needs nothing, even from someone like Alexander.

Secondly, the original idea of solitary autarkeia would later be crucial in the development of Christian monasticism, and it was exactly the ascetic tendencies of Cynicism expressed in ideas such as *autarkeia* that were influential in Christian

---

[104] Epictetus, *Diss.* 1.9.9 (LCL 131:65). Cf. Dio Chrysostom, *Serv.* 10.16 (LCL 257:429): "Consider the beasts yonder and the birds, how much freer from trouble they live than men, and how much more happily also, this much healthier and stronger they are, and how each of them lives the longest life possible, although they have neither hands nor human intelligence. And yet, to counter-balance these and their other limitations, they have one very great blessing — they own no property."

[105] Diogenes Laertius, *Vit. phil.* 6.104 (LCL 185:109).

[106] Rich, "The Cynic Conception," 234.

rhetoric. However, the reason we have chosen to use *autarkeia* instead of "self-sufficiency" throughout this brief exposition is because "self-sufficiency" is inadequate for signifying all the nuances of the Greek term and, additionally, has negative connotations. As Doyne Dawson has argued, *autarkeia* also signifies "spontaneity" and a sense of freedom that comes both from helping others and through askesis.[107] It can therefore be a communal, as well as an individual, concept. As it relates to the life of the individual, *autarkeia* often serves as a defence mechanism "against the vicissitudes of life and the fickleness of fate."[108]

Thirdly, while *autarkeia* was not the central Cynic value, it was essential for proceeding to the two essential virtues, freedom and *parrhesia*.[109] The Cynic ideal of *autarkeia* would later influence other philosophical schools and their related concepts, such as the Stoic and Sceptic *apatheia* or the Epicurean *ataraxia*.[110] It also influenced a number of Christian authors, John Chrysostom among them, and it is this influence we will attempt to trace in what follows.

ii. Chrysostom on Christian autarkeia

Chrysostom's definition of *autarkeia* is very close to that of the Cynics: he defines it as "the using [of] those things which it is impossible to live without. I say food, not feasting; raiment, not ornament."[111] If humans simply asked just for food and shelter,

---

[107] Doyne Dawson, *Cities of God: Communist Utopias in Greek Thought* (Oxford: Oxford University Press, 1992), 145-46.

[108] Philip Bosman, "Ancient debates on autarkeia and our global impasse," *Phronimon* 16.1 (2015), 13.

[109] Robert Bracht Branham, "Defacing the Currency: Diogenes' Rhetoric and the Invention of Cynicism," in *The Cynics*, ed. Branham and Goulet-Caze, 97: "[For the Cynics] *Autarkeia* ("self-sufficiency") is a desideratum, but freedom is imperative." Different scholars have made various propositions as to what was the core idea that best sums up Cynicism. *Autarkeia* has been one of them, along with negative freedom, *askesis*, and critique of wealth. For the scholars representing each of these views see Desmond, *Cynics*, 245.

[110] Desmond, *The Greek Praise of Poverty*, 171.

[111] τροφὴν, οὐ τρυφὴν λέγω· σκεπάσματα, οὐ καλλωπίσματα. The wordplay is somewhat lost in the translation. *In 2 Cor. hom.* 19.3 (PG 61:534).

then they would be able to obtain much more than that.[112] The one who does not desire what others possess, but is satisfied with what they have, is the wealthiest of all.[113] However, this limitation of desire only applies to earthly things. "In heavenly things let our desire of more never be satiated, but let each be ever coveting more. But upon earth let everyone desire only what is needful and sufficient, and seek nothing more."[114] At the same time, being *autarkēs* does not mean that one cannot enjoy things but rather that one should enjoy everything in moderation.[115] *Autarkeia* is thus connected with certain practices that allow it to flourish. They include disregarding fancy clothing and excessive care of the body, focusing instead on caring for the soul and dressing it with virtue. As for the Cynics, primary examples of *autarkeia* are the animals, which do not exceed their limits whether they eat or drink. Chrysostom regrets that some humans have become worse than dogs and asses and always overcome the boundaries of moderation.[116] But *autarkeia* is not an end in itself. On the contrary, it leads to all things that make human life better: pleasure, health, ease of mind, freedom, vigour of body, sobriety and alertness of mind.[117] In fact, *autarkeia* is both nourishment and pleasure, health and acuteness of the senses, and nothing prevents disease better than that.[118] *Autarkeia* is then part of what Chrysostom sees as the health of the soul, and the best preventative medicines against sicknesses such as vainglory and anger.[119] It also offers security and honor to one's self and prevents us from seeking glory and approval from

---

[112] *In 1 Cor. hom.* 16.3 (PG 61:138).

[113] *De Laz. conc.* 2.1 (PG 48:982).

[114] *In 1 Thess. hom.* 10.4 (PG 62:462; NPNF 1-13:370).

[115] *Pasch.* (long recension) 4.4 (SC 561:286-87). According to the editor, Nathalie Rambault, Introduction to SC 561:235-40, the homily belongs among the ps.-Chrysostomica that are mosaic in composition, but contains substantial portions of authentic Chrysostomian material.

[116] *In Matt. hom.* 57.6 (PG 58:565).

[117] *In Act. apost. hom.* 27.3 (PG 60:207).

[118] *In Heb. hom.* 29.7 (PG 63:207).

[119] For a discussion of John as a "therapist of the soul" see Mayer, "The Persistence."

others when we have self-respect.[120] Christian *autarkeia* thus automatically "corrects" one of the errors that John Chrysostom condemns in the Cynics: *kenodoxia*.[121]

Chrysostom further adduces the idea of *autarkeia* in his various comments on social issues. For example, in the fourth *Homily on 1 Timothy* he describes the diverse ways we can glorify God through body and soul. He mentions specifically how women can do so: when they do not use perfumes, or paint themselves, but are satisfied with the way God made them, without any additional embellishments. When they do use such enhancements, it is as if they are thinking God's craftsmanship is insufficient and consider themselves as better artists than Him. When the women adorn themselves, it is only so that they can attract crowds of lovers and insult their Creator. Instead, they should be *autarkeis* with their natural appearance and adorn it with modesty and chastity instead of paints and jewellery.[122]

Chrysostom's connection between divine craftsmanship and *autarkeia* is not the only instance of establishing a link with the concept of creating something out of nothing. Chrysostom also uses the concept of *autarkeia* to construct a hierarchy of arts and their usefulness for human life. These arts are housebuilding, weaving, shoemaking, and agriculture. Chrysostom claims that the latter is the most useful one, since "without shoes and clothes it is possible to live; but without agriculture it is impossible."[123] He then brings up the examples of the Nomads and the Gymnosophists,[124] who utilized only agriculture from among these arts, and uses this argument to shame those in his

---

[120] *In Matt. hom.* 87.4 (PG 58:774).

[121] *Kenodoxia* stands as an obstacle to our journey towards the glory of God, the only true *doxa*. For the importance of *kenodoxia* in Chrysostom's thought see A.M. Malingrey, Introduction to SC 13:13: "Toute la vie morale de l'antiquité s'appuie ... sur la gloire qu'une bonne action rapporte à celui qui l'a faite. Si le mot *doxa* est un des plus usuels du vocabulaire grec, celui de *kenodoxia* prend, dans la langue des Peres, une importance qu'il n'avait jamais eue. Autant la *doxa* forme, pour un païen, l'atmosphère où il aime vivre, autant la *kenodoxia* est, pour un chrétien, la tentation qu'il faut fuir avant tout."

[122] *In 1 Tim. hom.* 4.3 (PG 62:524).

[123] *In 2 Cor. hom.* 15.3 (PG 61:506; NPNF 1-12.352).

[124] Interestingly, certain aspects of the Gymnosophists' lifestyle served as models in Cynic writings of the Imperial period. For a discussion of similarities and differences, see Claire Muckensturm, "Les Gymnosophistes étaient-ils des Cyniques modèles?" in *Le Cynisme Ancien*, 225-239.

audience who have introduced "vain refinements into life," such as "cooks, confectioners, embroiders." He claims that the reasons he mentions this is not to lay down a law so that they would live that way but to provide them with a proper hierarchy of the arts, which is the following: "First then comes agriculture; second, weaving; and third after it, building; and shoemaking last of all; for amongst us at any rate there are many both servants and laborers (οἰκέται καὶ γεωργοί) who live without shoes."[125] Both this example as well as the one mentioned in the previous paragraph are connected through a single theme: initially, God creates the woman in her natural beauty, and the humans create the art that is sufficient for them to survive. But in both cases, the humans exceed their limit and stop being self-sufficient: the woman insults her Maker by adding things that are unnecessary and not intended by Him, while humanity creates arts that are not fit for their survival, in order to satisfy their various pleasures, such as gluttony.

Unlike Cynicism's version of solitary *autarkeia*, Chrysostom's paradigm envisions a community of self-sufficient people who serve as lights to each other.[126] However, utter self-sufficiency is not in our nature, he argues; for this reason, marriage was instituted.[127] Through marriage humans supply what they lack as individuals to one

---

[125] All of the references in this paragraph derive from *In 2 Cor. hom.* 15.3-4 (PG 61:506-7; NPNF 1-12:352-53). In one of his *Baptismal Instructions* Chrysostom claimed that the simple rustic who spends his time farming and tilling the earth "has exact knowledge of things which the philosophers who take pride in their beard and staff have never even been able to imagine." In his eyes, these simple folks hold a "deep philosophy of virtue" whilst not paying attention to visible things but have faith and hope in the invisible and unseen things. See *Cat.* 8.6 (SC 50bis:250-51; trans. Harkins, *Baptismal Instructions*, 121). For a similar comparison between a theologically-knowledgeable widow and an idle talking philosopher, see *Mut. nom. hom.* 4.5 (PG 51:152-53). The tradition of placing common people in a higher sphere of knowledge than philosophers precisely because they focus on invisible things goes back to Origen, who in *Contra Celsum* 7.46 (trans. Chadwick, *Contra Celsum*, 434) responds to Celsus' accusation that common Christians do not understand Plato's metaphysics because they are ἀπαίδευτοι: "They look, as they have learnt, not at the things which are becoming, which are seen and on that account temporal, but at the higher things, whether one wishes to call them 'being', or things 'invisible' because they are intelligible, or 'things which are not seen' because their nature lies outside the realm of sense-perception."

[126] *Adv. opp. vit. mon.* 3.2 (PG 47:351).

[127] *In 1 Cor. hom.* 40.6 (PG 61:354) Chrysostom discusses the possession of slaves and claims that even though human beings were created to be self-sufficient, if someone cannot be without slaves, then one or two should be enough. For further discussion on slavery and self-sufficiency, see Chris L. De Wet, *Preaching Bondage: John Chrysostom and the Discourse of Slavery in Early Christianity* (Oakland: University of California Press, 2015), 56. Both marriage and slave possession then can be considered as

another and their incomplete nature becomes self-sufficient, which leads to its immortality through the succession of descendants.[128] It is interesting that when Chrysostom talks about the institution of marriage he chooses to emphasize the fact that humans are not self-sufficient on their own. Elsewhere, he declares that God did indeed create humanity to be self-sufficient in order to choose virtue and avoid vice.[129] Virtue is sufficient in itself and has no need for wealth, nobility, or anything else external to accompany it.[130] As with other cases in Chrysostom's writings, we cannot be certain whether one view is dominant over the other. It seems that, just as we noted earlier, here too he picks and chooses how he employs this concept, depending on the requirements of his argument, leading to the simultaneous exercise in his thought of different, but not incompatible, modes. On the one hand, he promotes *autarkeia* as communal, when he justifies marriage as an institution that provides the other half of *autarkeia* we lack as human beings. On the other, he promotes solitary *autarkeia* when he argues that our self-sufficiency only genuinely comes into play when we choose virtue over vice. At the same time, he had to make a convincing case for his claim that a solitary man/woman could indeed be *autarkēs* on his/her own, since otherwise he could not justify the choice of asceticism and the solitary life, which he had experienced himself.[131] In a sense, John Chrysostom's version of *autarkeia* is both solitary and communal, but even if solitary it would be useless without helping others, as the monks did at the time of the riots, and as Diogenes and the Cynics did not, because they were too preoccupied with their own

---

outcomes of Adam's original disobedience that stripped humanity of the *autarkeia* with which it was originally created.

[128] *In Ioh. hom.* 19.1 (PG 59:120).

[129] *In Rom. hom.* 5.6 (PG 60:429).

[130] John expressed this view in one of his rhetorical outbursts against Greek philosophy, where he also argues against philosophers who denied the idea of providence or the origin of the world from God: *De stat.* 19.4 (PG 49:189).

[131] But see Wendy Mayer, "What Does It Mean to Say that John Chrysostom Was a Monk?" *Studia Patristica* 41 (Leuven: Peeters, 2006), 451-5, for a reconsideration of the ancient biographies of Chrysostom and their descriptions of his ascetic regime.

vainglory. As always, Chrysostom considers the criterion of usefulness behind the motivation of every action.

Our study of Chrysostom's conception of *autarkeia* would not be complete if we did not refer to his commentary on the three NT occurrences of the word, two in the form of *autarkeia* and one as *autarkēs*, all three in Pauline writings.[132] It is particularly in these commentaries that Chrysostom connects the concept with other virtues and develops a fuller theory of what it entails when it comes to its application in human life. First of all, John argues on the basis of Paul's use of ἔμαθον, that *autarkeia* is something that we learn. It is therefore "a matter of teaching and exercise and care" which at the same time involves a great deal of difficulty and pain. Paul is *autarkēs* because he knows how to use little, to bear hunger and want, and his self-sufficiency is contrasted to abundance, which is without virtue.[133] Paul's prayer in 2 Corinthians 9:8 ("And God is able to provide you with every blessing in abundance, so that by always having enough of everything, you may share abundantly in every good work") is called an example of great philosophy, because Paul wishes neither wealth nor abundance for the Corinthians. Instead, he condescends to their weakness by not compelling them to give from their want and asks them to be sufficient with what they have.

In terms of his commentary on Paul, John connects his exhortation to *autarkeia* with the virtue of philanthropy. In his own exhortation to his audience, he utilizes Paul's condescension yet again to argue that he is not asking them to reach the heights of indigence, but rather to cut off the superfluous things and learn how to be self-sufficient.[134] Finally, John also uses 1 Timothy 6:6 ("there is great gain in godliness combined with contentment") as a lead in to a practical discussion of the value of

---

[132] Philippians 4:11, 2 Corinthians 9:8 and 1 Timothy 6:6. For the possible sources behind Paul's references to *autarkeia*, see Hans Dieter Betz, *Studies in Paul's Letter to the Philippians* (Tubingen: Mohr Siebeck, 2015), 91-112.

[133] *In Phil. hom.* 16.1 (PG 62:289; John Chrysostom, *Homilies on Paul's Letter to the Philippians*, trans. Pauline Allen, Atlanta: Society of Biblical Literature, 2013, 301).

[134] *In 2 Cor. hom.* 29.3 (PG 61:532-33; NPNF 1-12:369).

money and possessions. Εὐσέβεια and αὐτάρκεια are only great gains when we do not have wealth, not when we do. Possessions are worthless, Chrysostom argues, because when we leave this world they stay behind and do not follow us: "if we brought nothing with us, [then we] shall take nothing away with us."[135] In essence, God created humanity to be self-sufficient "so as to be able to choose virtue and avoid vice."[136]

e. Conclusion

Numerous other Cynic themes appear in Chrysostom's work, such as *anaideia, hēdonē, typhos (atyphia),* and others. A comprehensive study in which his and the Cynics' interpretation of these themes are compared would be beneficial of future research, if we are to shed some much-needed light on the complicated subject of Cynicism and its reception in patristic writings. Indeed, the frequency of a number of key Cynic terms in Chrysostom's writings leads one to suspect that his corpus in particular will prove in future to be a rich field for investigating in a more nuanced way how these ideas were assimilated and transformed.[137] Our suspicion, even on the basis of the preliminary exploration undertaken in this chapter, is that the outcome will reinforce our finding that John would hesitantly approve of certain Cynic ideas, but would certainly not accept them without reservation. But as W. Mayer pointed out, even these ideas would need to be filtered through their interplay with similar Scriptural concepts before becoming normative in Christian discourse.[138] Chrysostom's engagement with the Cynics as individuals and with their ideas in any case shows the

---

[135] *In 1 Tim. hom.* 17.1 (PG 62:592; NPNF 1-13:468).

[136] *In Rom. hom.* 5.5 (PG 60:429; NPNF 1-10:365).

[137] A simple TLG search of the word παρρησία brings up more than a thousand references to Chrysostom's works. We also know how important that concept was to the Cynics and the construction of Diogenes as the epitome of virtue.

[138] Mayer, "John Chrysostom on Poverty," 81: "The point to be made here is that in assessing the discourse of John and other eastern bishops on the topics of poverty, wealth, virtue, and evergetism one should not expect it to be either novel or uniquely Christian, but rather deeply rooted in the Greek philosophical tradition. Their distinction lies rather in the way that they filter long-existing philosophical tropes through the Christian Scriptures, transforming them in the process into a specifically Christian ethic."

continuing relevance of Cynicism in late antiquity even though its greatest representatives were long gone. Diogenes' presence in the rhetorical handbooks and his popularity was something that many Christians (as well as non-Christians) felt they should be responding to, particularly as the establishment of Christianity as the state religion highlighted the need for Christians to showcase their own philosophers, even if they could not have their texts taught in schools. Chrysostom rose to that challenge with his comparison of Paul and Babylas to Diogenes but did not limit himself to just that. He expanded the meaning of *autarkeia* and interpreted it as both an exercise of the self as well as a communal event. Furthermore, he describes it as a gift from God, although humanity could not hold onto it after its fall. He also agreed with Cynic critiques of Greek culture and civilization and the effect it had on virtue, critiques which argued that the Greeks had by no means a monopoly on wisdom, if in fact one could call their philosophy proper wisdom-at least by Chrysostom's standards.[139]

The "tension" in Christian attitudes to the Cynics means that some Cynic values came under suspicion, while others were assimilated, and, in order to showcase that, we examined an example of the particular assimilation/critique of the Cynics by John Chrysostom. Here we saw that Chrysostom criticizes Cynics for typical reasons: love of praise, indecency and indifference, uselessness, and not being "real" philosophers. At the same time, his criticism is mostly directed towards contemporary pagan assessments of Diogenes (particularly Julian's) and his refutation serves as another instrument in proving the superiority of Christianity over Cynicism.[140] Thus, in terms of the reception of Cynics in his writings, he exhibits little difference from Christian and non-Christian critics alike and like others before him, such as Julian, he does not consider someone who wears a cloak and carries a staff and has long hair and a beard to be necessarily a

---

[139] Cf. Ps-Anacharsis, *Epistle 2 To Solon* (trans. Anne McGuire, *The Cynic Epistles,* 39): "The Greeks are wise men, yet in no way are they wiser than non-Greeks. For the gods did not withhold from non-Greeks the ability to know the good."

[140] Krueger, "Diogenes the Cynics," 39.

philosopher. His expectations extend well beyond appearance to address the interior person instead. In terms of the nuances of his critique, he does praise Diogenes for re-evaluating the ideas of kingship and wealth and, if we were to apply Diogenes' *parrhesia* to Chrysostom's life, we could claim that the latter's tendency to "speak truth to power" was personally costlier. He does not, like Theodoret, distort the stories he refers to when talking about the life of Diogenes or Crates, but he does characterize their actions differently. Whereas Gregory of Nazianzus praises Crates for dispersing his wealth and becoming free from its bondage, Chrysostom applies the criterion of utility to the act, seeing instead a madman who could have put his money to better use.

Finally, we also explored how John nuances and modulates one particular Cynic virtue, *autarkeia*. Chrysostom was quite careful to define the parameters, similarities and differences of Christian *autarkeia*. His main agreement with the Cynics was on the core definition of the concept. Aristotle describes controversies on the subject, with two sides involved: "about this question there are many controversies, owing to those that draw us towards either extreme of life, the one school towards parsimony and the other towards luxury."[141] At one extreme were those "who understood self-sufficiency as being able to cater for any personal need that might arise;" at the other, those "who believed that self-sufficiency is about restricting need to what is truly necessary."[142] Both the Cynics and Chrysostom (with many others from the Christian tradition) strongly opposed the first definition, while promoting the second. It is in the implications of this within a specifically Christian empire and how *autarkeia* of this kind should be expressed in a person's way of life that the two movements differed. Even so: why did Chrysostom and other Christians need to get involved in this debate, although indirectly? I believe that the response to this is related to the development of Christian discourse in the fourth century and the appropriation of the two constituents of

---

[141] Aristotle, *Pol.* 7.1326b (LCL 264:561).

[142] Bosman, "Ancient debates on autarkeia," 7.

classical rhetoric: rhetoric as a technique ("a form of specialized knowledge") and "a means of institutional power."[143] From the later fourth century onwards there is a realization among Christian writers that they need to move beyond the *sermo piscatorius*, whilst maintaining their previous arguments in favor of simplicity and inclusivity[144] and their argument that a Christian did not necessarily need learning in order to philosophize. One way of doing this was through the appropriation of concepts that their audience would be aware of (such as *autarkeia*) combined with a transformation, sometimes radical but often not, of what they entailed and how they could fit into their lives as citizens of a Christian empire. But this appropriation does not necessarily imply usurpation as has previously been argued, and the argument that "the purpose was to change consciousness by changing language" falls flat when we see that the reception of *autarkeia* was within the previous philosophical tradition and not outside of it.[145]

For Chrysostom, this difference between Christianity and Cynicism became defined by the criterion of usefulness or utility. In this respect, our investigation into Chrysostom's response against Cynic philosophy has also contributed to a discussion on the use of exemplars. The use of non-Christian or "pagan" exemplars, such as Diogenes, in Chrysostom is more complex than it appears at face value. Chrysostom uses the Cynics—both Diogenes and Cynic contemporaries of Chrysostom—as negative examples to highlight the nature and uses of voluntary poverty and charity, and the dangers of vainglory and neglecting modesty. At face value, Christians and Cynics may appear similar to one another, as Julian thought. Many may have held similar opinions about the commonalities between Christians and Cynics. But the renunciation of wealth

---

[143] Cameron, *Christianity and the Rhetoric of Empire*, 87.

[144] "The consciousness that Christianity and Christian discourse could and should appeal to all was never forgotten." Cameron, *Christianity and the Rhetoric of Empire*, 111.

[145] Herbert Hunger, "The Classical Tradition in Byzantine Literature: The Importance of Rhetoric," in *Byzantium and the Classical Tradition*, eds. Margaret Mullett and Roger Scott (Birmingham: University of Birmingham Centre for Byzantine Studies, 1981), 41.

without caring for the poor is akin to madness and vainglory. For Chrysostom, this is the main difference between Christians and Cynics. The Cynic exemplars in this way become convenient to illustrate the importance of, on the one hand, the act of wealth renunciation and, on the other, the motivation for it. And it is the motivations for one's actions that receive priority in Chrysostom's moral philosophy.

In chapter 2 we described three primary modes of interaction in John's reception of Hellenism: positive, negative, and neutral. As we relate these modes to our discussion in this chapter, we see him praising Diogenes, especially when he compares him to secular rulers, but otherwise disparaging him for his vanity and his uselessness when compared to Christian saints like Babylas. Yet despite his negative predisposition towards Diogenes and even Crates, we do not see him fabricating stories about them. Therefore, in terms of his reception of individual Cynics his attitude is mostly negative, sprinkled with a few positive references. What is more interesting is John's reception of a concept particularly associated with Cynicism, that of *autarkeia*. Although we do not find any direct quotations from Cynics in his corpus, we can confidently assert that he was aware of the discussion related to the concept and a participant in it throughout his works. As we have shown, he would be willing to tentatively accept the Cynic conception of *autarkeia* with a few caveats, and would also include, as he did with many other concepts elsewhere, Paul and the monks as the most illustrious examples of someone who is perfectly *autarkēs*. In essence, his reception of the philosophic ideal behind *autarkeia* is generally positive, even if filtered through Christian discourse. What distinguishes him from other Christian writers is his particular reconfiguration and application of Cynic philosophical concepts such as the one we have been discussing and the way he integrates them in Christian popular discourse.

5. Conclusion

John Chrysostom's understanding of Christianity as a way of life is part of the patristic legacy that sought to present the Christian faith in practical as well as intellectual terms. It largely shares that feature with what we conventionally call "schools of ancient philosophy", that is, different forms of life "defined by an ideal of wisdom."[1] In the introduction to this thesis we indicated that Chrysostom's reception of Greek philosophy is sometimes used by scholars to fit grand master narratives on the relationship between Christianity and Hellenism, and, depending on the author's position on the matter (peaceful co-existence, hostility, symbiosis), one can find statements to support any of these narratives. At other times, John's name is conspicuous by its absence, even if he is sometimes classified alongside others either for his contribution to the project of "Christian Hellenism," or for the influence that his hostility toward philosophy had in Byzantium and its attitudes towards the classical tradition.[2] One has to wonder about this absence. Is it because the essentializing of two large concepts such as Christianity and Hellenism requires the formation of a canonical set of writers who can be considered representatives of each? And if Chrysostom was so influential in Byzantium and beyond, why is he not part of this set?

In our literature review (chapter 1) we identified two scholarly focal points in the Christian reception of Hellenism: one that focuses on the time from the Apologists to Origen, and another on the Cappadocians. Both have previously been treated as paradigmatic, which is not a problem in itself except for the fact that it leaves out

---

[1] Hadot, *Philosophy as a Way of Life*, 59.

[2] For example, we do not find a single reference to him in De Vogel's article on Platonism and Christianity and he is not classified under the five main types of attitudes of early Christian writers towards philosophy. De Vogel, "Platonism and Christianity," 19: "(a) total rejection and hostility, (b) a great open-mindedness and assimilation of philosophical thinking forms, (c) an extremely critical attitude, yet reception of certain elements, (d) far-going acceptance of philosophical thinking forms, sometimes in a spirit of syncretism, (e) far-going acceptance joined with transformation." Many of the scholars we analysed in the literature review would include Chrysostom under type a, while a few might have opted for b. We believe we have sufficiently demonstrated that type c would be the most appropriate option, a type that according to Vogel also includes the Apologists, Origen, the Cappadocians, and Augustine (ibid., 20).

authors that would not fit either of these receptions, even if one can always find points of agreement. The study of the interaction between Christianity and Hellenism in Late Antiquity has been advanced on many fronts lately, yet Chrysostom's role in it seems to be severely limited. This study is an attempt to overcome that limitation by bringing together a wide variety of texts from John's corpus and reading them in the context in which they appear. In this respect, we look at several modes of interaction. We started in chapter 2 with John's stark critique of the philosophers and their ideas, because this has often been the reason for sweeping scholarly judgments that dismiss his reception, thus allowing very little room for discussion of the actual subject matter. We have identified several reasons for this critique, including the fame of certain philosophers, the popularity of some of their ideas, and their role (as John understood it) as the intellectual masterminds behind paganism. We showed that in his polemic against Hellenism Chrysostom utilizes a method similar to that in his polemic against the Jews. He creates an anchor concept which is then used as a measuring stick against each group, although there is a major difference, as we shall explain below. The Jewish anchor concept is the Mosaic Law. In his attempt to argue against what he considers Jewish national pride, Chrysostom is not afraid to admit that he will use the prophets as weapons against them.[3] In the case of the Greeks, the problem is their intellectual pride and the anchor concept is, obviously, philosophy. This is not just speculation on our part. John himself brings the two groups together and attributes their respective practices to the Law and philosophy.[4] In fact, he assigns the first polemic against them to Paul.

The major difference we indicated before needs to be explained. In using the Law against the Jews, Chrysostom treats it as a sacred text which now belongs to the Christians since the Jews failed to live up to its ideals and despite the fact that they are

---

[3] *Adv. Iud. or.* 8.1 (PG 48:927).

[4] *In Col. hom.* 6.1 (PG 62:339).

obstinately clinging to it.[5] On the contrary, Greek philosophy is not treated as sacred anywhere in John's corpus. In fact, it is usually considered as the main reason behind what he considers the downfall of the Greeks from their place as the most rational of all humans. It was because of the philosophers, their disagreements, and the perverted use of *logismoi* that the "Greeks" fell into irrationality and ended up worshipping sticks and stones. In this scheme, Hellenic religion often equals worship of creatures, either animate or inanimate. Chrysostom is never in doubt as to whether the Greeks were wise, at least from a secular point of view. In some issues, the Greeks are actually to be admired for their philosophical stance, because they did not have any expectations for any sort of future life. But an essential difference is related to the teachers each side could claim. Chrysostom had no issue with admitting that the Christians were first taught by a tentmaker, a publican, a fisherman, alongside exemplars such as the thief on the cross, the prostitutes, and even the Magi. For him, the insignificance of these individuals, at least according to worldly perceptions, was a cause célèbre and pointed to the divine origins of the Gospel. In this battle, he is willing to admit every argument the Greeks would use. Yes, Plato, Pythagoras and the others were philosophers, eloquent men of stature amongst their countrymen, glorious in their predecessors and honoured by everyone. Yet the hustlers beat the philosophers, the illiterate beat the rhetoricians and to prove this he would always ask, "Where is Plato now?" One has to wonder whether anyone in Chrysostom's audience ever pointed out to him that Plato seems to be right here, as you keep mentioning him again and again. But we digress.

Chrysostom's doubts are mainly focused on the outcomes of Greek wisdom, one of which was the prevalence of idolatry. The question remains: why does he often feel the need to demarcate Greek philosophy and Hellenism from Christianity? I would argue that the answer to this is Chrysostom's audience, regardless of his method of delivery

---

[5] *De Sac.* 4.4 (SC 272:256).

(oral/written or treatise/sermon).[6] When Chrysostom speaks (or writes) he has in front of him (or envisions) a Christian audience which needs to be educated. Part of this education is the argument that philosophy is not necessary for salvation. If we see the problem through this lens, his argument is not against philosophy *per se* but rather its soteriological role.[7] Chrysostom's most important argument against Greek philosophy is that, unlike faith, it has no salvific value. Someone who is well versed in philosophy has no advantage over someone who is illiterate in regard to their salvation as individuals, and Chrysostom could point to numerous examples to the effect of the illiterate prevailing over the educated, from Paul's victory over Plato and other Greek philosophers to the monks exhibiting real philosophy during the statues riots, unlike the allegedly brave Cynics.[8] John is also willing to exploit the Greek intellectual tradition from within, as when he refers to the animosity between philosophers and sophists or when he uses the disagreements of the philosophers as an argument against the unity of philosophy. His polemic against philosophy must also be related to the specific context of Greek philosophy in the fourth century, and particularly the role of the philosophers as theurgists.[9] One might offer the counterargument that this was not the aim of philosophy in general, and even more so before the Neoplatonists. But Chrysostom has intertwined it with religion to such a degree that for him their separation would be unthinkable. One avenue of further research which has emerged from our study is the

---

[6] For the debate on the composition of Chrysostom's audience, particularly in terms of issues such as social class and gender divisions, see Wendy Mayer, "Who Came to Hear John Chrysostom Preach? Recovering a Late Fourth-Century Preacher's Audience," *Ephemerides Theologicae Lovanienses* 76:1 (2000),73-87. Cf. Maxwell, *Christianization and Communication*, 65-87 for the actual composition of the audience.

[7] Papadopoulos, *John Chrysostom vol. 2*, 9 (my translation): "He does not deal with the problem of the value, beauty, or power of philosophy in itself, elements that he silently accepts, since he uses its structures and shapes."

[8] For an example of Paul being victorious against Plato see *In Rom. hom.* 3.3 (PG 60:414). For the monks' exhibition of true philosophy in Antioch see *De stat.* 17.2 (PG 49:173-4).

[9] Limberis, ""Religion" as the Cipher for Identity," 380: "For most of the fourth century, philosophers at the best schools gained their reputations much less from their dialectic skill than from their daemonic powers that manifested their greatness through supernatural signs. The philosopher's authority resided in his ability to manifest holiness, and his ability to prove that holiness is genuine, rather than in his skill at rational disputation."

desirability of a more detailed examination of this theme. It is exactly because of this that he also traces the influence of philosophy to Christian heresies of his own time and thus sometimes treats Hellenism (in the sense of paganism) as the originator of Marcionism, Manicheanism, Sabellianism, and Arianism.[10] The common basis is not at the level of ideas, however, but rather in that in all these cases the mistake he attributes to them is an excessive reliance on their own reasonings (*logismoi*) that can only lead to wrong belief. In terms of his own contribution to the anti-philosophical discourse, Chrysostom has been credited as the first author who used the term "Christian philosophy" (or simply "our philosophy") in contrast to Greek philosophy, as a concept by which he just meant a Christian way of life.[11]

Chrysostom's attacks on philosophy and pagan religious practices have also been interpreted as markers of identity, primarily by I. Sandwell and J. Maxwell. The assumption is that Chrysostom was chiefly interested in erecting boundaries between his group of Christians and every other religious group, and that he tried to do so by establishing clear-cut definitions and constructing an exclusive religious identity. Sandwell particularly emphasises that at that time Christianity was not something that was absolutely defined, and that its boundaries could still be very fluid. This is all well and good, minus the fact that the Christian community in Antioch had a history of more than 300 years before Chrysostom was born and one would assume that in the meantime it would have formed some sort of identity, even if it was not as "clear-cut" as Chrysostom's; this point of view also leaves aside the fact that Chrysostom is neither the first nor the last Christian attacking philosophy and paganism, and that in fact he provides no concrete systematic definitions for them other than that they were practices

---

[10] E.g. *In Gen. hom.* 2.3 (PG 53:30).

[11] Hubertus R. Drobner, "Christian Philosophy," in *The Oxford Handbook of Early Christian Studies*, eds. Ashbrook Harvey and Hunter, 678. The reference is to Chrysostom, *Homily on the Kalends* (PG 48:953-62). Malingrey's definition is still unrivalled: "L'incarnation de la foi chrétienne avec toutes les exigences qu'elle comporte, indépendamment d'une forme de vie particulière." Anne Marie Malingrey, *Philosophia: Étude d'un groupe de mots dans la littérature grecque, des présocratiques au IV* siècle après J.-C.* (Paris: Klincksieck, 1961), 288.

involved with a different way of life. If we take his polemic against paganism as a fight against a clear-cut concept, we disregard the varieties of Hellenism and paganism present in his very own works, unless one thinks that references to onion worship among the Egyptians or to the cult of Helios are part of one and the same thing. Chrysostom's constant attack on isolated elements from paganism was not just a part of his strategy to use it as a contrast to Christianity and thus as part of his "construction" of Christian identity. It was literally what Paul and tens of other Christian writers before Chrysostom did as well. When Chrysostom attacks blood sacrifices, he is not constructing an identity. He just follows Paul's thought in 1 Corinthians 10:20 to its logical conclusion.

This point of view is also overlooking the fact that, just like "pagans" such as Porphyry, Chrysostom had both praise and blame for the Greeks, and just like Porphyry he could be extremely critical of both the gods and pagan religious practices. Do we imply that their intentions were the same then? Absolutely not. What we are arguing is that not every attack on certain religious practices is due to a hypothetical construction of an identity and/or the erection of boundaries. If Chrysostom was interested in erecting boundaries, which we think he was not, then Hellenic philosophical schools did as well. After all, they too relied on assimilation and memorization of the dogmas and way of life of the school, which was presumably John's aim for the Christians as well.[12] In his case he did not even have to argue that he was following tradition. In his mind, as we have shown, the first and ultimate demolisher of the philosophers and of paganism was Paul. Despite this, scholarly discussions of identity have not particularly paid attention to John's dependence on the New Testament and Pauline examples, at the expense of losing sight of his biblical influences. In essence, the argument comes down to the purpose of Chrysostom's preaching: was it primarily an exercise in identity

---

¹² Hadot, *Philosophy as a Way of Life*, 59.

formation? Or simply the exercise of a priest's (and later bishop's) duty to interpret the Bible in order to bring salvation to those whom he is preaching? And why could it not be both? We would argue that a combination of these is the only solution to this problem and the tendency to read Chrysostomic material as a constant positioning on a battleground between different groups. Familiarity with the whole of Chrysostom's corpus would show that there never was a sense of any great conflict.

One of Chrysostom's points of contention was what he perceived as the Greek philosophers' support of the ancient religion. The chain of philosophers who acted as enablers of paganism is a long one and goes back all the way to the pre-Socratics. But to these he would add quite a few from his own time, particularly Libanius, and the one he calls the most impious of all: Julian the Emperor. Julian should be always kept in mind, and not just because Chrysostom wrote a treatise against him. Although he is writing long after Julian's death, the latter's memory, along with the possibility that someone like him might reach the imperial throne again, is very much alive in his mind. This is important not only because Julian made the strongest case for uniting Greek learning and religion in an unbreakable bond, but also because of his claims that Christianity is "antithetical to the civilized life."[13] In terms of Chrysostom's description of pagan cultic practices, at points they seem to resemble similar descriptions from Libanius' *Julianic* orations,[14] and can thus be contextualized more as a description of late antique paganism than an actual knowledge of classical or even Hellenistic religious practices. Likewise, we cannot dismiss the possibility that John was superimposing the attitude of contemporary philosophers towards religion back to the philosophers of the classical era. Nonetheless, John's understanding of paganism was not the most refined: idolatry is often reduced to the worship of sticks and stones, an inability to distinguish between the Creator and his creation, and the divinization of mortals and natural elements.

---

[13] Limberis, ""Religion" as the Cipher for Identity," 385.

[14] Cf. Libanius, *Or.* 18.126 (LCL 451:361) with *De capt. Eutr.* 14 (PG 52:409; NPNF 1-9:261).

But to focus on depictions of the philosophers as mere enablers of paganism is missing the point: their image throughout Chrysostom's corpus shows a multivalence of approaches[15] that help Chrysostom make specific arguments. At one end of the spectrum, as we saw in Chapter 2, Plato is a shameless pimp who wants women to be common to all and to fight naked in public: he is also an advocate for pederasty and the epitome of a failed philosopher. At the other end, Plato is a quiet ascetic who spends his days tending to his garden and sustains himself with olives and herbs. One might wonder: how could both images be written (or spoken about) by the same person? The answer goes back to a point we made in Chapter 1. All too often scholars look for consistency where none is to be found; but one wonders why it was expected in the first place. Chrysostom is able to use both images of Plato in different places because he is trying to make two different and unrelated points. By focusing on the negative images, scholars have misinterpreted Chrysostom as a pathological enemy of Hellenism. The same misinterpretation applies to a number of other issues. For example, his opinion on the value of rhetorical education has been interpreted as an all-out attack on *paideia*.[16]

And yet, as we have shown, it was no such thing. The opposite interpretation can also be applied, with certain passages treated in isolation in order to show that Chrysostom had no issues with education in his day and that he could easily recommend a reading of the classics without feeling that it would threaten Christian beliefs in any way. This interpretation would also miss the point. Chrysostom definitely had issues with the educational system of his day, specifically with its outcomes and the danger of

---

[15] It would be amiss if we did not point out that the same multivalence applies to Chrysostom himself: in his time, he was accused of being too friendly with the Greeks and of being too forgiving towards sinners (Socrates, *Hist. Eccl.* 6.21, GCS NF 4:345, for the first accusation; Photius, *Bibl.* 59, ed. Henry, 56, for a report of the charges brought against him by the monk Isaac at the Council of the Oak). Today, he is called the archenemy of Hellenism and his expectations from Christians are considered to have been too demanding.

[16] A similar interpretation has been proposed in relation to his attacks against "paganism." But these, as Liebeschuetz pointed out previously, were only occasional and sporadic because he realised that without public support it would inevitably fade away: *Ambrose and John Chrysostom*, 152. For this view see Athanassiadi, *Julian and Hellenism*, 19.

someone mastering rhetorical training without sufficient spiritual preparation. Essentially, this was a fear that an exclusive focus on the classics could lead one to disregard the Bible.[17] This acknowledgment, however, should not be taken as indicative that he was on a mission to take the whole system down or that this was even his secret aim. When he recommends reading the books of those "outside," he does this as a concession to his audience. He knows that some of them find pleasure in reading philosophy, and thus exhorts them to read it in a paradigmatic fashion. One should not be surprised to not find Chrysostom recommending a program of studies based on the classics.[18] Besides the fact that he was a priest, not a school teacher, he did not do that with Christian books either. In fact, the only book he ever recommended to an audience, other than the Bible, was Athanasius' *Life of Anthony*, and we would argue that this was not accidental.[19] Chrysostom's links to Egypt, both through his connections with individuals with first-hand experience of Egyptian asceticism like Palladius and John Cassian, and through some of the concepts he shares with ascetic writings (such as νῆψις), need to be further examined, and we believe this is another fruitful avenue for research emerging from our study. The classic distinction between the Antiochene and Alexandrian schools and their assumed opposition might be the reason this research has not yet been undertaken, but, as with his biblical exegesis, Chrysostom was no standard Antiochene, even if he is treated as such.

What about his actual engagement with philosophy itself? As we have seen, in a few instances he engages with cosmological ideas. At the same time, there is not much focus on metaphysical concepts. In general, we should be cautious when reading texts referring to the philosophy of those "outside," since, as we saw in chapter 2, John could

---

[17] Papadopoulos, *John Chrysostom vol. 2*, 13. See n. 60 in Chapter 1 for analysis of a complete misinterpretation of a passage from *Against the Opponents of Monastic Life*.

[18] Even if other Christian bishops and intellectuals, like Basil of Caesarea, did. The point needs to be repeated. The Christian response to Hellenism was neither uniform nor identical, and sometimes the local context could make all the difference.

[19] *In Matt. hom.* 8.7 (PG 58:88).

be quite flexible with the application of the term Hellenes to all pre-Christian non-Jews and the attribution of their religious practices to "paganism." His acquaintance with certain ancient texts cannot be doubted, even if sometimes his knowledge of them came through Eusebius, as in the case of *Timaeus*. In other cases, as we have demonstrated, his reception of different texts (such as Plato's *Republic*) or individuals (such as Plato or Pythagoras), shows a monomania with certain concepts to which he repeatedly returns. Severe criticism of a number of recommended practices from the *Symposium* and of Pythagorean and Platonic eschatological ideas is abundant. This engagement can tell us a few things, not only about the popularity of some texts and certain ideas, but also about one of the issues we questioned in the beginning of this thesis. Often, Christianity and Hellenism have been treated as entities that are either compatible or incompatible.

In Chapter 1 we asked why this question is asked in the first place. This is a false dilemma, because it assumes that the only interaction Christianity could have with Hellenism would be to either absorb it or discard with it. If this premise is accepted, it also creates a dead end: if it was absorbed, then Christianity was Hellenized—which for certain strands of scholarship would mean that it was corrupted. If it was discarded, then Hellenism died, or at least was in limbo. In light of Christianity's interaction with various other cultures in antiquity, why did it particularly have to be compatible or incompatible with Hellenism? Chrysostom would opt for a model of symbiosis, with certain caveats. On issues like faith and salvation, compatibility is not even a question. On other issues, he could be more flexible and allow for inquiry outside the Christian modes of discourse. This application to religious ideas is very important and it should be kept in mind because we will return to it later.

An exclusive focus on Chrysostom's negativity towards the Greeks and their philosophy also does a disservice to the fact that neither the Greeks nor the Jews were the constant target of his ire. He would often reproach some Christians about the way they behaved in public: for example, their reaction to losing a loved one, or their pub crawls after martyr festivals or their dressing in church. Let us briefly consider just one of those, which we examined in more detail in Chapter 2: Chrysostom's issue with some Christians' mourning customs because they resembled the mourning of those "without hope," i.e. the Greeks. Their long cries showed disbelief in the resurrection, something that was harmful to both themselves as well as to the person that was dead, or rather, asleep. One of his concerns was that the Christians would be mercilessly mocked by other groups for their behaviour, especially when they behaved like Greeks. This trope is always accompanied by a number of examples, the most common being women (pagan or Christian) chanting incantations or Christians attending the theatre or horse races.[20] John was a strong believer in the power of public behaviour, and to this extent he found many examples of Christians behaving shamelessly, which he was not hesitant to criticise, and many examples of Greeks (both past and present) behaving philosophically, which he commends. The dynamic of this kind of social behaviour is hard to imagine in a culture where religion is essentially a private matter that is considered too rude to be discussed in public.

At the same time, and as we saw in Chapter 2, Chrysostom often finds common ground on specific religious ideas, such as a last judgment and a retribution for our human deeds on earth. On this, he would claim, everyone agrees: poets and philosophers, Greeks and barbarians, and of course, the Christians. We cannot confidently say why he felt the need to refer to this common ground. One might speculate that this was because many from his audience would be familiar with these ideas. Others might say that at times he was prone to showcase his extensive classical education by evoking images from his student days. He is also willing to praise certain philosophers who rejected what both he and they considered as false values: wealth,

---

[20] See e.g. *Illum. Cat.* 2.5 (PG 49:240).

excessive pleasures, and fame. Yet this was no uncritical acceptance. In most cases, the praise was concluded with a critique of the philosophers' motive, principally vainglory. We should also consider John's pastoral considerations. He could very well have been trying to address concerns from his audience. Perhaps they were the ones who questioned how much 'Hellenism' they could have in their lives while yet remaining Christians, and he could have been trying to show them how they could properly integrate the two. His first concerns, as others have mentioned before, were always pastoral.

Vainglory is connected with the other major theme of Chrysostom's critique of philosophy: its usefulness and the way it is connected to the title of the philosopher. According to Chrysostom, Christian philosophy is based on a different premise, one that is more inclusive about who is eligible for the title of philosopher. Oftentimes, the philosopher is someone who knows a trade and is employed to do manual labour, contrary to those "who are brought up to nothing and are idle, who employ many attendants, and are served by an immense retinue,"[21] an image that brings to mind the philosopher as an idle aristocrat who spends his days thinking while others take care of his needs. By contrast, for John hard work is definitely "a kind of philosophy" that keeps the soul pure and the mind sharper.[22] The man that has nothing to do is by definition lethargic and spends his days doing either nothing or useless things. On the contrary, the manual worker is busy with useful enterprises, whether in deeds, words or thoughts and so is not to be despised. Chrysostom's argumentation is not just about the distinction between idlers and workers, however: it extends to the right use of one's leisure, and the subsequent rewards or punishments one will receive based on one's use of it; that is, whether you are living your life as you should, or if you are wasting it

---

[21] *In 1 Cor. hom.* 5.6 (PG 61:47; NPNF 1-12:28).

[22] Ibid.

away.[23] With this discussion in mind, we can gain a much better understanding of Chrysostom's comment that Peter was more philosophical than Plato and his emphasis on the exhibition of philosophical attitudes by anonymous individuals. John even refers to the example of a crippled widow begging outside the Church.[24] If she is examined on things such as the immortality of the soul, the resurrection of bodies, divine providence, the last judgment, punishment of sinners, etc., she will respond with precision. This is not the case with the philosophers who thinks that their hairstyle and staff make them great, and whose long speeches are garrulous and meaningless. This type of criticism is not unknown to Hellenic tradition, as we saw in the example of Julian and the Cynics or Diogenes' comment that Plato's lectures were "a waste of time."[25] But, as we have shown, Chrysostom employs it to particular effect in contrasting Christians and Greek philosophers, both famous and anonymous.

In order to highlight the virtues of what he considered Christian philosophy, Chrysostom was keen to use exemplars representing each side. As we have shown in a series of comparisons studied in detail in Chapter 3, his aim was to show the superiority of Christians through the use of specific themes, especially the visible success of Christianity and the fact that the philosophers failed in all their enterprises. John is also involved in re-appropriating derogatory terms directed against Christians, such as Galileans, and turning them on their head by emphasizing that in the end it was the Galileans who won. The *ad hoc* nature of these comparisons should also be mentioned again. The repetitive nature of certain accusations shows that John had a number of stock paradigms in mind, which he could flexibly apply to the individual he was talking about, whether he was referring to a pagan or a Christian. We also argued (although cannot conclusively prove) that the exception to the use of these stock paradigms are the

---

[23] *In 1 Cor. hom.* 5.6 (PG 61:47; NPNF 1-12:28).

[24] *Mut. nom. hom.* 4.5 (PG 51:152-3).

[25] Diogenes Laertius, *Vit. phil.* 2.6 (LCL 185:27).

first in his series of homilies on Matthew, where he discusses the various *politeiai* written by Greek philosophers and points to their failure by establishing the success of Christ's *politeia*, and the *Discourse on Babylas*, which we analysed extensively in chapter 3. The reason these two texts seem exceptional is due to their carefully crafted arguments, literary references and direct quotations from Libanius' corpus. The reasoning behind these *synkriseis* is best explained by John himself. Firstly, if someone wants to adopt the greatest way of life, then the emulation of one's example acts as an education. Secondly, when the soul is sick from belief in false doctrine, then the application of words becomes an emergency treatment, in order both to safeguard the Christians and to respond to attacks from those "outside."[26] By comparing Greeks and Christians then, John achieves both aims: he showcases examples that can be emulated, but also points out the effects false doctrines had on the lives of the Greeks in order both to prevent the Christians from emulating them and also to counterattack the ἔξωθεν for their high regard of these individuals.

Our study concluded in Chapter 4 with an example of how Chrysostomic scholarship can move forward when examining his reception of Hellenism and philosophy. First, we looked into Chrysostom's reception of Cynicism by situating it within the context of previous Christian assessments of the Cynics. We showed the extent to which his reception was similar to other Christian writers and we analysed the differences in his assessments of individuals like Diogenes and Crates. We then looked into a philosophical concept related to ethics and closely associated with Cynicism: *autarkeia*. There is a characterization of Chrysostom repeated *ad nauseam* in scholarship: that he was a moralist preacher/minister, but not a theologian or philosopher. Even if the terms are not exactly clarified, it is true that Chrysostom was very much concerned with practical ethics. As we saw, John commended certain

---

[26] *De sac.* 4.3 (SC 272:250).

philosophers (Diogenes, Crates, Anacharsis) for spending their lives concerned with the ethical part of philosophy, which was the reason they lived brilliant lives and also became very famous. This rare endorsement led us into looking at various ethical concepts within Cynicism. We chose *autarkeia* because the three references to the word in the New Testament would surely not provide enough material for Chrysostom's points, even though his primary example of *autarkēs* is, to no-one's surprise, Paul. We then compared the exegesis of the term in both the Cynics and John. What we found were two competing modes of discourse that shared enough similarities to be considered part of a discussion within the same intellectual tradition. We argued that in his use of the term *autarkeia* Chrysostom is exhibiting a method of reception which is complex and subtle and which falls outside the models of either outright hostility or complete approbation. To some extent, this conclusion coheres with the work of scholars such as Wendy Mayer, who have been working with a similar model for some time. Nevertheless, through our in-depth examination of the term *autarkeia*, we have shown that Chrysostom's use of other key Cynic concepts such as *parrhesia* or *tuphos* would be worth examining. Our detailed study of the Cynics also shows that the fact that John did not engage with Platonic metaphysics as much as others did does not mean that his engagement with Greek philosophy was limited.

All too often Chrysostom's comments towards philosophy have been interpreted as casual disparagement and deliberate mocking, without sufficient consideration of the precise content of the comments. Let us examine one example of John criticizing specific philosophical doctrines for being wrong: "that the things existing was destitute of a providence, and that the creation had not its origin from God; that virtue was not sufficient for itself, but stood in need of wealth, and nobility, and external splendour, and other things still more ridiculous."[27] Are these legitimate philosophical opinions or

---

[27] *De Stat.* 19.1 (PG 49:189; NPNF 1-9:465). Our citation of this passage deliberately omits its context. John's critique in this case, as in many others, does not appear out of nowhere. The context is a

just plain straw men that John introduces as such? And do they constitute what someone might consider an unthinking disparaging of all Greek philosophy?

Yet this sort of commentary sometimes comes from unrealistic expectations. How could someone possibly expect John to praise philosophy *when comparing it to Christianity*? Is there even one example of a Christian ever doing that? On the contrary, as we have shown, John's is an engagement with a complex set of ideas in mind. The variety of themes and concepts in ancient philosophy enabled not only a diversity of thought but also a plurality of modes of interaction by those traditionally thought of as its opponents. Some of these interactions have been well documented, but this study has aimed to demonstrate the complexity of the interaction in more detail. Still more remains to be done and one hopes that this will indeed be part of the future of Chrysostom studies.

Chrysostom's contribution to the patristic relation between Hellenism and Christianity was to bring certain ethical concerns that have been part of the philosophical tradition for a very long time to the forefront of Christian discourse. By virtue of that he reclaimed a Hellenic tradition of social justice which not only went on to have an enormous influence in Byzantine homiletic literature and practice, but which also, through his writings, became synonymous with authoritative orthodox biblical exegesis. In the end, his overall reception of Hellenism is not so different to that of many of his Christian counterparts. He is, at times, very critical; at other times, neutral; and, occasionally, he can praise the Greeks and their philosophy too. What is *different*, as we hope to have shown, are the specific aspects of Hellenism he chooses when utilising any of these three modes of interaction. Aaron Johnson described Hellenism in late antiquity as a sort of rhetorical and conceptual toolbox from which the educated

comparison between these philosophers and the monks and the opinions each group holds over these issues. However, this is not the important issue. Chrysostom uses it as a lead to the real point he wants to make: what good was all this schooling to these pagan philosophers since when the crisis hit the city (the statues riots) all they did was vanish into thin air? And how were the illiterate monks harmed by their lack of knowledge since they were the only ones to brave the elements and face the situation headstrong?

drew in order to articulate their own identity as well as that of others.[28] Anthony Kaldellis then posits Hellenism as existing in limbo for about 600 years (400-1000 AD).[29] I think the most appropriate metaphor for the way Chrysostom and other Christian intellectuals in late antiquity saw Hellenism is that it resembles Schrödinger's cat. Is Hellenism alive or dead? Or is Hellenism *both* alive and dead? From John's point of view, it was the latter, for he was always willing to embrace a paradox. In one of John's most brilliant paradoxical statements, the apostles overcome the Greeks' wisdom by becoming wiser than those considered wise. Hellenism may or may not have been dead. Either way, Chrysostom had to deal with it.[30]

---

[28] Johnson, "Hellenism and Its Discontents," 439.

[29] Kaldellis, *Hellenism in Byzantium*, 173-88.

[30] In our case the metaphor works like this: people who look at individual bits of Chrysostom's corpus and even overlook the context of some of these bits remind us of the observers of the cat, giving a status to Hellenism that is only fixed at an individual moment of observation. I would like to thank Dr. Richard Flower for this excellent point.